Deconstructing
Legal Analysis

ASPEN PUBLISHERS

Deconstructing
Legal Analysis
A 1L Primer

Peter T. Wendel

Professor of Law
Pepperdine University

Wolters Kluwer
Law & Business

AUSTIN   BOSTON   CHICAGO   NEW YORK   THE NETHERLANDS

Aspen Publishers
Attn: Permissions Department
76 Ninth Avenue, 7th Floor
New York, NY 10011-5201

To contact Customer Care, e-mail customer.care@aspenpublishers.com, call 1-800-234-1660, fax 1-800-901-9075, or mail correspondence to:

Aspen Publishers
Attn: Order Department
PO Box 990
Frederick, MD 21705

Printed in the United States of America.

3 4 5 6 7 8 9 0

ISBN 978-0-7355-8475-4

Library of Congress Cataloging-in-Publication Data

Wendel, Peter T., 1956-
   Deconstructing legal analysis : a 1L primer / Peter T. Wendel.
     p. cm.
   Includes index.
   ISBN 978-0-7355-8475-4
   1. Law students — United States — Handbooks, manuals, etc. 2.   Law — United States — Methodology. I.   Title.

KF283.W46 2009
340.071'173 — dc22

                                                                    2009033954

About Wolters Kluwer Law & Business

Wolters Kluwer Law & Business is a leading provider of research information and workflow solutions in key specialty areas. The strengths of the individual brands of Aspen Publishers, CCH, Kluwer Law International and Loislaw are aligned within Wolters Kluwer Law & Business to provide comprehensive, in-depth solutions and expert-authored content for the legal, professional and education markets.

CCH was founded in 1913 and has served more than four generations of business professionals and their clients. The CCH products in the Wolters Kluwer Law & Business group are highly regarded electronic and print resources for legal, securities, antitrust and trade regulation, government contracting, banking, pension, payroll, employment and labor, and healthcare reimbursement and compliance professionals.

Aspen Publishers is a leading information provider for attorneys, business professionals and law students. Written by preeminent authorities, Aspen products offer analytical and practical information in a range of specialty practice areas from securities law and intellectual property to mergers and acquisitions and pension/benefits. Aspen's trusted legal education resources provide professors and students with high-quality, up-to-date and effective resources for successful instruction and study in all areas of the law.

Kluwer Law International supplies the global business community with comprehensive English-language international legal information. Legal practitioners, corporate counsel and business executives around the world rely on the Kluwer Law International journals, loose-leafs, books and electronic products for authoritative information in many areas of international legal practice.

Loislaw is a premier provider of digitized legal content to small law firm practitioners of various specializations. Loislaw provides attorneys with the ability to quickly and efficiently find the necessary legal information they need, when and where they need it, by facilitating access to primary law as well as state-specific law, records, forms and treatises.

Wolters Kluwer Law & Business, a unit of Wolters Kluwer, is headquartered in New York and Riverwoods, Illinois. Wolters Kluwer is a leading multinational publisher and information services company.

*To each student who had the courage
to share his or her analytical process with me;*

and

to my daughter, Carolyn, the law student

Summary of Contents

Contents

Preface

It is with some trepidation that I undertake this project. Greater minds than I have addressed this subject,[1] all with varying degrees of success. Traditionally, virtually all lawyers and law professors agreed that the crux of the law school experience — "learning how to think like a lawyer" — cannot be explained, it can only be experienced. While there is much truth in that statement, there is a growing school of thought that the legal analysis process can be described, at least conceptually, so as to facilitate a student's mastery of it. This book adopts that school of thought and will attempt to do just that: to offer a conceptual description, and visualization, of what it means to think like a lawyer that will facilitate your transition from thinking like a layperson to thinking like a lawyer. The material will then take that abstract, conceptual understanding and translate it into a series of practical recommendations about how to read and analyze cases, how to brief cases, how to outline, and how to write a law school exam that will help you succeed in law school.

This conceptual description and visualization of what it means to think like a lawyer, and the practical study and exam writing recommendations that flow from that conceptualization, are well-tested ideas. They were first developed from working one-on-one with students at risk to help them transition from college to law school. The ideas and techniques were so well-received on an individual basis that we were asked to develop a workshop that would convey the same information to a group of incoming law students. The challenge was taking the ideas and information that had worked so well on a one-on-one basis and converting that material into a workshop format for a group of students. Fortunately, the resulting academic success workshop proved successful in helping the group transition successfully from thinking like a layperson to thinking like a lawyer.

Armed with the feedback that the academic success workshop helped students at the school where I teach, the natural question was whether the ideas and techniques were "exportable" — would they work at other law schools as well? At first we were invited to conduct the workshop for students at risk at other law schools in California. Again, the feedback we received was positive. In light of that response, the following year we made the workshop available to students at risk across the country. To date, the workshop has been conducted at

---

1. Karl Lewylln, BRAMBLE BUSH; ON OUR LAW AND ITS STUDY (Oceana Press 1981); William L. Prosser, *Lighthouse No Good*, 1 J. Legal Educ. 257 (1948), reprinted in 28 Stetson L. Rev. 1017 (1999).

over 50 law schools and academic retreats across the country. The law schools run the academic gamut, including some of the top ranked law schools. At many of the law schools the workshop has become an annual event. Based on the success of the workshop, it appears as though (1) the essence of legal analysis is universal, and (2) the ideas and techniques in the academic success workshop help many law students transition from thinking like a layperson to thinking like a lawyer.

The positive response to the academic success workshop gave rise to the present challenge: could the material presented in interactive form in the workshop be translated into narrative form and still be effective? I leave you to be the judge of that. By presenting the information in written form, we hope to reach as many students as possible.

I wish to express my thanks and appreciation to the many people who contributed one way or another to the production of this book: to the Pepperdine alumni, Pepperdine University, and my Dean, Dean Kenneth Starr, who financially supported exporting the workshop to students at risk at law schools across the country; to the students who attended the workshop and provided feedback on it, and through their comments and constructive criticism, helped to identify where the workshop could be improved; to my research assistants, Courtney Kohout, Tamara Kagel, and Taurean Brown, and my daughter, Carolyn Wendel, for their comments and contributions on prior drafts; and to Barbara Roth and the rest of the editorial and production staff at Aspen Publishing, particularly Troy Froebe, for their invaluable efforts that ensured that this final product was the best it could be.

I wish you the best with your law school experience. More than just academic success, I hope you *enjoy* law school. Armed with the information in this book, I believe both are possible.

Peter Wendel
August 2009

Deconstructing
Legal Analysis

Deconstructing Legal Analysis: Learning How to Think Like a Lawyer

The key to "doing well" in law school is doing well on law school exams. The key to doing well on law school exams is clear and effective legal writing. The key to clear and effective writing is clear and effective legal analysis.

Part I of this book sets forth a conceptual and analytical model of what constitutes clear and effective legal analysis, i.e., what it means to "think like a lawyer."

CHAPTER 1

Introduction

Law school is different from any other academic experience you have had or will have. It is a life altering experience. Ask any law student or lawyer. You come out a different person than when you started.[1] You *think* differently. While lay people think the primary purpose of law school is to teach you the law, anyone who has attended law school knows better. You do not practice law based on the *law* you learn in law school: you practice law based on the *skills* you learn in law school. The most important skill is knowing how to "think like a lawyer."[2]

While virtually all lawyers and law professors agree that the primary purpose of law school is to teach you how to think like a lawyer, they also agree that it is difficult to articulate what that means. Thinking like a lawyer is an active process, like riding a bike. Because it is an active process, the assumption is the best way to learn it is by doing it. Just as you learned how to ride a bike by getting on the bike and riding it — learning through repetition, through trial and error, through falling and getting back on the bike again — most law professors teach students how to think like a lawyer by asking them, from the first day of law school, to think like a lawyer — to read and analyze cases with the expectation that students will learning through repetition, through trial and error, through making mistakes but learning from those mistakes. That explains why law students are asked to perform the same task on the first day of law school that they are asked to perform on the last day: read and analyze cases. Just as you learned how to ride a bike by *riding* the bike, you learn how to think like a lawyer by *thinking like a lawyer* — by reading and analyzing cases.

Some law *students* will tell you, however, that the proper analogy for how law schools teach you how to think like a lawyer is not by putting you on a bike and asking you to ride, but rather by throwing you in the deep end of the pool and telling you to "swim." Some students believe that law school does not provide enough guidance with respect to *how* to read and analyze a case, *how* to brief a case, *how* to outline, and *how* to write a law school exam. Some students complain law schools appear to assume that the smart students will figure it out and the students who do not, they do not belong in law school. Darwin would have loved this traditional approach to legal education; and this

---

1. The hope is that when you graduate you are still as good a person as when you started.
2. The rules of law are just the tools law professors use to teach you how to think like a lawyer.

"survival of the fittest" philosophy is still alive and well at some law schools, particularly the so-called "elite" schools.[3]

At most law schools, however, the traditional Darwinian approach has been replaced by a "kinder and gentler" approach to legal education. Most law schools offer some type of academic assistance to students. Part of the orientation program is used to introduce students to legal analysis. Sessions are held on *how* to read and analyze a case, and *how* to brief a case. During the semester, academic support programs are held on *how* to create an outline and *how* to write a law school exam. Such programs can be of great value, and you should take advantage of them as much as possible.

But even with this kinder and gentler approach to law school, many students continue to struggle with what it means to think like a lawyer and how to use that skill to succeed in law school. Orientation is a hectic time with so many different activities going on; there is a great deal of information for students to digest in such a short period of time. For some students, the sessions on legal analysis just do not take hold. During the semester, so many different organizations hold sessions on outlining and exam taking that some students are overwhelmed by the different approaches. At some schools, participation in the academic support program is limited, and even if all students are able to participate, sometimes the way the professor presents the material is different from the way a student thinks.

In addition, many law students have a difficult time mastering what it means to think like a lawyer because they think they already know everything they need to know to succeed in law school. Most law students did well in college. They automatically assume that what worked for them before will work for them again — they assume they should use the same study habits and exam writing style they used in college. But law school *is* different. You read cases, not textbooks. Your professors use the Socratic method of teaching; they do not lecture. The final exam is a fact pattern where you need to spot the issues and analyze them, not questions you answer by regurgitating material you learned through rote memorization. *To be successful in law school most students need to change their analytical skills, their study habits, and their exam writing style.* Unfortunately many law students do not realize this until after they receive their first semester grades — at which point they realize they have dug themselves a deep academic hole that they spend the rest of law school trying to climb out of.[4] So for various reasons, the transition from college to law school is a difficult one for many students.

---

3. I have never understood the logic behind the traditional Darwinian approach to legal education. Even with other forms of knowledge that are experiential based (learning how to swim, learning how to sail), guidance is still offered as to what the process is like to facilitate the learning process.

4. This is particularly damaging in light of the traditional way many law firms — particularly larger law firms — hire new associates, a process in which a student's first semester grades play an integral role. Many law firms hire out of their summer program, the program they run each summer for law students typically between their second and third year of law school. For all practical purposes, to be considered by that firm, you need to be a part of their summer program. The law firms interview for that summer program during the fall of your second year of law school. The only grades you will have at that time are your first-year grades, half of which, obviously, are your first semester grades. It is not

The purpose of this book is to offer an alternative way of thinking about what it means to think like a lawyer and how to use that skill to perform better in law school. It is based upon an academic success workshop that has proven successful for several years now for many different students at many different law schools across the country, especially for students who are the first in their family to attend law school. The success of the workshop led to the conclusion that maybe, just maybe, there is something about the ideas and techniques developed in the workshop that make a difference in a student's success in law school. Substantively, there is little, if anything, new about the material in the workshop, so the logical assumption is that the presentation makes the difference for many students. Often hearing the same information, but from a different perspective, helps make it resonate better. The hope — and expectation — is that this will be equally true for you with respect to the way the material is presented in this book.

Organizationally, the first part of the book provides a conceptual understanding and a model of what it means to think like a lawyer. That understanding will facilitate your transition from thinking like a layperson to thinking like a lawyer. The second part of the book takes that conceptual understanding and translates it into a series of recommendations for *how* to read and analyze a case, *how* to brief a case, *how* to outline, and *how* to use those skills to write your law school exams. The final section of the book builds upon the basic analytical skills and introduces some more sophisticated legal analysis techniques that are essential to being a successful law student and lawyer.

It is time to begin the process of transitioning from thinking like a layperson to thinking like a lawyer. Remember, learning how to "think like a lawyer" is analogous to learning how to ride a bike. Do not expect to be successful from the first case you read and analyze. Ask any law student, the first few weeks of law school the class discussion is full of examples of students who "fall off the bike" in class and skin their knees. That is natural. The students may not expect it, but the professors do. But just like when you fell off your bike, the expectation is you will go home that night and get back on the bike — you will read and analyze another case. And with each case, with each class, your "sense of *legal* balance" will improve. Each day your legal analysis skills will improve incrementally. And just as when you finally learned how ride a bike you could not articulate what it was you were doing differently, so too with legal analysis. When you finally learn how to think like a lawyer, you will have difficulty articulating what it is you are doing differently, but you will sense it. Then you can begin the process of honing and perfecting that skill, for that is the skill you will use the rest of your professional career on your law school exams and in the practice of law.

It is time to get on the bike.

---

wise to leave those grades to chance — to the *assumption* — that you are reading and analyzing cases, that you are outlining, and that you are writing exams the way you should be. You want to do your best to determine how law school differs from college and make the necessary changes in your analytical skills, your study habits, and your writing style before your first set of finals.

CHAPTER 2

The Traditional "Darwinian" Approach

A. INTRODUCTION

There is no doubt that the best way to learn *how* to read and analyze cases is *by reading and analyzing* cases. Analyzing a case is an active process that is best learned by doing. The only issue is whether some meaningful guidance can be provided to assist and facilitate that process. Traditionally, at most law schools, the answer was "no." The traditional thinking was that the best, and *only*, way to teach students how to read and analyze cases was by having them read and analyze cases on their own.

This material will start by letting you try your hand at the traditional approach to learning how to think like a lawyer. The case that has been selected for you to read and analyze on your own is a well-known Property case that works well for this purpose. It is one of the first cases in many Property casebooks and has been for decades. Generations of lawyers have started the process of learning how to think like a lawyer by reading the case of *Pierson v. Post*. It will give you a genuine feel for what it is like to be a first-year law student on his or her first day of law school.

B. "SWIM"

Congratulations. Assume you have been admitted to the law school of your choice. When you show up for orientation, you hear that there is an assignment board where your professors post their reading assignments for the first day of class. Your Property professor has posted the following assignment:

> **Property, Section A**
> Professor Wendel
>
> Welcome to law school.
>
> Please read, analyze, and be prepared to discuss *Pierson v. Post*, the first case in the casebook.

You open your casebook to read the case.

C. *PIERSON v. POST*

Pierson v. Post

SUPREME COURT OF JUDICATURE OF NEW YORK

3 Cai. R. 175 (1805)

This was an action of trespass on the case commenced in a justice's court, by the present defendant against the now plaintiff.

The declaration stated that Post, being in possession of certain dogs and hounds under his command, did, "upon a certain wild and uninhabited, unpossessed and waste land, called the beach, find and start one of those noxious beasts called a fox," and whilst there hunting, chasing and pursuing the same with his dogs and hounds, and when in view thereof, Pierson, well knowing the fox was so hunted and pursued, did, in the sight of Post, to prevent his catching the same, kill and carry it off. A verdict having been rendered for the plaintiff below, the defendant there sued out a certiorari, and now assigned for error, that the declaration and the matters therein contained were not sufficient in law to maintain an action.

TOMPKINS, J., delivered the opinion of the court:

This cause comes before us on a return to a certiorari directed to one of the justices of Queens County.

The question submitted by the counsel in this cause for our determination is, whether Lodowick Post, by the pursuit with his hounds in the manner alleged in his declaration, acquired such a right to, or property in, the fox as will sustain an action against Pierson for killing and taking him away?

The cause was argued with much ability by the counsel on both sides, and presents for our decision a novel and nice question. It is admitted that a fox is an animal feroe naturoe, and that property in such animals is acquired by occupancy only. These admissions narrow the discussion to the simple question of what acts amount to occupancy, applied to acquiring right to wild animals.

If we have recourse to the ancient writers upon general principles of law, the judgment below is obviously erroneous. Justinian's Institutes (lib. 2, tit. 1, sec. 13), and Fleta (lib. 3, ch. 2, p. 175), adopt the principle, that pursuit alone vests no property or right in the huntsman; and that even pursuit, accompanied with wounding, is equally ineffectual for that purpose, unless the animal be actually taken. The same principle is recognized by Breton (lib. 2, ch. 1, p. 8).

Puffendorf (lib. 4, ch. 6, sec. 2 and 10) defines occupancy of beasts feroe naturoe, to be the actual corporeal possession of them, and Bynkershock is cited as coinciding in this definition. It is indeed with hesitation that Puffendorf affirms that a wild beast mortally wounded or greatly maimed, cannot be fairly intercepted by another, whilst the pursuit of the person inflicting the wound continues. The foregoing authorities are decisive to show that mere pursuit gave Post no legal right to the fox, but that he became the property of Pierson, who intercepted and killed him.

It, therefore, only remains to inquire whether there are any contrary principles or authorities, to be found in other books, which ought to induce a different decision. Most of the cases which have occurred in England, relating to property in wild animals, have either been discussed and decided upon the principles of their positive statute regulations, or have arisen between the huntsman and the owner of the land upon which beasts feroe naturoe have been apprehended; the former claiming them by title of occupancy, and the latter ratione soli. Little satisfactory aid can, therefore, be derived from the English reporters.

Barbeyrac, in his notes on Puffendorf, does not accede to the definition of occupancy by the latter, but, on the contrary, affirms that actual bodily seizure is not, in all cases, necessary to constitute possession of wild animals. He does not, however, describe the acts which, according to his ideas, will amount to an appropriation of such animals to private use, so as to exclude the claims of all other persons, by title of occupancy, to the same animals; and he is far from averring that pursuit alone is sufficient for that purpose. To a certain extent, and as far as Barbeyrac appears to me to go, his objections to Puffendorf's definition of occupancy are reasonable and correct. That is to say, that actual bodily seizure is not indispensable to acquire right to, or possession of, wild beasts; but that, on the contrary, the mortal wounding of such beasts, by one not abandoning his pursuit, may, with the utmost propriety, be deemed possession of him; since thereby the pursuer manifests an unequivocal intention of appropriating the animal to his individual use, has deprived him of his natural liberty, and brought him within his certain control. So, also, encompassing and securing such animals with nets and toils, or otherwise intercepting them in such a manner as to deprive them of their natural liberty, and render escape impossible, may justly be deemed to give possession of them to those persons who, by their industry and labor, have used such means of apprehending them. Barbeyrac seems to have adopted and had in view in his notes, the more accurate opinion of Grotius, with respect to occupancy. . . . The case now under consideration is one of mere pursuit, and presents no circumstances or acts which can bring it within the definition of occupancy by Puffendorf, or Grotius, or the ideas of Barbeyrac upon that subject.

The case cited from 11 Mod. 74, 130, I think clearly distinguishable from the present; inasmuch as there the action was for maliciously hindering and disturbing the plaintiff in the exercise and enjoyment of a private franchise; and in the report of the same case (3 Salk. 9), Holt, Ch. J., states, that the ducks were in the plaintiff's decoy pond, and so in his possession, from which it is obvious the court laid much stress in their opinion upon the plaintiff's possession of the ducks, ratione soli.

We are the more readily inclined to confine possession or occupancy of beasts feroe naturoe, within the limits prescribed by the learned authors above cited, for the sake of certainty, and preserving peace and order in society. If the first seeing, starting or pursuing such animals, without having so wounded, circumvented or ensnared them, so as to deprive them of their natural liberty, and subject them to the control of their pursuer, should afford the basis of actions against others for intercepting and killing them, it would prove a fertile source of quarrels and litigation.

However uncourteous or unkind the conduct of Pierson towards Post, in this instance, may have been, yet this act was productive of no injury or damage for which a legal remedy can be applied. We are of opinion the judgment below was erroneous, and ought to be reversed.

LIVINGTSON, J. My opinion differs from that of the court. Of six exceptions, taken to the proceedings below, all are abandoned except the third, which reduces the controversy to a single question.

Whether a person who, with his own hounds, starts and hunts a fox on waste and uninhabited ground, and is on the point of seizing his prey, acquires such an interest in the animal as to have a right of action against another, who in view of the huntsman and his dogs in full pursuit, and with knowledge of the chase, shall kill and carry him away.

This is a knotty point, and should have been submitted to the arbitration of sportsmen, without poring over Justinian, Fleta, Bracton, Puffendorf, Locke, Barbeyrac, or Blackstone, all of whom have been cited: they would have had no difficulty in coming to a prompt and correct conclusion. In a court thus constituted, the skin and carcass of poor Reynard would have been properly disposed of, and a precedent set, interfering with no usage or custom which the experience of ages has sanctioned, and which must be so well known to every votary of Diana. But the parties have referred the question to our judgment, and we must dispose of it as well as we can, from the partial lights we possess, leaving to a higher tribunal the correction of any mistake which we may be so unfortunate as to make. By the pleadings it is admitted that a fox is a "wild and noxious beast." Both parties have regarded him, as the law of nations does a pirate, "hostem humani generis," and although "de mortuis nil nisi bonum" be a maxim of our profession, the memory of the deceased has not been spared. His depredations on farmers and on barnyards, have not been forgotten; and to put him to death wherever found, is allowed to be meritorious, and of public benefit. Hence it follows, that our decision should have in view the greatest possible encouragement to the destruction of an animal, so cunning and ruthless in his career. But who would keep a pack of hounds; or what gentleman, at the sound of the horn, and at peep of day, would mount his steed, and for hours together, "sub jove frigido," or a vertical sun, pursue the windings of this wily quadruped, if, just as night came on, and his stratagems and strength were nearly exhausted, a saucy intruder, who had not shared in the honors or labors of the chase, were permitted to come in at the death, and bear away in triumph the object of pursuit? Whatever Justinian may have thought of the matter, it must be recollected that his code was compiled many hundred years ago, and it would be very hard indeed, at the distance of so many centuries, not to have a right to establish a rule for ourselves. In his day, we read of no order of men who made it a business, in the language of the declaration in this cause, "with hounds and dogs to find, start, pursue, hunt, and chase," these animals, and that, too, without any other motive than the preservation of Roman poultry; if this diversion had been then in fashion, the lawyers who composed his institutes, would have taken care not to pass it by, without suitable encouragement. If anything, therefore, in the digests or pandects shall appear to militate against the defendant in error, who, on this occasion, was the fox hunter, we have only to say tempora mutantur; and if men themselves change with the times, why should not laws also undergo an alteration?

It may be expected, however, by the learned counsel, that more particular notice be taken of their authorities. I have examined them all, and feel great difficulty in determining, whether to acquire dominion over a thing, before in common, it be sufficient that we barely see it, or know where it is, or wish for it, or make a declaration of our will respecting it; or whether, in the case of wild beasts, setting a trap, or lying in wait, or starting, or pursuing, be enough; or if an actual wounding, or killing, or bodily tact and occupation be necessary. Writers on general law, who have favored us with their speculations on these points, differ on them all; but, great as is the diversity of sentiment among them, some conclusion must be adopted on the question immediately before us. After mature deliberation, I embrace that of Barbeyrac as the most rational and least liable to objection. If at liberty, we might imitate the courtesy of a certain emperor, who, to avoid giving offense to the advocates of any of these different doctrines, adopted a middle course, and by ingenious distinctions, rendered it difficult to say (as often happens after a fierce and angry contest) to whom the palm of victory belonged. He ordained, that if a beast be followed with large dogs and hounds, he shall belong to the hunter, not to the chance occupant; and in like manner, if he be killed or wounded with a lance or sword; but if chased with beagles only, then he passed to the captor, not to the first pursuer. If slain with a dart, a sling, or a bow, he fell to the hunter, if still in chase, and not to him who might afterwards find and seize him.

Now, as we are without any municipal regulations of our own, and the pursuit here, for aught that appears on the case, being with dogs and hounds of imperial stature, we are at liberty to adopt one of the provisions just cited, which comports also with the learned conclusion of Barbeyrac, that property in animals feroe naturoe may be acquired without bodily touch or manucaption, provided the pursuer be within reach, or have a reasonable prospect (which certainly existed here) of taking what he has thus discovered with an intention of converting to his own use.

When we reflect also that the interest of our husbandmen, the most useful of men in any community, will be advanced by the destruction of a beast so pernicious and incorrigible, we cannot greatly err in saying that a pursuit like the present, through waste and unoccupied lands, and which must inevitably and speedily have terminated in corporeal possession, or bodily seisin, confers such a right to the object of it, as to make any one a wrong-doer who shall interfere and shoulder the spoil. The justice's judgment ought, therefore, in my opinion, to be affirmed.

Judgment of reversal.

D. READ, ANALYZE, AND BE PREPARED TO DISCUSS

1. Read

What is the case about? If you had to tell someone who had not read the case what the case is about, what would you say? You might want to take a moment to write down on a separate piece of paper a few sentences about what *you think* the case is about (some people recommend that you think about it as a story about real people that you need to explain to someone else). You will come to learn that *how* you express your analysis — the precise words you use — tells you more than you might think about the *quality* of your analysis.

2. Analyze

What does it mean to *analyze* a case? Notice the professor's assignment was to "read, analyze, and be prepared to discuss" the case. You know how to read (though that is part of the problem — you probably assumed you read a case the same way you read other texts when in fact you should not — but that is for later). You have read the case, but what does it mean to *analyze* a case? Take a moment to reflect upon that question (1) generically, and (2) as applied to *Pierson v. Post*. You might want to take a moment to write down (1) what you think it means to analyze a case in general, and (2) your analysis of *Pierson v. Post*. Again, *how* you express your analysis — the precise words you use — tells you more than you might think about the *quality* of your analysis. Later the material will offer a methodology and a model that you can use to critique your analysis.

Most lay people struggle to articulate what it means to analyze a case and to articulate their analysis of *Pierson v. Post*. Yet that is what first-year law students are asked to do from the very first day of law school, with varying degrees of guidance regarding what it means to "read and analyze" a case. Now you have a better understanding of why some law students say that the traditional approach to learning how to think like a lawyer is like being thrown into the deep end of a pool and being told to swim. Under the traditional approach, you were expected to learn by doing, through repetition, through trial and error, with minimal guidance. "Reading" a case is self-evident, but analyzing a case is not. It is a skill that must be developed and mastered.

3. Be Prepared to Discuss

Most law professors, particularly those who teach first-year classes, use the Socratic teaching style. The essence of the Socratic approach is that it is the students' responsibility (individually and collectively) to teach each other; it is not the professor's responsibility to teach the students. The professor is there simply to guide the discussion. You may find this definition strange — until you experience it.

Consistent with the Socratic approach, the professor begins the "analysis" of the case by questioning one or more students about *their* understanding of the case. Regardless of what the student says, the professor's response tends to be another question challenging the student's statement. From the students' perspective, the Socratic discussion resembles a rambling debate. The professor challenges the students' understanding of the case with little guidance as to when a student has given a "good" or "bad" answer. Many students complain they are confused about what to take away from the class discussion. Students tend to take either copious notes (hoping that they will figure out later what to do with them) or no notes (further evidence of their bewilderment).

"Do you think the court got it right or wrong? Do you prefer the majority opinion or the dissenting opinion? Why?" These questions are representative of the type of questions a professor may include in his or her analysis of a case on the first day of class. Notice the questions are open ended, intended to start a discussion. Students are asked to put forth *their* thoughts about the case, *their* analysis, for the class' consideration and then to be prepared to defend those thoughts and analyses from attack by either the professor or other students in the class. So if the students are leading the discussion, and the students do not really know what they are doing, is the Socratic approach just an example of the blind leading the blind?

How's the water?

E. CASE BRIEFING

To help prepare for class, many students "brief" each case they read. Briefing a case is covered later in greater detail, but in a nutshell briefing a case is analogous to dissecting a case. The case is broken down into its most important parts. While briefing a case *facilitates* analyzing the case, briefing a case is *not* analyzing the case. Analyzing a case requires more aggressive, critical thinking about the case. Still there is much benefit to case briefing when done properly.

There are different approaches to briefing a case. In the spirit of the traditional approach to teaching law school, you might want to take a shot at briefing *Pierson v. Post*. One of the more traditional approaches to case briefing asks the student to complete, at a minimum, the following template:

CASE NAME
(Court and Date as Well)

FACTS (what happened):

PROCEDURAL POSTURE (what has happened to the dispute in the court system before this opinion — how did the dispute get before the court that issued you the opinion you are briefing):

ISSUE (what the issue is):

HOLDING (the court's ruling):

RATIONALE (why the court ruled the way it did):

CRITIQUE (your chance to add your comments, criticisms, and/or analysis of the court's opinion):

Again, *how* you express your case brief — the precise words you use — tells you more than you might think about the *quality* of your analysis. Later the material provides a model brief for *Pierson v. Post* that you can use to analyze the quality of your brief if you choose to write one out (which is strongly recommended).

F. CONCLUSION

Now you know how a law student feels before he or she attends his or her first class under the traditional approach to teaching law school. Have you properly "read and analyzed" the case? What are you supposed to take away from the case? How are you supposed to know? Now you have a sense of the uncertainty and frustration that the traditional Darwinian approach to legal education bred in many students (and still does at some of the more elite law schools where it still prevails).

Having exposed you to the issue — what does it mean to think like a lawyer and how does one learn how to do it — it is time to contrast the traditional approach with a different approach, a more contemporary, kinder and gentler approach that offers some guidance as to what it means to think like a lawyer and how to use that skill to perform better in law school. As with the traditional approach, it begins with how to read and analyze a case. But instead of throwing you in the deep end of the pool and telling you to swim, the material will put you on a bike — with training wheels at first to help ease the transition.

CHAPTER 3

The Evolution of a Case from an Analytical Perspective

Your law school professors will ask you to read and analyze cases, but rarely do they stop to cover "the evolution" of a case. Most of you have heard about a case before. You have seen TV shows and movies where different stages of a case have been depicted. It is understandable that you would start law school *thinking* that you know what a case is and how it develops. But the material below is going to ask you to view the evolution of a case from a different perspective, an *analytical* perspective. The analytical perspective involves translating the story about the dispute between the particular parties to the case into a rule of law, with a rationale that can be applied to other scenarios and parties. The analytical perspective begins by playing off of the *temporal* evolution of a case, by chronologically answering the question "what happened"?

The temporal evolution of a case can be diagrammed on a timeline:

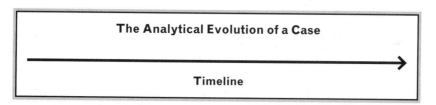

The particular case the material will use to study the analytical evolution of a case is *Pierson v. Post*, the case you just read.

A. THE GENESIS OF A CASE

How does a case begin? How did *Pierson v. Post* begin? Assume you are Post. You get up one morning and decide to go hunting. You get your dogs and hounds together.[1] You head out with them for the hunt. It is a hot and sunny

---

1. Historically, the gentleman's way of catching foxes was to sic your hounds on a fox till they caught it.

day. You have been hunting for several hours with no luck. You are starting to get tired and frustrated when all of a sudden your dogs and hounds spy a fox. They take off after the fox, chasing the fox down an un-owned beach. You take off after your dogs and hounds. You are closing in on the fox. You are about to capture the fox, when Pierson, who is walking up the beach in the other direction, seeing all of this unfold before him, pulls out a gun and shoots and kills the fox.[2]

If you were Post, what would you have said to Pierson out there on that beach that day? Do not respond like a law student; respond like Post would have that day: role play. You might even want to take a moment to write down your arguments on a separate piece of paper.[3]

If you were Pierson, what would you have said in response? Again, do not respond as a law student; respond like Pierson would have that day: role play. Again, you might want to write down your responses on a separate piece of paper.

Who ends up with the fox that day? (Hint—who had the gun?!) Pierson ends up with the fox. If you are Post, are you happy with that result? Of course not, you had been chasing that fox for hours. In our society, if we are not happy, what do we tend to do? We sue.

Notice the typical case starts out as *a dispute* between two parties[4]—a dispute that the parties cannot resolve on their own to their mutual satisfaction. Returning to the timeline, put a dash towards the left end, intersecting the timeline to represent the start of the case. It starts as a dispute between two parties:

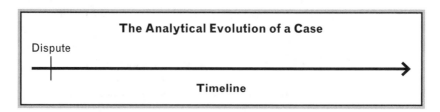

If the parties cannot resolve the dispute to their mutual satisfaction, often one of the parties sues the other. How do you sue someone? Take it one step at a time. If you are a layperson, how do you sue someone? You go to a lawyer.

---

2. The opinion does not indicate how Pierson "killed" the fox, but for purposes of this material assume he shot and killed it.

3. Again, *how* you express Post's arguments—the precise words you use—will help provide insights into what it means to think like a lawyer. The material will come back to this question and the typical student answer so you can contrast and critique your arguments with the typical student's arguments.

4. Obviously there can be, and often are, more than two parties, but the material will assume a *typical* case. In the typical—or paradigm—case there are two parties just as there are in *Pierson v. Post.*

B. THE ROLE OF THE LAWYER

Assume you are a lawyer.[5] Post walks into your office. At this point you know nothing about what has happened or why he has come to your office. After exchanging greetings and small talk, what is the first question you would ask Post? *What happened? Why are you here?* No doubt Post would relay what happened as best he understood it from his perspective. To the extent the story is incomplete, you, the lawyer, would ask additional questions about what happened.

After you, Post's lawyer, get all of the information that you think might be relevant, what do you do next? The lawyer researches *the law*, looking for a rule of law[6] that when applied to the facts entitles his or her client to the relief he or she is seeking. The rule of law the lawyer chooses for the case is called the "cause of action."[7] After the lawyer finds a rule of law that can serve as his or her cause of action, he or she writes it up in a document typically called a complaint (or a petition, or a declaration—the terminology varies by jurisdiction). Then the lawyer files the complaint with the court. The evolution of the case proceeds. Add another dash to the timeline:

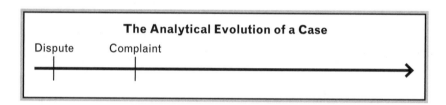

The Analytical Evolution of a Case

Dispute   Complaint

The party who files the complaint in a civil action typically is called the plaintiff (or the petitioner). In addition to filing the complaint, the plaintiff (or more appropriately, his or her lawyer) serves it on the defendant (the opposing, or responding, party in a civil action).

Now assume you are Pierson. You have just been served with a complaint. How do you feel? What—or more appropriately *who*—do you need? You need a lawyer. Change roles again. Now assume you are an attorney and Pierson walks into your office. As the attorney at this point you know nothing about what has happened or why he has come to your office. After exchanging greetings and small talk, what is the first question you would ask Pierson? *What happened? Why are you here?* No doubt Pierson would relay what happened as he understood it from his perspective. To the extent the story is incomplete, you, Pierson's lawyer, would ask additional questions.

---

5. Role play again.
6. Or rule*s* of law, but keep it simple to start. Assume there is only one applicable rule of law.
7. There may be one more than one cause of action. Parties can plead in the alternative, which means the parties can plead multiple causes of action (all possible causes of action—any cause of action that can be asserted in good faith). The parties can even plead inconsistent causes of action. The lawyer does not care which cause of action the court adopts to rule in his or her client's favor, just that the court rules in the client's favor.

As Pierson's lawyer, after you get all of the information you think might be relevant, what would you do next? You would research the law. You would research the cause of action(s) that the plaintiff's lawyer has asserted to see if you agree that the cause of action(s) applies. You would also research the law to see if there are any "affirmative defenses" that the defendant could assert which would counter or bar the plaintiff's cause of action(s).[8]

When you are done with your research, you would write up the defendant's reply to the complaint in a document typically called an answer (or response). As Pierson's lawyer, you would file the answer with the court. Filing the answer constitutes another step in the evolution of the case. Add another dash to the timeline:

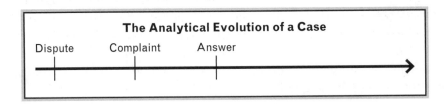

The Analytical Evolution of a Case

Dispute   Complaint   Answer

C. THE "VERTICAL" ANALYTICAL EVOLUTION OF A CASE

1. The Factual Plane

In addition to the timeline (which depicts the evolution of the case on the horizontal axis), the evolution of a case can also be depicted conceptually as the interaction of several abstract planes. The first plane is the factual plane. Everything that occurs in the real world—all actions, all events—occurs on the factual plane. The factual plane can be depicted as a two-dimensional plane with an "F" in the corner for "Factual":

The dispute that arose between Pierson and Post arose on the factual plane: Post was chasing the fox down an un-owned beach, in hot pursuit of the fox,

---

8. An affirmative defense is a rule of law that can be invoked to negate, bar, or otherwise defeat a competing legal claim. For example, if a plaintiff has a cause of action against a defendant, he or she must file the claim in a timely manner or it will be barred by the statute of limitations. The applicable statute of limitations is an example of a possible affirmative defense.

when Pierson killed it. All of those actions, all of those words, belong on the factual plane. The dispute can be depicted as an "x" on the factual plane:

But you implicitly knew this. Back on page 16 the material asked what you thought Post would have said to Pierson out there on that beach that day, and what Pierson would have said to Post. If you are like most students, the words you used to describe what they would have said belong primarily, if not exclusively, on the factual plane.[9] The words used in the argument between the parties would have been primarily about the *facts*, about what happened out there on the beach that day. The dispute typically arises on the factual plane.

Notice also when Post went to his lawyer, what were the first meaningful questions the lawyer asked him? *What happened? Why are you here?* Notice those questions are seeking information on the *factual* plane—in response to those questions Post told to his attorney what happened *factually* out there on the beach that day.

2. The Rule Plane

After Post's attorney gathered all the relevant factual information from his or her client, what did the attorney do? The attorney researched *the law*. He or she moved off the factual plane and on to the *legal plane*, the *rule plane*. The rule plane floats above the factual plane:

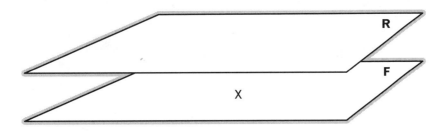

Post's attorney went to the rule plane looking for a rule of law that when applied to the facts of his or her particular case entitled his or her client to

---

9. If you wrote out what you think the parties would have argued, go back and look very carefully at the exact words used. Analyze those words. The typical student, and almost all students, uses almost exclusively words that invoke the facts of the dispute.

the relief he was seeking. One can visualize the rule Post's attorney selected as a circle on the rule plane:

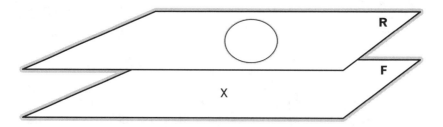

The argument the plaintiff's attorney is making is that the scope of the rule (the rule's shadow on the factual plane) covers the facts of the case in question, entitling his or her client to the relief he or she is seeking:

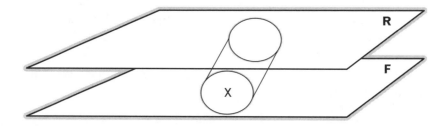

If this is true — if the facts *are* governed by the rule — then the plaintiff should prevail.

But rarely does the defendant agree that the dispute is governed by the rule. Typically the defendant's answer will dispute the plaintiff's version of the facts and/or the assertion that the rule applies to and governs the facts. The defendant's version of the dispute can be visualized on the planes as follows:

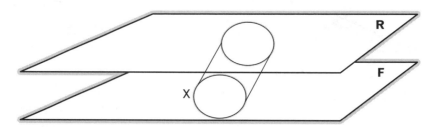

Not surprisingly, the defendant's version of the dispute is that the plaintiff is not entitled to the relief he or she is seeking. It is for the legal system to decide which party's version of the dispute is the more accurate one. The evolution of a case can be depicted on both the timeline and on the abstract planes.

Returning to the timeline, after the defendant files his or her answer, what is the next big event on the timeline? Assuming the matter is not settled, it typically will go to trial. Going to trial constitutes another dash on the timeline:

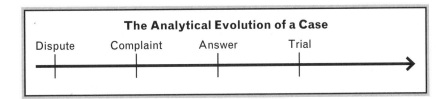

The period of time after the defendant files his or her answer and before trial is called pre-trial.

D. PRE-TRIAL

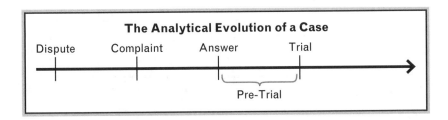

During pre-trial, what do the parties typically engage in? Discovery.

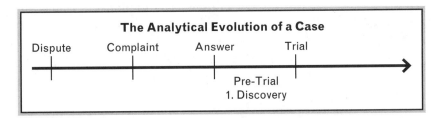

What is discovery? Depending on whether you are a law student yet, and even if you are, what year law student you are, you may not be comfortable with that question. Another way to think about discovery is to ask "what are the three most common forms of discovery"? Depositions, interrogatories, and requests for the production of documents.[10] What are all of these forms of discovery trying to

---

10. Put each one of these forms of discovery under the analytical microscope to make sure that you are thinking about them from the proper perspective. Depositions are the form of discovery with which most law students and prospective law students are most familiar with (because they appear on TV or in movies the most). In a deposition, one party (or witness) is under oath and the other party's attorney asks him or her questions. It is a fluid give-and-take where the questions asked depend, to a large degree, on the answers given. On the other hand, Interrogatories are written questions one party submits to the other to be answered in writing under oath. And the third

discover? The other party's version of *the facts*. Discovery is the legal process by which one party is permitted to learn the other party's version of *what happened*. Discovery occurs almost exclusively on the factual plane.

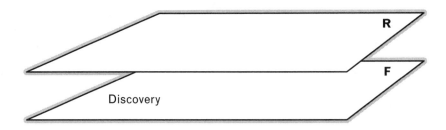

In addition to discovery, during pre-trial what else do the parties typically do? What can they file? The parties typically file motions during pre-trial:

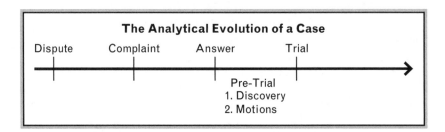

What are the two most common motions? The motion to dismiss and the motion for summary judgment. The motion to dismiss basically asks the court to dismiss the cause of action because, *as a matter of law*, it fails to state a valid claim.[11] When a party, typically the defendant, files a motion to dismiss, the defendant is basically arguing that even if all the facts as alleged by the plaintiff are true and can be proved, the plaintiff is still not entitled to any relief because the facts as alleged do not satisfy the elements of the cause of action — they do not entitle the plaintiff to the relief he or she is seeking; the plaintiff is not entitled to the relief he or she is seeking *as a matter of law*.

The motion for summary judgment basically asserts that in light of the parties' pleadings (the complaint and the answer), and uncontested evidence produced

---

most common form of discovery is the request for the production of documents. If there is any paperwork related to the dispute (police reports, insurance reports, doctor's reports/bills, etc.), one party can request the other party to produce all such paperwork.

11. Sometimes a motion to dismiss can be — and *must* be — filed in lieu of filing an answer. *When* a motion to dismiss should be filed in lieu of filing an answer is a matter of civil procedure law that is beyond the scope of this material. The point to remember is that the evolution of a case the material is presenting, and the timeline is diagramming, is that of a *typical* case, and it is the *analytical* evolution of a case. You will learn the technical *civil procedure* evolution of a case when you take the civil procedure class.

during discovery, the moving party is entitled to relief *as a matter of law* and there is no need for a trial: there are no questions of fact that need to be answered at trial (everyone agrees on the relevant facts), and therefore the judge can decide whether the rule applies without the need for a trial.

Both the motion to dismiss and the motion for summary judgment basically say, assuming the facts as alleged by the opposing party, the moving party believes he or she is entitled to relief *as a matter of law* and no trial is necessary. While discovery occurs almost exclusively on the factual plane, motions occur almost exclusively on the legal plane:

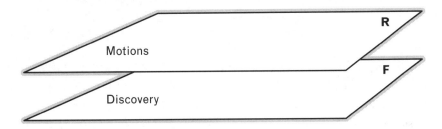

One way to conceptualize the evolution of a case is that it involves the inter-action of the planes.

E. THE TRIAL

Assuming the dispute is not settled and it is not resolved by motion, it will go to trial.

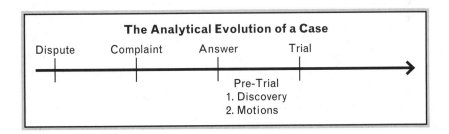

Put the trial under the microscope to make sure you are viewing it from the proper *analytical* perspective.

Who goes first at trial? The plaintiff. The plaintiff puts on his or her case — or proves his or her case — by calling his or her witnesses. What do the witnesses testify to? *The facts.* The witnesses cannot testify to the law, only *the facts.* After the plaintiff's witnesses testify, the defendant puts on his or her case by calling his or her witnesses. What do the defendant's witnesses testify to? They testify to *the facts.* Again, the witnesses cannot testify about the law, they testify to *the facts.*

Thinking about the trial from the perspective of the abstract, analytical planes, on which plane does the trial take place primarily? *The factual plane.*

After the defendant finishes his or her case, and assuming no rebuttal witnesses, there are closing arguments. The respective lawyers argue the case to the jury.[12] What can they argue? Do they argue the facts or the law? The lawyers are not permitted to argue the law to the jury. They can only argue the evidence — *the facts* — to the jury. The trial occurs primarily on *the factual plane.*

After closing arguments, what happens next? Jury instructions. Who gives them? What are they? The judge instructs the jury on *the law*. The trial is primarily about the facts until the very end, when the judge instructs the jury on *the law.*

The evolution of a case involves the interaction between the factual plane and the rule plane.

After the judge instructs the jury, the jury goes back and "deliberates." Put that term under the microscope to make sure you understand it from the proper *analytical* perspective. What does is mean to say the jury "deliberates?" Assume you are on the jury in *Pierson v. Post.* After you pick a foreperson, what would you do first? Take a moment to think about that question.[13]

Most students answer that first they would figure out what happened factually — what happened on the factual plane. If you were on the jury in *Pierson v. Post,* do you believe Post? Do you believe Pierson? Do you believe both of them, but you also know they are human, and as humans their minds may play tricks on them? Do you believe they may see the world from their own self-interested, flawed perspective so what actually happened may be some combination of what each one individually thinks happened?

After you determine what you think happened factually, what would you do next?[14] When first-year law students are asked if they were on the jury, what they would do after determining the facts, most students give one of two answers. Some students answer "I would apply *the facts to the law* to determine the outcome in the case." Other students answer "I would apply *the law to the facts* to determine the outcome in the case." Notice the subtle but critical difference between those two answers. Which of these answers is the answer you would give?

At one level, both of those answers are correct. But at another level, one of these answers is much better than the other. Which answer is better and why?

The better answer is that after determining the facts, the jury *applies the law to the facts* to reach a verdict in the case. Why is that the better answer? Two

---

12. Not all cases are tried to a jury. Some cases are tried by a judge. But the norm is a jury trial, and that is the model most students come to law school with in their heads, so we will use that in our paradigm case.

13. Again, you might want to take a moment to write down your answer because *how* you express it may provide some insights later into the quality of your analytical skills.

14. Again, you might want to take a moment to write down your answer because *how* you express it may provide some insights later into the quality of your analytical skills.

reasons: one abstract, one practical. First, go back to the two planes. Notice that the rule plane floats above the factual plane; it casts its shadow down onto the factual plane. Legal analysis applies the rule to the facts, not the facts to the rule.

The more important reason why it is better to think you apply the rule to the facts is because the way you *think* is the way you will *write* your legal analysis. If you *think* legal analysis means you *apply the facts to the law*, you will likely *write facts to law* on your law school exams. Writing "facts to law" typically results in a conclusory writing style (meaning you have not adequately explained *why* you have reached the conclusions you have reached) that will cost you points.[15] If you *think* that legal analysis means you apply *the law to the facts*, you will likely *write law to facts* on your law school exams. Writing "law to facts" is much more likely to result in a writing style that your law professors will like and will produce better grades.[16] *Lead with the law, both analytically and in your writing.*

Many students do not consciously think about which answer is better: whether they should apply the law to the facts or the facts to the law. They apply the facts to the law because they assumed, without thinking about it, that that is what they should do. It seems more "natural" to them. They are more comfortable with the facts. They have spent their whole lives dealing with facts, relating what happened factually. In addition, when a professor covers a case in class he or she typically starts with the facts. It just seems natural to lead with the facts. Learning rules of law and knowing how to apply and analyze them is new. It is difficult. While it is understandable that you would prefer to lead with the old and more comfortable way of thinking, with the facts, you need to shift your focus to lead with the new, and at least initially more difficult material, the rules.

Back to *Pierson v. Post*. Who prevailed at the trial court level? Post did — the jury found for Post. If you are Pierson, are you happy with the verdict? Of course not. What do you authorize your attorney to do? You authorize your attorney to appeal. Add another dash to the timeline:

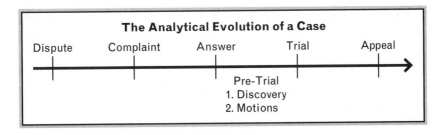

---

15. The material shows *why* writing facts to law results in a conclusory writing style later in Chapter 13. For now, if your answer was that if you were on the jury you would apply the facts to the law, I *strongly recommend* that you revise your analysis and lead with the law. Apply the law to the facts.

16. For now I ask you to accept these assertions. Later the material will show you why they are true.

F. THE APPEAL

Again, you probably have a general understanding of what it means to appeal a case, but put it under the microscope to make sure you see if from the proper analytical perspective. As a general rule, what can you appeal, and what can you *not* appeal? (Hint: think of the two planes.) As a general rule, you cannot appeal questions of fact. The facts are determined by the trial court, not the appellate court. The trial court determines the facts and sends them up to the appellate court as part of the record on appeal. As a general rule, you can only appeal questions of law.

Reflect upon that point for a moment. At first blush it does not appear to be that important, but again, put it under the microscope to make sure that you are thinking about it from the proper analytical perspective. In law school, you read cases day in and day out. What level cases do you read—are they trial court opinions or appellate court opinions? They are virtually all appellate court opinions (from either the intermediate court of appeal or the appellate court of last resort, typically called the supreme court).

Because you read appellate opinions in law school, it means that every opinion you read started out as a question of law on appeal. What should the court of appeals do to that question? Keep it simple. The court should *answer* the question. And in an overwhelming majority of the cases you read in law school, the court will tell that you that the question on appeal is a certain *type* of question. Go back to *Pierson v. Post*. In discussing the question on appeal, how did the court describe the question? The court said that the question was "a novel and nice question." Other courts may describe the question as "a new question," "a unique question," or "a question of first impression." When the court uses one of those phrases, what is the court telling you? Most first-year law student gloss over the phrase, not really appreciating the significance of the subtle but important message the court is sending.

If the question on appeal is a question of law, and it is a new question—a question of first impression—when the court answers the question, what is the court really doing? *The court is making law.* The court is not just deciding a dispute between the parties before it. *The court is making law, new law.*

If *you* were on the court of appeals in *Pierson v. Post*, and you realized that in answering the question on appeal you would be *making law*, what should you take into consideration before you make law?[17]

Some students answer that if they were an appellate judge deciding the case, and they knew they were making law in the case, they would take into consideration existing law. If that was your answer, or part of your answer, make sure that you understand the limited relevance of that answer. Is the court bound by

---

17. Again, you might want to take a moment to reflect upon that question and write down your thoughts. What you write—*how* you express it—may give you some insights later into your analytical skills.

existing law? Must the court follow the existing law? No. The new law has to "fit" into the existing legal framework (the existing rules in the area), but the existing law does not bind the court. If the court were bound by existing law, the question would not be a question of first impression. By saying that the question is a new question, a novel question, a question of first impression, the court is telling you that it has determined that existing law does not answer the precise question on appeal. The court is free to create whatever law it thinks best.

So if you were sitting on the court of appeals in *Pierson v. Post*, and you realized that the question on appeal was a question of first impression, what should you take into consideration before you create new law? You should take into consideration *who* will be affected by this new law. Not only will Pierson and Post be affected, this new law will also directly affect all similarly situated parties in society, and indirectly affect all of society. You should take into consideration *the consequences* of any new law — how people will be affected by it *in the future*.

Moreover, in thinking about what law you should create, you should take into consideration *public policy*. What is public policy? Public policy is an abstract concept that is rather open ended. One way to think about public policy is to ask "with respect to this particular issue, what do we as a society value and why"? What type of society do we want and why? What type of behavior do we want to encourage; what type of behavior do we want to discourage?

Notice what we have done to both our timeline and to our abstract planes. First, on the timeline, up until now this case has been about a dispute between two parties, Pierson and Post. A dispute that occurred in the past:

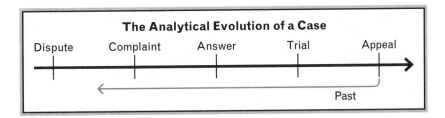

Now that we realize we are not just resolving a dispute between two parties but that we are *making law* in this case, suddenly this case is not about them at all. This case is about all of society; this case is about what type of law we want to affect people's behavior in the future:

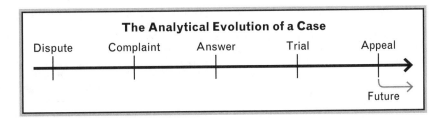

And before the court adopts this new law, it needs to take into consideration relevant public policy considerations. What type of society do we want and why? What do we value? What should be encouraged, and conversely, what should be discouraged? Before the court adopts the new law, it needs to go to *the public policy plane*:

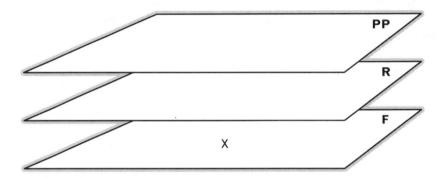

Notice the public policy plane floats *above* the rule plane, which floats *above* the factual plane. The dispute arose on the factual plane. The lawyers went to the rule plane looking for a rule of law which when applied to the factual plane resolved the dispute. On appeal, if the parties disagree on what the rule of law is, and if the question of law is a question of first impression, before the court can answer the question it has to go to the public policy plane. What rule of law does society want and why? After the court analyzes the relevant public policy considerations, it comes back down to the rule plane and adopts a rule of law, which it then applies to the facts of the case on the factual plane to reach the holding in the case — to resolve the dispute before the court.[18]

This conceptual, analytical perspective of how a case evolves, both from a timeline perspective and from the perspective of the three planes, offers a way to classify the different arguments and points a court makes in an opinion that should help you read and analyze a case. It also provides the conceptual framework for how to "think like a lawyer."

---

18. Be careful not to overuse the public policy plane. It often is of relevance in reading and analyzing the cases in the casebook, but how much relevance to the exam will depend on a number of variables. A very high percentage of cases in a casebook are usually cases of first impression where public policy is critical, but not all issues on an exam will be of first impression. In going from the factual plane to the rule plane, if there is a rule that clearly applies the fact pattern, there is little to no need to resort to the public policy plane. The analysis will be simply applying the rule of law to the facts. The public policy plane is most useful when there is a legal issue of first impression, or there are two competing rules of law and arguably both could be applied to the facts, or there is only one rule that applies but the facts fall near the edge of the rule and it is unclear whether the facts come within the scope of the rule. Depending on the class, the professor, and the issues on the exam, it may be of more importance in reading and analyzing the cases than it will be on the exam.

CHAPTER 4

"Thinking Like a Lawyer"

A. A CONCEPTUAL UNDERSTANDING

Many law professors and lawyers argue that you cannot *explain* what it means to think like a lawyer, that you can only *experience* it. I respectfully submit that we have just explained, at least at a conceptual level, what it means to think like a lawyer. On the vertical axis, you need to be able to think on three planes at the same time: the factual plane, the rule plane, and the public policy plane.

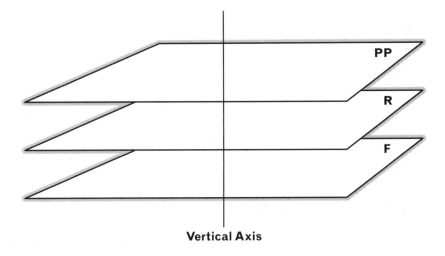

Vertical Axis

And on the horizontal axis, the timeline, you need to be able to think in two directions at the same time:

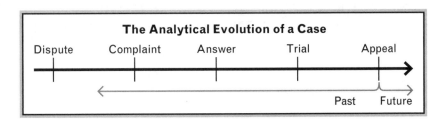

Sometimes you need to be thinking *backwards* about the facts of the case in question, and sometimes you need to be thinking *forwards* about the future consequences of the rule of law you are thinking about adopting.

Every word written in a judicial opinion belongs on one of the three planes. Think about the court's opinion in *Pierson v. Post* for a moment. The court spent most of its opinion discussing the writings of ancient Roman writers: Justinian, Puffendorf, Barbeyrac, and Grotius to name a few. On which plane does that discussion belong? The rule plane. The court was discussing different possible phrasings of the rule statement as articulated by the ancient Roman writers. The issue was *which* rule statement the court should adopt—or whether it should create its own. See how you can break down a judicial opinion differently now when you read it. You can read it from the perspective of the three planes. As you are reading an opinion, ask yourself which plane the court is on at any given time.

Likewise, if you could tape a classroom discussion and analyze each statement made in class, each statement would belong on one of the three planes. Anyone who has experienced law school will tell you that the first week of law school the class discussion appears to be bouncing off the walls, going in all different directions, jumping from point to point. But that is the nature of legal analysis. Sometimes the discussion will be focusing on the factual plane, sometimes it will be focusing on the public policy plane, and sometimes it will be on the rule plane, discussing different possible articulations of the rule statement the court is considering adopting. Sometimes the discussion will be looking backwards at the facts of the dispute, and sometimes the discussion will be looking forwards at different possible consequences of the different possible rule statements under consideration. When you go to class and listen to the discussion, you can analyze it from the perspective of the three planes. Do not listen to the discussion holistically. Classify the nature of the point being made—which plane it is on—and analyze it.

Proper legal analysis requires you to be on the right plane, looking in the right direction, at the right time. No professor is going to tell you which plane you should be on when, but through repetition, through trial and error, by experiencing it through reading and analyzing cases, and through the class discussion, you will master it. Now that you are more conscious of the conceptual nature of the process, however, that will greatly facilitate the transition from "thinking like a layperson" to "thinking like a lawyer." It will also make you better at "thinking like a lawyer" because you will be more conscious of, and confident about, the process.

B. RANKING THE PLANES

1. Which Plane Is the Most Important?

Now that you understand the three planes—the factual, the rule, and the public policy plane—which one is the most important? Admittedly, that question is a bit unfair because it is not a single plane that is the most important; *it is the interaction of the three planes that is the key to legal analysis.* But if you had to identify just one plane to lead with, which plane is the most important? (Hint: why do you read cases in law school?) For the most part, you read cases first and foremost to learn *the rule of law* in the case. If you had to pick one plane to lead with, the most important plane is the rule plane.

What was the case of *Pierson v. Post* about? It was about the rule of *occupancy.* The question of law on appeal was "what constitutes occupancy?" The bulk of the opinion was about what *should* be the rule of occupancy and why.

Back on page 12, the material asked you to think about what you thought *Pierson v. Post* was about. When most students are asked that question, they answer that it is about a person hunting with dogs, Post, who is in hot pursuit of a fox and who was about to catch the fox when another person, Pierson, steps in and kills the fox.[1]

If you are like the typical student, notice the analytical significance of the answer. It over-focuses on the factual plane. If that is consistent with your answer, do not worry. That is natural, classic, first-year law student thinking. Your mind naturally gravitates to the factual plane because that is the part of the case with which you are most familiar and most comfortable. But you want to shift your focus. Lead with the rule plane. That will force you to work harder on your legal analysis skills. Again, why do you read cases in law school? *To learn the rule of law in the case.* The case starts out as a question of law on appeal. When you read and analyze a case, do not read it holistically; instead aggressively dissect it to its different analytical components — its facts, its rule, and its public policy considerations. In particular, find the rule of law the court created in the case.

Moreover, do not accept a *general* understanding of the rule the court adopted. That is what most students accept — a general, conceptual understanding of the rule. They can tell you all sorts of interesting comments *about* the rule, but they have a tough time telling you *the rule. Look for the sentence in the opinion where you think the court answers the question of law on appeal. Find that sentence — the sentence that you think, more than any other sentence in the opinion, constitutes the rule of law that you are to take away from the case.* Write that sentence down (ideally in your brief — we will discuss briefing later in greater detail). Take that sentence to class. Listen carefully to the class discussion. You can use that sentence to help critique the class discussion, but more importantly, you can use that sentence to evaluate the development of your analytical skills. Is that the sentence that the professor and the class discussion seem to be focusing on as the rule of law from the case? If so, you are doing a good job of developing your analytical skills. If not, you need to work harder

---

1. If you wrote down your thoughts, focus carefully on the words you used. Did you include the word "occupancy" in you description of the case? Or does your description look more like the typical student description — does it include references to the fox and the hunters and what they were doing?

on thinking about what is *a* rule of law in the abstract and what is *the* rule of law you should be extracting from each case you read.

2. Which Plane Is the Second Most Important?

If the rule plane is the most important plane, which plane is the second most important plane? Again, this question is a tad unfair, because *the key to legal analysis is the interaction of the three planes*. But if you had to identify one plane as the second most important, which plane would you select? Think about it analytically. Once you find the sentence that you think is the rule the court adopted in the case, what should you ask yourself? *Why? Why* did the court adopt the rule it did? That question should direct you to which part of the court's opinion? The court's discussion of the relevant public policy considerations. The public policy plane is the second most important plane. Even if your professor does not focus on it much, analytically it will help you understand the rule if you know and understand *why* the court adopted the rule it did.

3. Which Plane Is the Least Important?

Each plane has its relevance, but at least for now, the least important plane is the factual plane. Yet that plane is the plane most students lead with. Think back to the question on page 12 that asked you to think about what the case was about.[2] Which plane did you lead with? If you are like most students, you led with the facts of the case — you led with the factual plane. If you did, you are leading with the least important plane. *Shift your focus.* When you think of a case now, think first of rule of law you learned in that case, the rule of law you are supposed to take away from that case. *Pierson v. Post* is about the rule of occupancy, not about a fox on the beach.

If your answer to the question "what is *Pierson v. Post* about?" back on page 12 included a reference to occupancy, your analytical skills are off to a good start. Keep it up, and be more conscious of it. But do not settle with saying that the case is about the rule of occupancy. Can you *state* what the rule of occupancy is? The whole rule? Can you state it in one, succinct sentence? You need to know the rule statement just as well as you know the name of the rule. On the exam, you will apply *the rule statement* to the facts, *not the name of the rule.* Your goal is to know the full rule statement and to be able to write it, and apply it, on the exam.

To say that the factual plane is the least important plane is *not* saying that the factual plane is unimportant. Comparatively speaking, it is the least important, but it is still important. After the court adopts the rule of law, it applies the rule of law to the facts of the case to reach *the holding* in the case (the outcome of this particular dispute in this particular fact pattern). You want to carefully critique

---

2. If you wrote down your thoughts, focus carefully on the words you used. Analyze them relative to the different planes that the material has introduced you to.

the court's application of the rule of law to the facts. Which part or parts of the rule, or *elements* as the different parts of the rule are commonly called in law school, are satisfied by the facts? Which parts of the rule, or elements, are "in dispute" — are subject to good faith arguments on both sides of the element? If the plaintiff's claim fails, *why* does it fail?

Notice how analysis of the case revolves around the rule plane. Answering the question "*why* did the court adopt *the rule* it did?" requires you to be able to analyze the relationship between the *rule* plane and the *public policy* plane — the rule statement adopted by the court in light of the relevant public policy considerations. Answering the question "*why* did the court reach *the holding* it did?" requires you to be able to analyze the *rule* plane and the *factual* plane — the particular rule statement adopted by the court and how it applies to the facts of this case.

The facts of the case are also important because they help you develop the skill of knowing how to "spot an issue," the first step to doing well on the typical law school exam. We will discuss that skill in greater detail in a later chapter on exam taking. For now, remember that while comparatively the factual plane is the least important of the three planes, it is still an important plane.

Legal analysis is the interaction of the three planes, but lead with the rule plane first, the public policy plane second, and the factual plane last. If you are like the typical student, you need to shift your focus. If you do, it will help you master what it means to think like a lawyer.

CHAPTER 5

Re-analyzing *Pierson v. Post*

Now that you have a better understanding of what a case is and how it evolves analytically, re-analyze the court's opinion in *Pierson v. Post*.

A. APPELLATE OPINION = QUESTION OF *LAW*

Remember that *Pierson v. Post* is an appellate opinion. As such, it is about a question of law. The particular question of law that was on appeal in *Pierson v. Post* was what constitutes occupancy.

Do you think Pierson and Post are going to agree on what the answer to the question of law should be? Of course not. If they did, there would be no appeal. Post wants a rule of occupancy that when applied to the facts will result in him prevailing. Pierson wants a rule of occupancy that when applied to the facts will result in him prevailing. The court of appeals will always have at least two different rule statements to choose from when trying to decide how to answer the question on appeal — the rule statement offered by the plaintiff and the rule statement offered by the defendant. This can be visualized on the three planes by picturing more than one rule of law on the rule plane:

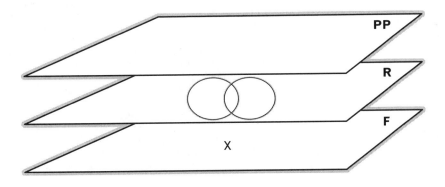

B. FIND THE ANSWER—THE RULE OF LAW

Take a moment to re-read the majority opinion and the dissent in *Pierson v. Post*.[1] Who won on appeal? Pierson. So the majority adopted a rule of occupancy that favors Pierson. The dissent preferred a rule of law that would have favored Post.

See if you can find the sentences in the respective opinions that constitute the respective rule statements. You probably will find this task harder than it sounds. Reading an opinion and being able to extract the rule of law from it is an art, a skill, that is learned by doing (like learning how to ride a bike). You should not expect to be able to do it well on the first day of law school, and the ease with which you can identify the sentence varies with the quality of the opinion (yes, some judicial opinions are better written than others).

First, re-read the dissent in *Pierson v. Post*, this time looking for *the sentence* where you think the dissent sets forth the rule it would have adopted if it had been the majority opinion (in this particular case it is easier to pick the proposed rule sentence out of the dissent; that is why it is recommended you start with the dissent in this case). In re-reading the dissent, remember the issue is what constitutes occupancy, i.e., what is necessary to acquire a property interest in a wild animal?[2]

---

1. What is the relevance of the dissenting opinion? From a technical legal perspective, a dissenting opinion has absolutely no value. The majority opinion constitutes the opinion in the case, it sets forth the rule of law adopted in the case and the holding in the case. The majority opinion is binding authority on all lower courts in the jurisdiction. If "the same" fact pattern arises again, the lower courts are required to apply the same rule and come to the same holding. The dissenting opinion constitutes, at best, persuasive authority. If the same case comes up in another jurisdiction, the court in that jurisdiction may be persuaded by the dissent's reasoning to adopt the dissent's proposed rule of law and opinion as opposed to the majority's rule of law and opinion. (The court would not literally adopt the dissent's opinion; it would write its own opinion, but it would adopt the reasoning and proposed rule of law in the dissent's opinion.) But while a dissenting opinion carries no weight as a technical legal perspective, from an analytical perspective, a dissenting opinion is of great value because it gives you greater insights into the court's analysis. One way to think of a dissenting opinion is it is an alternative opinion—an opinion that if it had been the majority opinion typically would have adopted a different rule of law that typically would have favored the party who lost on appeal.

The fact that a dissenting opinion has no precedential value is reflected in the different wording used to describe the majority opinion versus the dissenting opinion. When talking about the majority opinion, it is appropriate to refer to it as "the court's opinion" since a majority of the court sided with it. You would never describe a dissenting opinion as "the court's opinion"—it is only a dissenting opinion, something less than a majority. Moreover, in describing the majority opinion you would say "the court held . . ." or "the court ruled. . . ." You would never say "the dissent held . . ." or "the dissent ruled . . ." because the dissenting opinion has no legal authority. Instead you would say "the dissent *argued*. . . ."

2. Again, you might want to write down on a separate piece of paper the sentence where you think the dissent answers the question of what is necessary to acquire a property interest in a wild animal. Writing it down will permit you to come back later and evaluate how well you did when the material answers the question.

Then re-read the majority opinion looking for *the sentence* where you think the majority sets forth the rule of law it is adopting for occupancy—where it answers what is necessary to acquire a property interest in a wild animal.[3]

The dissent wanted a rule of law, a rule of occupancy, that basically said that one can acquire a property interest in a wild animal as long as (1) one has manifested an intent to appropriate the animal to his or her individual use; and (2) he or she is within reach or has a reasonable prospect of capturing the animal.[4]

The majority adopted a different rule of law. The majority ruled that to acquire a property interest in a wild animal, to establish occupancy, one must prove that he or she had an intent to appropriate the animal to his or her individual use, deprive the animal of its natural liberty, and bring it within his or her certain control.[5]

While these two rule statements may not have been the exact rule statements the respective parties argued for on appeal, it is easy to see how one rule statement favors one party while the other rule statement favors the other. Post

---

3. Again, you might want to write down on a separate piece of paper the sentence where you think the majority answers the question of what is necessary to acquire a property interest in a wild animal. Writing it down will permit you to come back later and evaluate how well you did when the material answers the question.

4. See the dissent's opinion where it argues as follows: "[P]roperty in animals feroe naturoe may be acquired without bodily touch or manucaption, provided the pursuer be within reach, or have a reasonable prospect (which certainly existed here) of taking what he has thus discovered with an intention of converting to his own use." *See supra* page 11, last sentence of the second to last paragraph of the dissenting opinion.

5. The majority ruled that occupancy is established when "the pursuer manifests an unequivocal intention of appropriating the animal to his individual use, has deprived him of his natural liberty, and brought him within his certain control." *See supra* page 9, second full paragraph, middle of the paragraph.

Students tend to have a much more difficult time finding the rule sentence in the majority opinion. Some students think it is the sentence where the court says "Justinian's Institutes . . . and Fleta . . . adopt the principle, that pursuit alone vests no property or right in the huntsman; and that even pursuit, accompanied with wounding, is equally ineffectual for that purpose, unless the animal be actually taken." There are two problems with that sentence as a rule statement. First, the court is only telling us what those commentators say; it does not tell us that the court has *adopted* their approach. More importantly, that sentence tells you what does *not* qualify as occupancy. A rule statement typically will contain elements that must be established to invoke the rule. Some students like the sentence where the court says "That is to say, that actual bodily seizure is not indispensable to acquire right to, or possession of, wild beasts; but that, on the contrary, the mortal wounding of such beasts, by one not abandoning his pursuit, may, with the utmost propriety, be deemed possession of him. . . ." Again, the first part of that quote tells you what is *not* necessary to establish occupancy, so it is not a good candidate to be the rule statement; and the second half of that quotation gives *examples* of what constitutes occupancy but is not a generic statement of the rule that could be applied to a variety of fact patterns to determine whether the party has established occupancy. Some students like the sentence where the court says "So, also, encompassing and securing such animals with nets and toils, or otherwise intercepting them in such a manner as to deprive them of their natural liberty, and render escape impossible, may justly be deemed to give possession of them to those persons who, by their industry and labor, have used such means of apprehending them." Again, however, this sentence is more about *examples of what constitutes* occupancy than what *is* occupancy.

wanted the rule of "hot pursuit plus reasonable prospect of capture"; Pierson wanted the rule of "certain control." The choice the court had to make on appeal was whether to adopt Post's proposed rule, Pierson's proposed rule, or some other rule statement that it created.

Issue Statement	Proposed Rule Statements
	Intent to appropriate to individual use, plus either have the animal within reach or have a reasonable prospect of capturing it
What constitutes occupancy?	
	Intent to appropriate to individual use, deprive the animal of its natural liberty, and bring the animal within certain control

At a generic level, in every appellate opinion the court must choose between at least two different possible rule statements. The parties will be proposing different answers to the question of law on appeal in the form of their different proposed rule statements. Legal analysis inherently involves being able to analyze the appellate court's decision-making process. The court has to pick between the two proposed rule statements (or create one of its own), and explain why it picked it. Put the court's decision-making process in *Pierson v. Post* under the microscope.

C. FIND THE RATIONALE FOR THE RULE: THE PUBLIC POLICY

Assume you are on the court of appeals and the case of *Pierson v. Post* is being argued before you. Which rule statement *should* you adopt? Again, the competing rule statements can be visualized as circles on the rule plane:

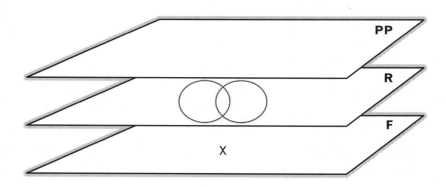

Analytically, whenever you have to choose between two items, which one should you pick? You pick the *better* one. How does a court determine which rule statement is the better one? The court has to go to the public policy plane. With respect to the legal issue in question, the court has to ask what are the relevant public policy considerations and why? What type of society do we want and why? The relevant public policy considerations can be depicted on the public policy plane as a set of asterisks:

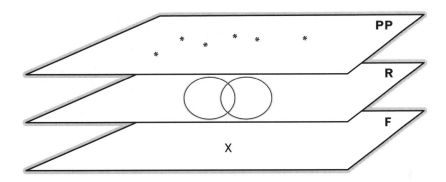

Notice *first* the court should identify all the relevant public policy considerations, and then it must *analyze* the different public policy considerations to determine which are *the most important.* Then the court has to decide which rule statement does the better job of promoting the more important public policy considerations. If you are going to analyze a rule of law fully, you must start by identifying and analyzing the relevant public policy considerations: what purpose does the law serve in our society.[6]

What were the principal public policy considerations in *Pierson v. Post?* What policy arguments did the dissent advance in favor of its rule of occupancy? What policy arguments did the majority advance in favor of its rule of law? Take a moment to re-read the opinions to see if you can find the policy arguments. See if you can find what were the primary public policy arguments advanced by the dissent and the majority.[7]

The dissent describes the fox as what type of an animal? A *noxious* beast. Why is the fox a noxious beast? Foxes eat farmers' chickens, thereby reducing the supply

---

6. That, however, is a very time-consuming process. Do not expect your professors to analyze fully each and every rule of law in the course. If he or she did so, you would not cover very many rules. Your professor will pick and choose which rules he or she wants to analyze fully and which rules he or she will analyze in a more abbreviated manner.

7. Again, you might want to write down on a separate piece of paper the sentence the public policy arguments advanced by the majority opinion and the dissenting opinion in support of their respective positions. Try to write down the exact wording used in the respective opinions. Writing it down will permit you to evaluate how well you did when the material provides the respective public policy arguments.

of chickens that can be brought to market, thereby driving up the cost of chickens for consumers. From a societal perspective, is that good or bad? Bad. So what does the dissent say society would prefer with respect to the fox? Maximize the kill of foxes. Does that statement belong on the factual plane, the rule plane, or the public policy plane? The public policy plane. The dissent's paramount public policy consideration is that the rule of occupancy should be one that maximizes the kill of foxes because foxes are noxious beasts that harm farmers and consumers.

What did the majority say were its paramount public policy considerations? Another way of asking that question when analyzing the court's opinion is to ask *why* the court adopted the rule statement that it did. In *Pierson v. Post*, the court said it adopted the rule it did to promote peace and certainty, and to reduce quarrels and litigation. At first blush one might depict the analysis the court performed on appeal as follows:

Issue Statement	Proposed Rule Statements	Public Policy Considerations
	Intent to appropriate to individual use, + either have the animal within reach or have a reasonable prospect of capturing it	Maximize kill of foxes
What constitutes occupancy?		
	Intent to appropriate to individual use, deprive of natural liberty, + bring within certain control	Promote peace + certainty, minimize quarrels

1. Did the Court Get It Right?

Did the court get it right? Many professors like to ask that question, but notice that question is ambiguous. Did the court get it right on which plane? To properly analyze whether the court got it right, first you must analyze whether you think the court properly identified and analyzed the relevant public policy considerations. Assuming the court did a good job of analyzing the relevant public policy considerations, then you must analyze whether the rule of law the court adopted does a good job of promoting the paramount public policy considerations. Assuming the rule of law the court adopted does a good job of promoting the relevant public policy considerations, then you must analyze whether the court did a good job of applying the rule it adopted to the facts of the case. Proper analysis of a case requires proper analysis of all three planes.

2. Justice and Fairness

How come neither the majority nor the dissent identified and analyzed justice and fairness as relevant public policy considerations? Should not the law be concerned with justice and fairness? The public policy considerations of justice and fairness beg the question: justice and fairness *to whom*? To the parties in the case or to society? As between the parties, Pierson arguably was a jerk (the point implicitly made by the court when it admitted that "[h]owever uncourteous or unkind the conduct of Pierson towards Post, in this instance, may have been, yet this act was productive of no injury or damage for which a legal remedy can be applied"). Pierson knew that Post was in hot pursuit of the fox and was closing in on the fox, but instead of being courteous and letting Post play out the chase, Pierson stepped in and killed the fox. If justice and fairness *between the parties* were the controlling consideration, Post arguably should have prevailed.

But in this case the court is *making law*. The court's primarily concern is what is in *society's* best interest. The court needs to focus more on the rule and public policy planes than on the dispute between the two parties — i.e., than on the factual plane. As simple as that sentence sounds, it may be one of the most important points to remember in reading and analyzing cases. Law students tend to see the case as a dispute between the parties and tend to over-focus on the factual plane. Because the cases selected for study in law school typically involve a "question of first impression," however, the court of appeals sees it as a case where the court will be *making law*. Because it is making law, the court has a responsibility to focus more on the rule and public policy planes.

Inasmuch as most of the cases you read in law school are cases of first impression, you too should shift your focus more to the rule and public policy planes. That focus is critical to learning how to "think like a lawyer." Once you shift your focus to the rule and public policy planes, the questions of justice and fairness become more difficult because these considerations typically are subsumed in the analysis of the *particular* public policy considerations raised by the *particular* legal issue. The law is very much concerned with justice and fairness — only it is a question of justice and fairness *to whom* and how that is intertwined with the *particular* public policy considerations raised by the issue.

Back to the choice the court was facing in *Pierson v. Post*. The court had to choose between two competing proposed rules and sets of policy considerations:

Issue Statement	Proposed Rule Statements	Public Policy Considerations
	Intent to appropriate to individual use, + either have the animal within reach or have a reasonable prospect of capturing it	Maximize kill of foxes
What constitutes occupancy?	Intent to appropriate to individual use, deprive of natural liberty, + bring within certain control	Promote peace + certainty, minimize quarrels

The court adopted the rule favored by Pierson:

Issue Statement	Proposed Rule Statements	Public Policy Considerations
	Intent to appropriate to individual use, + either have the animal within reach or have a reasonable prospect of capturing it	Maximize kill of foxes
What constitutes occupancy?	Intent to appropriate to individual use, deprive of natural liberty, + bring within certain control	Promote peace + certainty, minimize quarrels

You can visualize the rule of law the court selected by bolding one of the circles on the rule plane, the rule statement that the court concluded did a better job of promoting the more important public policy considerations:

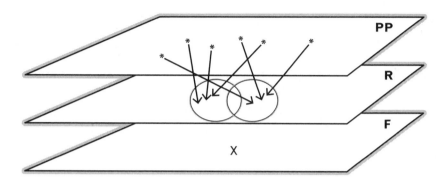

The exact size and scope of the circle depends upon the wording in the rule statement. Which leads to the question: how precise should you be in your wording of the rule of law? Should you sweat the words that you put in your rule statement or are you free to paraphrase it — put it in your own words — so that it is easier to recall? Is a general understanding of the rule in the case sufficient or do you need to know the precise wording of the rule?

The general answer is that you need to be very careful about how you word your rule statements. The words in the rule statement can be broken down into two types of words, the operative words (the key terms) and the filler words. The operative words define the scope of the rule, the size of the circle on the rule plane. You need to sweat the details of the operative words and be as precise as possible. If you change any of the key, operative words, you are potentially changing the rule of law. The filler words do not matter (as long as your final rule statement reads like a well-written sentence), but the key, operative words are critical. Your goal is to write the perfect rule sentence; write your rule statement just like a court would write it.

Once you find the sentence in the opinion that you think is the rule sentence, ask yourself *"why* did the court adopt that rule of law"? That question will naturally lead you to the court's discussion of the relevant public policy considerations surrounding the particular issue on appeal. Even if your professor does not emphasize public policy, you should at least think about it. You will quickly learn in law school that you can *know* a rule without *understanding* it. You may know the words that make up the rule statement, but if you do not understand the rule, you probably will have a difficult time applying it on the exam to a new fact pattern.

Your goal is *not* just to *know* a rule; your goal is to *understand* the rule: to have complete command of the rule. Complete command of a rule requires an understanding of the public policy considerations pertaining to it (pro and con). If you understand the public policy considerations that underlie a rule of law, you will understand the rule of law. If you understand the rule of law, not only will it facilitate your application of it to a fact pattern, you will also find that it will help you recall the rule of law. If you understand a rule of law, it will make sense, it will be logical, and it will be easier to recall and apply on an exam.

D. THE HOLDING

After you find the rule statement in a case, and the public policy considerations that support it, ask yourself "*how* did this case come out"? The outcome of the case — the application of the rule to the facts of the case before the court — is the holding in the case. How is the *particular dispute between the parties in the case* resolved?

E. THE RATIONALE FOR THE HOLDING

After you determine the holding, ask yourself "*why* did this case come out the way it did"? That will shift your focus to the court's application of the rule to the facts of this case — to the relationship between the rule plane and the factual plane.

In *Pierson v. Post*, why did Post lose? The court ruled that to establish occupancy in a wild animal, the claimant must show that he or she had the intent to appropriate the animal to his or her individual use, he or she must deprive the animal of its natural liberty, and he or she must bring the animal within his or her certain control.

1. Analyze Each Element

In analyzing the relationship between the rule plane and the factual plane, start by breaking the rule statement into its elements. How many elements are there in the rule of occupancy? Three: the claimant must prove that he or she (1) had the intent to appropriate the animal to his or her individual use; (2) deprived the animal of its natural liberty; and (3) brought the animal under his or her certain control. Analysis of each element means pairing up the element with the relevant facts from the fact pattern.

2. See Both Sides

How would you *analyze* the first element — whether the claimant had the intent to appropriate the animal to his individual use? Do not play judge too fast. Do not jump to a conclusion. Instead *think about the facts from the perspective of each of the parties*. In particular, ask yourself whether the party who bears the burden of proving the element can make a good faith argument based upon the facts that the element has been satisfied. Then, ask yourself whether the opposing party can make a good faith element based on the facts that the element has not been satisfied.

With respect to the *first* element, Post can make a good faith argument that the element of the intent to appropriate the animal to his individual use is satisfied because he was chasing the animal with his dogs and hounds, attempting to capture it. Those actions manifest his intent to appropriate the fox to his individual use. Does Pierson have a good faith argument that Post did not satisfy the element? Not really. So the analysis of the first element is pretty straightforward.

What about the second element? How would you analyze the second element — that he deprived the wild animal of its natural liberty? Most students say that Post cannot show that he deprived the fox of its natural liberty. But *do not jump to a conclusion*. Instead ask yourself if the party who bears the burden of proof has a good faith argument that it was satisfied. Can Post make a good faith argument based on the facts that he satisfied the element? Post can argue that because he was chasing the fox down the beach with his dogs and hounds, the fox was not free to go wherever it wished, evidence that he had deprived the fox of its natural liberty. Does Pierson have a counterargument? Sure. Pierson will argue that because the fox was still running up and down the beach it still had its natural liberty. Whether Post's argument or Pierson's argument is the winning argument depends on what constitutes "depriving the animal of its natural liberty." But that issue is moot[8] because of the third element.

Does Post have a good faith argument that he had the animal under his certain control? Not really. The fox was still running down the beach. While Post may have a good faith argument that he deprived the fox of its natural liberty, he does not have a good faith argument that he had the fox under his *certain* control. Because Post cannot prove all three elements, he cannot establish occupancy. Without occupancy, he does not have a property interest in the fox. Without a property interest in the fox, he has no cause of action against Pierson for trespass on the case (wrongfully interfering with Post's *property* interest). By applying the rule to the facts of this case, you have come to, and properly analyzed, the holding in this case.

The holding in the case can be visualized on the three planes. Based on the court's holding, should the "x" on the fact pattern fall within the shadow the rule casts on the factual plane or outside of the shadow?

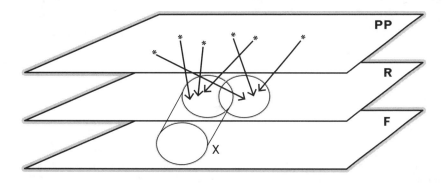

---

8. Moot means it is of no significance or importance.

The "x" falls just outside the shadow the rule casts on the factual plane because the court concluded that not all of the elements of the rule were satisfied; the rule did not entitle Post to the relief he was seeking.

Notice that proper *analysis* of the facts *requires* a *complete and accurate rule statement*. You apply the rule to the facts. While legal analysis requires you to analyze the relationship between and among all three planes — the rule, the public policy, and the factual plane — at most law schools most professors will focus primarily on the relationship between the lower two planes, both in class and on the exam.[9] You need to be comfortable with that degree of legal analysis at a minimum. Often the class discussion gives students the impression that the factual plane is the most important plane. But do not be mislead: the rule plane is the most important because it is the starting point for proper analysis of the factual plane. The factual plane is important, but lead with the rule plane.

F. RECAP

Almost every opinion you read in law school will be an appellate opinion. The court's opinion should answer the question on appeal by adopting a rule. Before the court can decide which rule to adopt, it should raise and analyze the public policy considerations that are relevant to the issue on appeal. After adopting the rule of law, the court reaches the holding in the case by applying the rule to the facts of the case. In *Pierson v. Post*, at the factual level, Pierson prevailed because Post could not satisfy the elements required to establish what is required to have a property interest in the fox.

G. GET COMFORTABLE WITH THE RULE

Inasmuch as the rule plane is the most important plane, you should spend some time with each rule to get comfortable with it. Along these lines, go back to the two proposed rule statements that were being debated in *Pierson v. Post*.

---

9. Under the traditional approach to law school, most of your professors will assume that you are smart enough to analyze and understand the rule and factual planes on your own and they will spend most, if not all, of their time in class on the public policy plane. But do not be mislead. Come exam time they will expect you to show on the exam that you know and understand all three planes, and in particular, how the rule and factual planes interact.

Issue Statement	Proposed Rule Statements
What constitutes occupancy?	Intent to appropriate to the animal to individual use, deprive the animal of its natural liberty, and bring the animal within certain control
	Intent to appropriate to individual use, + either have the animal within reach or have a reasonable prospect of capturing it

Whenever you learn a new rule of law, I encourage you to ask two questions about the rule to help you get more comfortable with it.

1. The Scope of the Rule

First, what is the *scope* of the rule? This is a rather abstract question. First-year law students often have some difficulty thinking about it. One way to think about the question is if you were to draw a circle on the rule plane that represented the rule, what would be the *size* of that circle? This type of analysis is tough, particularly when dealing with a single rule in isolation. But that is part of the beauty of *Pierson v. Post*. Because there is a dissenting opinion with its own proposed rule statement, you can perform the analysis comparatively.

Between the two possible rule statements (the dissent's and the majority's), which one is broader andwhich one is narrower? Another way to think about that question is to ask which one encompasses more fact patterns? To the extent the circle on the rule plane casts a shadow down onto the factual plane, and all fact patterns that come within that shadow come within the scope of the rule, which rule casts a broader shadow and which rule casts a narrower shadow?

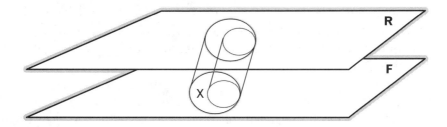

The dissent's proposed rule statement is broader than the majority's rule statement. Post arguably came within the scope of the dissent's rule statement. He arguably had demonstrated the intent to appropriate the animal to his individual use by chasing it, and he arguably had a reasonable prospect of capturing it. Post did not, however, come within the scope of the majority's rule statement. He did not have the fox within his certain control. Thus, the majority's rule statement is narrower.

Why is the scope of a rule relevant? First, the analysis of the scope gives you a better understanding of the rule, which is always important. Second, the broader the rule statement, the easier it is for a professor to create a fact pattern on the exam that raises the issue — but the material will discuss that in more detail later when it covers issue spotting.

2. The Sharpness of the Rule

In addition to analyzing the scope of a rule, you should also analyze whether the rule is a "bright-line rule" or a "soft, fact-sensitive" rule. One way to think about that question is to visualize the rule as a circle on the rule plane. Focus on the line that constitutes the outer edge of the circle. Is that line a "bright" line so that it is relatively easy to tell if a fact pattern is inside or outside the circle, or is that line a soft, fact-sensitive line so that it is difficult to tell if a fact pattern is inside or outside the circle? Bright-line rule statements tend to be rather black and white, relatively easy to apply and analyze. Soft, fact-sensitive rules tend to have a lot of "grey" area around their edges so that often it is difficult to tell if a fact pattern is inside or outside the rule.

Look back again at the two possible rule statements at issue in *Pierson v. Post*:

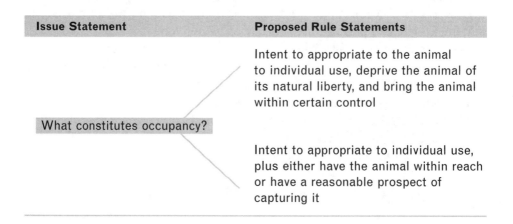

Issue Statement	Proposed Rule Statements
	Intent to appropriate to the animal to individual use, deprive the animal of its natural liberty, and bring the animal within certain control
What constitutes occupancy?	
	Intent to appropriate to individual use, plus either have the animal within reach or have a reasonable prospect of capturing it

Which rule is more bright-line and which rule is more soft, fact-sensitive? The dissent's rule (the second rule above) is the softer, more fact-sensitive. What constitutes "within reach" and what constitutes a "reasonable" prospect of capturing? Those terms are more open-ended and ambiguous compared to "certain" control.

What is the relevance of whether a rule is bright-line or soft, fact-sensitive? In general, bright-line rules tend to be more open and shut, giving rise to less of a chance to raise and analyze counterarguments on an exam (though given the appropriate fact pattern, *any rule* can be fact-sensitive). If a bright-line rule applies to an issue on the exam, assuming a rather typical fact pattern, you should probably get in and out of the issue fairly quickly. On the other hand, if the rule is a soft, fact-sensitive rule, in general such rules tend to lend themselves to a good faith argument-counterargument discussion on an exam. Proper analysis of a soft, fact-sensitive rule tends to take more time. If the rule is a soft, fact-sensitive rule you should expect to raise and include the proper counterarguments on the exam. Being aware of the nature of the rule before the exam will help you identity those issues on the exam that are more likely to entail counterarguments.

H. CONCLUSION

Legal analysis stretches your analytical skills. On the vertical axis, you need to be able to think on three planes simultaneously — the rule plane, the public policy plane, and the factual plane. On the horizontal axis, legal analysis requires you to be able to think in two directions simultaneously — backwards at the facts of the case in question and forwards to possible consequences of any proposed rule.

Now that you have a better understanding of how to read and analyze a case, this will help you understand how you should brief a case.

CHAPTER 6

Briefing a Case from an Analytical Perspective

A. INTRODUCTION

Why do law students brief cases? Most law students brief cases because of "herd mentality." They brief cases because they heard they are supposed to brief cases; they brief cases because they heard that is what everybody else is doing. But they do not know *why* they are supposed to brief cases. This problem is compounded by the fact that most law students are given relatively little instruction on *how* to brief. Any guidance a student does receive tends to be so general and vague that it is of little help.

The result is most law students *start* law school spending countless hours briefing cases, but not too long into law school they *stop* briefing cases. Why do they stop? Because they realize they are not getting much out of their briefs. They do not see how briefing fits into the big picture; they do not understand *why* they are briefing or *how* they are supposed to brief. They are just going through the motions — a very labor-intensive and time-consuming process. But briefing can, and does, play an important role in developing your legal analysis skills when properly understood and properly performed.

B. TYPICAL BRIEF

First and foremost, you brief a case to help you analyze the case. The problem is most law students fail to see the connection between briefing and legal analysis. This failure means most law students who attempt to brief cases end up developing bad habits that are only reinforced the longer they brief. And bad briefing habits typically lead to and reinforce bad legal analysis habits. The only silver lining to the fact that most law students stop briefing rather early on in law school is that this minimizes the damage done by the bad briefing habits.

You can test the hypothetical that bad briefing reinforces bad legal analysis by thinking back to page 14 where the material encouraged you to brief *Pierson v. Post*. Whether you wrote out that brief or just thought about it (mentally briefed it), you created that brief before you understood what it meant to analyze a case — to think like a lawyer. You created that brief under the same conditions most law students write briefs — with very little understanding of *why* you were briefing the case or *how* to brief it. If you are like the typical student, your brief probably reads something like the following:

PIERSON v. POST
(New York Supreme Court 1805)

FACTS: Post was hunting with his dogs and hounds when he spied a fox. He and his dogs and hounds were in hot pursuit of the fox, and apparently were about to catch the fox, when Pierson, who was walking by and saw all of this, killed the fox.

PROCEDURAL POSTURE: At the trial court level, the jury found for Post. Pierson appealed.

ISSUE: Who gets the fox?/Who has a stronger claim to the fox?/Is Post entitled to the fox?/Did Post acquire a property interest in the fox?/Did Post have occupancy of the fox?

HOLDING: Pierson prevails./Post loses.

RATIONALE: Pierson prevails because Post did not have occupancy./ Pierson prevails because Post did not have actual possession of the fox.

CRITIQUE: Post should have prevailed because he put forth all the work and it is unfair for Pierson to reap the benefit.

No doubt the brief you created (mentally or in written form) does not look exactly like this, but again, if you are like the typical student, it probably is not that different — it probably is more like this brief than not. The key question, for both this brief and your brief, is how much "good" legal analysis does it reflect?

You should *brief* cases to practice and develop your legal analysis skills, your ability to think like a lawyer. Thinking like a lawyer requires you to think on the rule plane, the factual plane, and the public policy plane at the same time, and in two temporal directions at the same time, forwards and backwards. To the extent you should lead with one plane, you want to lead with the rule plane first, the public policy plane second, and the factual plane third. Why do you read cases? *You read cases to learn the rule of law adopted in the case, to learn* why *the court adopted that rule, and then to understand the holding in the case* — the application of the rule to this particular fact pattern. How much legal analysis is reflected in the typical brief set forth above?[1]

As the typical brief above evidences, most student briefs over-emphasize the factual plane. The typical student briefs the case *almost exclusively* on the factual plane. If you quickly re-read the representative student brief, you will notice there is no rule statement *anywhere* in it. At best the typical student brief may

---

1. If you wrote out your brief, how much legal analysis is reflected in your original brief?

make a passing reference to the name of the rule, but typically the brief will not contain a statement of the rule the student is expected to learn and take away from the case.

Go back and compare the typical student brief to your brief. Did you brief the case primarily on the factual plane? Does your brief refer to occupancy or actual occupancy? If so, does it reference it in such a way that you clearly understand the rule the court adopted — the rule you are expected to take away from the case — or does your brief make only passing reference to the doctrine when talking primarily about the facts of the case? *Does your brief contain a rule statement*: a statement of the rule you should take away from the case; a statement of *the rule, the whole rule, and nothing but the rule*? If you are like the typical student, the chance that your brief contains the rule statement for occupancy is low. Does the brief include a discussion of *why* the court adopted that proposed rule and not another rule statement? Does it include any reference to the relevant public policy considerations? Again, if you are like the typical student, the chance that you have any references to the relevant public policy considerations is low. A well-written brief should include a discussion of the rule plane and the public policy plane, but most students tend to brief almost exclusively on the factual plane.[2]

So *why do* students brief cases? And *how* should they brief them?

C. WHY YOU SHOULD BRIEF YOUR CASES

You should brief the cases you read to help develop your legal analysis skills — your ability to think like a lawyer.

First, writing clarifies one's thinking. After reading a case, most law students will tell you they understand the case. But they understand it at a very general, holistic level. That does not mean they have *analyzed* it. Forcing yourself to write out your analysis in a brief will force you to be more critical of your understanding of the case.

Second, briefing a case forces you to take a stand, to state your analysis of the case. That may not sound that important, but you need a tangible record of your analysis so that later you can critique and assess it. Students who do not brief the cases they read often fool themselves into thinking they are doing a better job of reading and analyzing than they actually are. This is because all they have is a general understanding of the case in their heads. When they go into class and hear what the professor and class discussion have to say about the case, they say

---

2. If you did brief the case, and if your brief did not include the rule statement or the relevant public policy considerations, do not be too harsh on yourself. You were not given much guidance as to *why* or *how* to brief the case. In that respect you were in the same position as many new law students who fail to see the connection between briefing and analyzing cases.

to themselves "yeah, that is what I got out of the case." They employ "revisionist" analysis, unconsciously assuring themselves that is what they got out of the case when they read it when in reality they did not. If, however, you write out your brief of the case, you have a fixed record of what you thought the case was about when you read it—before you go into class. You can compare your analysis to the class' analysis. If you are honest with yourself, by listening carefully to the professor's comments and to the class discussion, you should be able to critique how well you analyzed the case—how well you are developing your legal analysis skills.

That is why in theory when you brief a case, it is important to write out your brief. The problem is that in practice most law students' briefs provide little opportunity for self-critique because the students receive such little guidance as to *why* and *how* to brief that they have no way of evaluating their briefs. The typical student briefs the case only on the factual plane. The typical class discussion tries to shift the focus more to the rule and public policy plane. Because there is so much disjoint between the typical student's brief and the typical class analysis, most students see little relationship between their brief and what happens in class. Hence the reason most students stop briefing relatively early on in law school.

Third, you should brief the cases you read because it helps to prepare you for the Socratic discussion in class. One way to think about the Socratic discussion is that the students are responsible for presenting the case, for analyzing the case. Most law students find the Socratic approach a bit intimidating. Having a written summary of the case helps the typical student handle the Socratic approach when called upon. The problem is their brief helps them only to the extent they have properly briefed the case. The typical student brief helps a student present the facts of the case, but after that, how much it helps depends on how well the student has briefed the case. The typical student brief is of marginal benefit because it has briefed the case almost exclusively on the factual plane; it has over-focused on the factual plane. The typical brief usually has a great statement of the facts so the student can start the Socratic dialogue, but it is of limited use after that. First-year law students realize the deficiencies of their briefs fairly quickly, but they do not know how to improve them—hence the reason most law students stop briefing relatively early on in law school.

You need to understand *why* you should brief cases to understand *how* you should brief cases. First and foremost you brief cases to develop your legal analysis skills—your ability to think like a lawyer. Thinking like a lawyer means you need to be able to think on all three planes simultaneously: the rule plane, the factual plane, and the public policy plane. Legal analysis is the interaction of the three planes. All of this should be reflected in your case brief for each case (to the extent the court opinion covers all three planes). Now that you have a better appreciation for *why* you brief cases, you should have a better appreciation for *how* you should brief cases.

D. HOW TO BRIEF

1. Identify the Case

A brief dissects and summarizes a case. It makes sense to start the brief by identifying the case. For most professors, the relevant information they want about the identity of the case is the name of the case, the court that rendered the opinion (jurisdiction and level), and the date:

```
                        PIERSON v. POST
                   (New York Supreme Court 1805)
```

2. The Facts

It also is rather self-evident that you should include the facts of the case in your brief. Logically it makes sense to put the facts up front. The facts are what led to the dispute, which is what started the case. The problem with putting the facts up front is that this reinforces the typical law student's tendency to over-focus on the facts. Nevertheless, logically it makes sense in writing your brief to put them up front. If you are called upon in class, most professors like to start the discussion about a case with the facts. So it makes sense in your brief to lead with the particular facts of the case, but analytically remember that is probably the least important part of the brief:

```
                        PIERSON v. POST
                   (New York Supreme Court 1805)

FACTS: Post was hunting with his dogs and hounds on an un-owned
       beach when he spied a fox. He and his dogs and hounds were in
       hot pursuit of the fox, and apparently were about the catch the fox
       when Pierson, who was walking up the beach from the opposite
       direction and saw all of this coming towards him, killed the fox.[3]
```

Most students intuitively understand what they should include in their statement of facts, but two suggestions might be useful. First, as a general rule, you should write your fact statement *in chronological order*. It is usually easiest to understand and recall a fact pattern when it starts with the first relevant fact and then proceeds from that point in time in chronological order — just as if you

---

3. You should feel free to re-word the facts, particularly if necessary to put them in chronological order. But be very careful when re-wording not to drop any of the key facts. You should keep the key words in their original words, though you can re-word the "filler" words.

were moving across a timeline. (This rule applies as well when you write your fact statements for your legal research and writing memos.)

Second, be sure to include all "outcome-determinative" facts in your statement of the facts. What is an "outcome-determinative" fact? If you change that fact, the outcome of the case would/may change. For example, go back to the typical student brief above.[4] Does the statement of facts include *where* the hunt occurred? It occurred on an un-owned beach. Depending on how much time your Property professor spends on this area of the law, you may learn later that if the hunt had occurred on private property a different rule would apply, which would result in a different outcome. So *where* the animal was when it was killed is an outcome-determinative fact that should be included in the statement of facts. Often you will not be able to determine the outcome-determinative facts until after you finish properly analyzing the case — or maybe even several cases — because the outcome-determinative facts often depend upon the scope of the rule(s) you are learning.

3. Procedural Posture of the Case

Some professors recommend that students include the procedural posture of the case in their briefs. The procedural posture is basically where the case is on the judicial timeline and what was its procedural history in getting to that point. Who prevailed at the trial court level? If there was an intermediate appellate court opinion, who prevailed at that level — what did the intermediate court of appeals decide — and why?

Whether you should include the procedural posture of the case in your brief is up to you. You should definitely include it for the cases you read in Civil Procedure because the procedural posture will often be directly related to the issue in the case. But for many of your other classes, you probably do not need to include it in your brief unless your particular professor asks about it on a regular basis. Most non-Civil Procedure professors do not. Because *Pierson v. Post* is a Property case, for most professors there is no need to put it in the brief.

4. Issue

Logically it makes sense to follow the facts with the issue. What is the issue in the case? Sometimes the court does a very good job of stating the issue, sometimes not. Sometimes even when the court does a good job of stating the issue, it is not worded properly for briefing and legal analysis purposes. You might wonder how that can be.

Issue statements can be worded one of two ways: more on the factual plane or more on the legal plane. Look back at *Pierson v. Post*. Remember that one way to

---

4. If you wrote our your own brief, you should critique it instead of the typical student brief.

think of the dissenting opinion is that it is an alternative opinion. It has its own issue statement. Compare the majority's issue statement to the dissent's issue statement.

The majority *started out* its discussion of the issue by saying the following:

> The question submitted by the counsel in this cause for our determination is, whether Lodowick Post, by the pursuit with his hounds in the manner alleged in his declaration, acquired such a right to, or property in, the fox as will sustain an action against Pierson for killing and taking him away?

Is that statement of the issue primarily on the factual plane or the legal plane? Notice how many references to the facts there are in the issue statement. It is a rather fact-based issue statement. But the majority did not stop there; it went on to discuss the issue, working its way to the following issue statement:

> These admissions narrow the discussion to the simple question of *what acts amount to occupancy*, applied to acquiring right to wild animals. (Emphasis added).

Is that issue statement primarily on the factual plane or the rule plane? It is almost exclusively on the rule plane. There are no references to the particular facts of the case in the sentence.

Contrast the majority's issue statement with the dissent's issue statement:

> Whether a person who, with his own hounds, starts and hunts a fox on waste and uninhabited ground, and is on the point of seizing his prey, acquires such an interest in the animal as to have a right of action against another, who in view of the huntsman and his dogs in full pursuit, and with knowledge of the chase, shall kill and carry him away.

Again, is that issue statement more on the factual plane or the rule plane? The factual plane. The dissent recognizes that it is making law in the case, so it should use generic terms when talking about the parties ("a *person* . . . against *another* . . . *the huntsman*"), but the issue statement is nevertheless still very fact sensitive in that it still has lots of references to the facts in it (*with his own hounds . . . hunts a fox . . . is on the point of seizing . . . the huntsman and his dogs . . .*).

How should the issue be stated, more on the factual plane or more on the rule plane? *It depends.* First, *why* are you stating the issue; *who* do you represent? The facts of *Pierson v. Post* favor which party, Pierson or Post? Post. At a minimum Pierson was inconsiderate — if not a jerk. If you represent Post, the facts are in your favor so emphasize them and use them as much as possible in the issue statement in your appellate brief. If, however, you represent Pierson, you know the facts put your client in a poor light. So in your appellate brief you want to de-emphasize the facts. If you represent Pierson you want to write an issue statement that presents the issue as almost a pure question of law.

The actual practice of the law requires you to be a zealous advocate for your client; being a zealous advocate often involves some gamesmanship. How an issue statement is worded is an area where you can exercise that gamesmanship. Keep this in mind when writing your legal research and writing memos as well.[5]

But which approach works best when briefing a case? *It depends.* Are you writing your brief primarily for classroom use or to help you prepare for the exam? Most professors prefer to start the discussion by stating the issue in the case from more of a case-specific, factual perspective. The problem with that approach is it is looking backwards on the timeline. You are not going to see that fact pattern ever again, particularly on the exam. If that issue comes up again on the exam, it is going to be raised by a different fact pattern. You want your issue statement to be forward looking. A more generic, rule plane–oriented issue statement will be more useful if the issue is on the exam. You want to lead with the rule on the exam, so leading with a more rule-oriented issue statement in your briefs will help you more when it comes time for the exam. Either type of issue statement is acceptable, as long as you are conscious of which type you are writing and why.

PIERSON v. POST
(New York Supreme Court 1805)

FACTS: Post was hunting with his dogs and hounds on an un-owned beach when he spied a fox. He and his dogs and hounds were in hot pursuit of the fox, and apparently were about the catch the fox when Pierson, who was walking up the beach from the opposite direction and saw all of this coming towards him, killed the fox.

ISSUE: Whether Post, by his hot pursuit of the fox with his dogs and hounds and being on the verge of capturing it, acquired a property interest in the fox?/What constitutes occupancy?[6]

In your brief, you might want to consider writing both styles of issue statements. Notice that is what the majority did.[7] The issue starts out on the factual plane based on the facts of the case, but the court needs to go to the rule plane to answer the question of law before it can come back down and answer the particular issue raised by the facts of the case.

---

5. But that will depend on whether you are writing an "internal" memo that should be an objective memo versus an "external" memo that is intended to be a persuasive instrument. The difference between the different types of legal instruments, and how that affects your writing style, is one of the topics you will cover in your legal research and writing course.

6. You should feel free to re-word the court's issue statement. But be careful when re-wording not to drop any of the key words or phrases. You should use the court's wording for the key words or phrasing, though you can re-word the "filler" words. The issue statements above are re-worded from the following respective sentences in the court's opinion: "[W]hether Lodowick Post, by the pursuit with his hounds in the manner alleged in his declaration, acquired such a right to, or property in, the fox as will sustain an action against Pierson for killing and taking him away?"/"[W]hat acts amount to occupancy, applied to acquiring right to wild animals."

7. *See* the discussion above.

That is what you will have to do analytically on the exam. You will spot an issue in the fact pattern. You will have to go to the rule plane to select the relevant rule. Then you will have to apply the rule back down to the facts and analyze. If you take a fact specific issue statement from the case you read, that typically will not help you as much on the exam. It will not help you think of the rule as easily. If, on the other hand, you word your issue statement more on the rule plane, that typically will help you identify the rule that you should apply to the issue on the exam.

For class discussion purposes you may find that many of your professors prefer a more fact specific issue statement. For exam purposes you may find that a more generic, rule-oriented issue statement will be more helpful.

5. Rule Statement

Some briefing templates ask the students to write the holding next. That type of briefing template implicitly encourages students to develop bad habits. It implicitly encourages students to brief the case almost exclusively on the factual plane because the holding is the application of the rule to the facts of the case. A better briefing template is one that shifts the students' analytical focus more to the rule and public policy planes. The third entry on your briefing template should be entitled Rule Statement. To complete that part of your brief properly, you must extract what you think is the rule statement the court adopted in the case and write it in your brief.

Extracting the rule statement from the opinion and writing it in your brief is important for several reasons. First, it forces you to focus on the rule plane while reading the case. When you first start reading cases, it is easy to understand the court's discussion of the facts. You know how to read and understand facts. What you need to develop is your ability to read and understand the court's analysis of the question of law and the rule it adopted. You need to force yourself to work on understanding that part of the opinion. Forcing yourself to extract the rule statement you think the court adopted will force you to develop your ability to read and understand a court's discussion and analysis of the question of law at issue.

Moreover, if you write in your brief the sentence that you think is the rule of law adopted in the case, and then take your brief to class, you can assess your legal analysis skills. Listen carefully to the professor and the class discussion. Do the professor and the class discussion appear to be focusing on the sentence that you extracted from the opinion? If so, you are doing a good job of developing your legal analysis skills. If not, that is a sign that you are still not comfortable enough with the rule plane.

Third, if you write the rule statement in your brief, it forces you to be more precise in your knowledge of the rule. Many law students think that a *general* understanding of a rule is all that is necessary. Unfortunately, that level of knowledge does not cut it when it comes to writing your exams. You need a more precise, detailed knowledge of the rule statement. Having to write the rule in your brief promotes that more detailed, precise knowledge of the rule.

Accordingly, be precise and careful about how you word your rule statement. Do not paraphrase it. Write it the same way the court wrote it. Then listen carefully in class to see if the professor modifies the wording.

Writing what you think is the rule statement in your brief will also help you learn to distinguish *the* rule statement from a statement *about* the rule. A court may spend several paragraphs talking *about* the rule, but in the end, the rule statement typically is just one sentence in that discussion. Learning to distinguish a rule statement from statements about the rule is an important skill that you need to develop fairly early in your law school career to be successful in law school, but it is one of the more subtle skills. Remember that a rule statement must be a sentence that you can apply to a dispute to resolve the dispute, not just the dispute before the court, but other similar disputes. A rule statement should not have any references to the parties to the dispute. It needs to be worded more generically to permit it to be applied to similar fact patterns in the future. A statement *about* a rule cannot be used to resolve the dispute before the court or other similar fact patterns.

And, finally, it is important to put the rule statement in your brief because if you are going to use any part of the opinion on your exam, more likely than not it will be the rule. You want to focus your analysis on that part of the opinion that typically will have the greatest relevance for your final—the rule plane.

PIERSON v. POST
(New York Supreme Court 1805)

FACTS: Post was hunting with his dogs and hounds on an un-owned beach when he spied a fox. He and his dogs and hounds were in hot pursuit of the fox, and apparently were about the catch the fox when Pierson, who was walking up the beach from the opposite direction and saw all of this coming towards him, killed the fox.

ISSUE: Whether Post, by his hot pursuit of the fox with his dogs and hounds and being on the verge of capturing it, acquired a property interest in it?/What constitutes occupancy?

RULE: To establish occupancy, the claimant must prove that he (1) had an unequivocal intention of appropriating the animal to his individual use, (2) deprived the animal of its natural liberty, and (3) brought the animal within his certain control.[8]

---

8. While you can re-word the rule statement, if you do, of all the parts of your brief you should be the most careful about how you do it. Key words or phrases in a rule statement often take on particular legal significance. The key words or phrases also define the scope of the rule—the size of the circle on the rule plane. If you change a key word or phrase in a rule statement and the wording you pick does not have the same meaning and legal significance, you are changing the rule. Be very, very careful when re-wording rule statements to ensure that you keep all the key terms and phrases, but feel free to re-word the filler words. The rule statement in the brief is a re-wording of the following clause in the court's opinion: "[To establish occupancy a claimant must show] an unequivocal intention of appropriating the animal to his individual use, has deprived him of his natural liberty, and brought him within his certain control." But if your professor re-words the rule statement in class, you should feel free to use the professor's wording.

6. Public Policy Considerations

After you find the court's rule statement and put it in your brief, ask yourself *"why did the court adopt this rule"?* That analytical question will take you to the court's discussion of the relevant public policy considerations. Just as a rule statement is of a different nature than a statement of fact, you will find that a public policy statement is of a different nature than a rule statement. That is a very abstract point, but if you keep it in mind it should help you learn to distinguish the court's discussion of the public policy considerations from the court's discussion of the rule.

The court's discussion of the relevant public policy considerations often includes a discussion of the following question(s): What did the court want to encourage, and why? What did the court want to discourage, and why? What type of society do we want, and why?

Write the public policy considerations in your brief. That way, when you take your brief to class it should help you if called upon to discuss the case. You can also use it to help critique your analytical skills by comparing your list of public policy considerations to the professor's comments and your classmates' comments.

You need to read the court's opinion carefully to find the court's discussion of the relevant public policy considerations, but you should be able to develop a knack for doing so fairly quickly. In *Pierson v. Post*, the court does a pretty good job of indicating *why* it adopted the rule that it did:

PIERSON v. POST
(New York Supreme Court 1805)

FACTS: Post was hunting with his dogs and hounds on an un-owned beach when he spied a fox. He and his dogs and hounds were in hot pursuit of the fox, and apparently were about the catch the fox when Pierson, who was walking up the beach from the opposite direction and saw all of this coming towards him, killed the fox.

ISSUE: Whether Post, by his hot pursuit of the fox with his dogs and hounds and being on the verge of capturing it, acquired a property interest in it?/What constitutes occupancy?

RULE: To establish occupancy, the claimant must prove that he (1) had an unequivocal intention of appropriating the animal to his individual use, (2) deprived the animal of its natural liberty, and (3) brought the animal within his certain control.

PUBLIC POLICY: To promote certainty and preserve peace and order in society, and to minimize quarrels and litigation.[9]

---

9. You should feel free to re-word the public policy. You will come to see that the same public policy considerations tend to arise with some frequency not only in the same class, but often even in different classes. When that is the case, you will come to learn either the generally accepted way of expressing that public policy consideration or the professor's favorite way of describing it. When you learn the generally accepted or professor's favorite way of expressing the public policy consideration, you should feel free to use it even if a particular court has re-worded it. The public policy considerations above are re-worded (to save words) from the following statements in the court's opinion: "for the sake of certainty, and preserving peace and order in society. If the first seeing, starting or pursuing such animals, without having so wounded, circumvented or ensnared them, so as to deprive them of their natural liberty, and

You will come to learn that not all courts will bother to include a discussion of the public policy considerations that support the rule of law it adopted. There are a variety of reasons why a court may not include such information. Sometimes the court will think the rule so self-evident there is no need to explain why it adopted that particular rule. Sometimes the court will write a conclusory or poorly written opinion that fails to include a discussion of why the court favored that rule. Whatever the reason, do not be surprised if you cannot find a discussion of why the court adopted the rule it did in every opinion. When that is the case, include the template entry in your brief, but leave it empty since the court failed to state why it was adopting that rule. When you come to class, pay particular attention to whether the professor covers that issue either in his or her comments on the case or through the Socratic dialogue. If both the court's opinion and the class discussion fail to address it, then it is probably safe to assume that you are not responsible for that material.

7. Holding

After extracting the rule of law from the case and the relevant public policy considerations, the next step in briefing a case is to apply the rule to the facts of that particular case to reach the holding. What was the court's conclusion after applying the rule it adopted to the facts of this case? Typically you should be able to state the holding in one rather concise sentence. It should be more of a fact-based sentence since it is the application of the rule to the facts which typically leads to a fact-specific conclusion regarding how this case is resolved (unless the case went up on appeal on a procedural matter).

Analytically the holding involves the interaction of the rule plane and the factual plane. Some professors may recommend that you include *why* the court reached the conclusion it did in the holding section of your brief. Most authorities recommend that you treat the holding and why the court reached its holding as two different components of your brief. *Why* the court reached the holding it did is typically referred to as the rationale for the holding.

Often the court will express its holding in rather technical, legal terms — not in plain English. The court may conclude that "the lower court's judgment is affirmed" or "the lower court's judgment is reversed." Such wording of the holding typically is of little value to you. You should re-word the court's technical holding so that it makes sense on the factual plane.

The court's holding in *Pierson v. Post* is a good example of where you should re-word the court's technical holding so that it is more understandable as applied to the case.[10] How would you re-word it?

---

subject them to the control of their pursuer, should afford the basis of actions against others for intercepting and killing them, it would prove a fertile source of quarrels and litigation."

10. The court ruled: "However uncourteous or unkind the conduct of Pierson towards Post, in this instance, may have been, yet this act was productive of no injury or damage for which a legal remedy can be applied. We are of opinion the judgment below was erroneous, and ought to be reversed."

PIERSON v. POST
(New York Supreme Court 1805)

FACTS: Post was hunting with his dogs and hounds on an un-owned
   beach when he spied a fox. He and his dogs and hounds were in
   hot pursuit of the fox, and apparently were about the catch the fox
   when Pierson, who was walking up the beach from the opposite
   direction and saw all of this coming towards him, killed the fox.

ISSUE: Whether Post, by his hot pursuit of the fox with his dogs
   and hounds and being on the verge of capturing it, acquired a
   property interest in it?/What constitutes occupancy?

RULE: To establish occupancy, the claimant must prove that he
   (1) had an unequivocal intention of appropriating the animal to his
   individual use, (2) deprived the animal of its natural liberty, and
   (3) brought the animal within his certain control.

PUBLIC POLICY: To promote certainty and preserve peace and order
   in society, and to minimize quarrels and litigation.

HOLDING: Post failed to establish occupancy in the fox and therefore
   has no cause of action against Pierson for trespass on the case.

---

8. Rationale

The term "rationale" is an ambiguous word that different professors — and even
courts — may use differently. Conceptually, the word rationale goes to the interaction of the different planes. The rationale is simply a technical term for asking
"why" the court did what it did; what was the court's explanation? Viewed from
that perspective, a well-written opinion really should have *two* rationales: one
explaining why the court adopted the rule that it did (the interaction between the
public policy plane and the rule plane); and one explaining why the court
reached the holding that it did (the interaction between the rule plane and
the factual plane). Because of this inherent ambiguity in the term, you should
distinguish between the two rationales by expressly referring to the first one as
the public policy considerations and save the term rationale for the explanation
of why the court reached the holding that it did.

Some professors — and even some courts — tend to compress the rule and public policy planes into one in their writing. Under this approach, the term "rationale"
may include not only an explanation of the holding but also of the public policy
considerations that gave rise to the rule/holding. If you pay close attention to how
your professor conducts the Socratic dialogue you will quickly come to realize in
what sense he or she is using the word "rationale" — if he or she uses that word at
all. Analytically, however, your analysis will be sharper and cleaner if you distinguish the rational for the rule from the rationale from the holding.

Sometimes the court will not give a detailed statement of its application of the
rule to the facts of the case. Even if the court does not, you should. It is good

practice for what your professor will expect you to do on the exam. Go through the rule element by element, pairing each element with the facts in the fact pattern that are relevant to that particular element. You will see that some facts are relevant to more than one element. Where the elements in the rule have a natural sequencing to them, address the elements in order. Where the elements do not have a natural sequencing to them, write out your analysis of each element separately, starting with the elements that are clearly satisfied and working your way to the element in dispute. Depending on why the element in question was in dispute, analysis of that element may need to include the respective parties' arguments with respect to the element (argument—counterargument). Resolution of the element in dispute typically will resolve the larger issue.

In *Pierson v. Post*, the court did not perform an element-by-element application and analysis of the new rule it had adopted. Instead it wrote a rather conclusory statement that Post did not have any property interest in the fox and therefore did not have a cause of action against Pierson.[11] How would you brief the application of the rule of law adopted in *Pierson v. Post* to the facts?

PIERSON v. POST
(New York Supreme Court 1805)

FACTS: Post was hunting with his dogs and hounds on an un-owned beach when he spied a fox. He and his dogs and hounds were in hot pursuit of the fox, and apparently were about the catch the fox when Pierson, who was walking up the beach from the opposite direction and saw all of this coming towards him, killed the fox.

ISSUE: Whether Post, by his hot pursuit of the fox with his dogs and hounds and being on the verge of capturing it, acquired a property interest in it? What constitutes occupancy?

RULE: To establish occupancy, the claimant must prove that he (1) had an unequivocal intention of appropriating the animal to his individual use, (2) deprived the animal of its natural liberty, and (3) brought the animal within his certain control.

PUBLIC POLICY: To promote certainty and preserve peace and order in society, and to minimize quarrels and litigation.

HOLDING: Post failed to establish occupancy in the fox and therefore has no cause of action against Pierson for trespass on the case.

RATIONALE: Post could establish that he had the intent to appropriate the animal to his individual use as evidenced by his hot pursuit of the fox with his dogs and hounds; Post arguably had deprived the fox of its natural liberty because the fox was not free to do as it wished because it was being chased by the dogs and hounds; but Post could not prove that he had the fox under his certain control because the fox was still running down the beach and there was still the risk that the fox could have gotten away.

---

11. *See supra* note 10.

9. Critique/Analysis

You should include in your brief a section entitled "Critique" or "Analysis." It is a good idea for several reasons. First, it is not uncommon for a professor to ask you what you thought of a court's opinion. Thinking about that ahead of time and writing it down will help in the event your professor calls on you and asks you your opinion.

You might wonder how you are supposed to critique an opinion when you are still trying to learn how to read and analyze cases. As a law student, you sit on the highest court in the land. You sit in review of every opinion written by every judge/justice. Part of the legal analysis process is learning how to distinguish a "good" opinion from a "bad" opinion. You will learn to evaluate opinions based on their result (their holding), on their analysis (the interaction of the three planes), and on how well they are written. A court may reach the "right" result but for the wrong reasons. A court may perform a good job of analyzing the issue on appeal but reach the "wrong" result. A court may reach the right result but the opinion may be poorly written. Just as legal analysis can be performed on several levels, an opinion can be evaluated on several levels.

Be careful when you read and analyze a case in the casebook. Just because a case is in the casebook that does not mean it is a "good" opinion. Because mastering legal analysis includes being able to recognize a "bad" opinion, many of the leading casebooks will include a handful of "bad" opinions. Do not automatically assume that just because an opinion is in the casebook it must be a "good" opinion.

The "critique/analysis" section of your brief is where you express *your opinion* about any part of the court's opinion. The most important part of that sentence may be its negative implications. In all the other sections of the brief, you should *not* express your opinion. In the rest of your brief, you are simply stating what *the court* did and why—*not* what you think about it. You need to be able to state and understand what *the court* did before you can *analyze* it. Most professors will apply a similar subtle distinction in class. You need to pay close attention to the professor and class discussion. Logically it makes sense to establish in class *what* the court did *before* evaluating and critiquing what the court did. The first purpose of the brief is to establish *what* the court did, to break down *the court's* analysis. Only after you fully understand what the court did and why the court did it are you in a position to critique what the court did. Some students are so eager to critique a court's opinion that they fail to stop and understand what the court did.

10. Dissenting Opinion

A dissenting opinion is an alternative opinion. In *that* jurisdiction it is of no legal value unless a higher court *subsequently* adopts it or the same court adopts it in a *subsequent* opinion. Absent such subsequent history, a dissenting opinion has no value in that jurisdiction. But in the jurisdiction of a law school classroom, dissenting opinions may have great weight. There are several possible reasons why a dissenting opinion may be included in a casebook.

A dissenting opinion may be included in the casebook to help you analyze the majority opinion. If that is the only reason it is included, after the class analysis you may conclude that the dissenting opinion is of no value for exam purposes.

A dissenting opinion may be included in the casebook because while it did not carry the day in that case, the rule it proposed may have been adopted in another jurisdiction. In such cases, the dissenting opinion is used to teach you a split in the jurisdictions. On the exam, if the professor does not tell you which jurisdictional approach to apply, the rule statement proposed by the dissent (and adopted by the other jurisdiction) is just as important as the rule adopted by the majority.

A dissenting opinion may be included in the casebook because although no court to date has adopted it yet, the academic community may think the arguments set forth by the dissent and the rule statement it proposed are the "better" arguments and the "better" rule. If the dissent is included in the casebook because the authors think it represents the modern trend even if no court has adopted it yet, you will be expected to raise and argue the dissenting approach on the exam just as if it were a rule of law (as *if* there were a split in the jurisdictions).

Bottom line, you should fully brief a dissenting opinion if it is in the casebook just as you would brief a majority opinion. Remember most casebook opinions are heavily edited opinions. If the dissenting opinion has been included in the casebook, there is probably a good reason why it has been included. When you go to class, pay particular attention to the professor's and the class' discussion of the dissenting opinion to see what relevance, if any, it has for exam purposes.

When you brief the dissenting opinion, you should modify your template to make sure that you indicate it is a dissenting opinion. In particular, you should clearly indicate that the dissent has set forth a "proposed" rule statement. The dissent's proposed rule statement is not a rule unless another court has adopted it, a subsequent development you should not assume unless the note material in the casebook so indicates or the professor so indicates in the course of the class discussion.

How would you brief the dissenting opinion in *Pierson v. Post*?

PIERSON v. POST— DISSENTING OPINION
(New York Supreme Court 1805)

FACTS: Post was hunting with his dogs and hounds on an un-owned beach when he spied a fox. He and his dogs and hounds were in hot pursuit of the fox, and apparently were about the catch the fox when Pierson, who was walking up the beach from the opposite direction and saw all of this coming towards him, killed the fox.

ISSUE: Whether a person who, with his own hounds, starts and hunts a fox on waste and uninhabited ground, and is on the point of seizing his prey, acquires such an interest in the animal as to have a right of action against another, who in view of the huntsman and his dogs in full pursuit, and with knowledge of the chase, shall kill and carry him away?

PROPOSED RULE: Property in animals *feroe naturoe* may be acquired without bodily touch or manucaption, provided the pursuer be within reach, or have a reasonable prospect (which certainly existed here) of taking what he has thus discovered with an intention of converting to his own use.

PUBLIC POLICY: To maximize the kill of foxes.

PROPOSED HOLDING: Post established occupancy in the fox through his actions and therefore has a cause of action against Pierson for trespass on the case.

RATIONALE: Under the dissent's proposed rule statement Post would have a property interest in the fox because his action of pursuing the fox indicates that he had the intention of converting to his own use the fox that he and his dogs and hounds had discovered, and because he was in hot pursuit of the fox and on the verge of capturing it, he was either within reach of it, or if not, he had a reasonable prospect of capturing it.

E. CONCLUSION

Having read, analyzed, and briefed the case, you are now ready for class.

CHAPTER 7

The "What if..." Game

A. THE SOCRATIC APPROACH

Most law professors, particularly first-year law professors, use some variation of the Socratic teaching style. The Socratic teaching style comes in many different shapes and styles, so it is difficult to describe. In its pure form, the professor asks only questions about the material. He or she provides no answers. Students are left to present the case—and their analysis of the case—on their own. Understandably most first-year law students find this method of teaching maddening—hence the proliferation of commercial outlines (to be discussed in greater detail later).

Most law professors, however, do not use the pure Socratic approach. Most use some combination of Socratic and lecture. The exact mixture varies by professor. Most law professors expect the students to make at least a good faith attempt at presenting their understanding and analysis of a case, and then the professor, either through his or her questioning or through his or her comments, implicitly provides feedback on both the quality and accuracy of the students' comments.

The best preparation for class is to read and brief each case. A well-written brief should contain all of the relevant information about a case. It takes time to develop the skill of briefing a case, and even longer to develop the skill of being able to critique/analyze a case. But just like with riding a bike, practice makes perfect.

At first the Socratic approach will seem confusing. You should err on the side of taking copious notes. Often you will not understand the significance of a point made in class for days, sometimes weeks. A good set of class notes gives you the flexibility to go back and review the material with the benefit of additional knowledge. Do not, however, be a stenographer. You need to listen to the class discussion and think critically about it. Pay close attention to *both* sides of the Socratic discussion. Not just the professor's questions, but just as importantly, your classmates' answers—and questions.

One year about half way through the first semester, a first-year law student stopped me in the hall after class and said: "Prof. Wendel, I think I'm getting the hang of this 'thinking like a lawyer' thing." When I asked him why, he said, "At the beginning of the semester, I couldn't answer hardly any of the questions you asked in class. But now, I can answer almost all of them." I could tell how proud he was of his achievement. I congratulated him, and smiled, and told him while it was a good sign that he could answer almost all of the questions, the key to mastering the process of "thinking like a lawyer" is being able to *ask the question* before I do, not simply answer the question. When you hear a classmate make a comment, and you immediately think of a question that puts the comment under the analytical microscope and questions its validity, and then you hear the professor ask that question, then you have crossed over; *then* you are truly beginning to "think like a lawyer."

The purpose of the Socratic dialogue is to develop that critical thinking voice that you will need to be a successful lawyer. When you graduate and start to practice, there will not be a professor there to ask the right questions. *You* have to play both sides of the Socratic dialogue. You have to ask the right questions and then be able to analyze them. Simply being a stenographer in class will not develop that critical thinking voice. You need to pay close attention to and *analyze* each and every comment made in class, while doing your best to take notes.

You will also quickly realize that while the class discussion often starts with the analysis of a case you read, often that case simply serves as a springboard for the professor to play the "what if . . ." game.

B. THE "WHAT IF . . ." GAME

Assume you are sitting in class. The class has been discussing *Pierson v. Post* in great detail. The professor asks, "Why, then, in the end, did Post lose?" A student raises his or her hand and explains that Post lost because of the rule of occupancy the court adopted. That while Post clearly had the intent to appropriate the animal to his individual use, and maybe his pursuit had deprived the fox of its natural liberty, Post had not brought the fox under his certain control because the fox was still running down the beach when Pierson killed it. That exchange between the student and the professor appears to signal that the professor is wrapping up the discussion of *Pierson v. Post*. You assume that the professor will move on to the next case. Instead, the professor throws out a hypothetical for the class' consideration.

1. "What if . . ." — First Hypothetical

"*What if*, a week after the opinion in *Pierson v. Post* has been published, in the same jurisdiction Cheney decides to go out hunting. Cheney no longer hunts with a gun (after an unfortunate little incident); he now hunts only with dogs and hounds. He gets his dogs and hounds together and goes out hunting on an un-owned beach. It is a hot and sunny day, and he has been hunting for several hours without any luck. He is starting to get frustrated and tired, when all of a sudden his dogs and hounds spy a fox. They take off down the beach after the fox. Cheney takes off down the beach after his dogs and hounds. He is in hot pursuit of the fox. He is closing in on the fox. It appears as though he is about to catch the fox when Obama, who is walking up the beach from the other direction and who is watching all of this unfold before his eyes, takes out a gun and shoots and kills the fox right before Cheney can get it. Same case or different case?"[1]

Most students intuitively analyze that this first hypothetical is basically the same case as *Pierson v. Post* and should come out the same way. To establish occupancy the claimant must prove that he or she had the intent to appropriate the animal to his or her individual use, deprive it of its natural liberty, and brought it within his or her certain control. Cheney can prove that he had the intent to appropriate the animal to his individual use by his action of chasing the fox. He has an argument that he deprived the animal of its natural liberty because it is not free to do what it wanted because Cheney is chasing it. But he cannot prove that he brought it within his certain control. The fox was still running down the beach and there was the possibility that the fox could escape. Same case as *Pierson v. Post*, same outcome.

But the professor does not let the class off the hook that easily. He or she has a follow-up hypothetical.

2. "What if . . ." — Second Hypothetical

"*What if*, two weeks after the opinion in *Pierson v. Post* is published, *you* decide to go out hunting. You get your dogs and hounds together and go out hunting. It is a hot and sunny day, and you have been hunting for several hours without any luck. You are starting to get frustrated and tired, when all of a sudden your dogs and hounds spy a fox. They take off after the fox. You take off after your dogs and hounds. You are in hot pursuit of the fox. You are closing in on the fox. It appears you are about to capture the fox when Wendel comes onto your property and shoots and kills the fox right before you can get it. Same case or different case?"[2]

Most first-year law students intuitively say this second hypothetical is a "different case." When asked "Why?" the typical student answer is "Because Wendel came onto my property." Assuming that was your answer as well, take a moment to analyze that answer.

Which plane is that comment on? If you had to put that comment on one of the three planes, which plane would you put it on? The factual plane. Most students believe there is a factual distinction in this second hypothetical — Wendel came onto your property — that should make a difference in the outcome. But notice, at a technical level, there was a factual distinction in the first

---

1. I.e., if Cheney were to sue Obama, should the case come out the same way as *Pierson v. Post* or differently? You might want to take a moment to write out your answer. If you think the case is different, be sure to say why. If you write out your analysis, you can compare and contrast it with the analysis in the material to come.

2. Again, you might want to take a moment to write out your answer. If you think the case is different, be sure to say why. If you write out your analysis, you can contrast it with the analysis in the material to come.

hypothetical. In the first hypothetical, the parties are different from the parties in *Pierson v. Post*. Technically, Cheney is not Post, and Obama is not Pierson. But most students intuitively analyze that those factual distinctions (that the names of the parties are different) made no difference. The first hypothetical is basically the same case as *Pierson v. Post* because the factual distinction in question, that the names of the parties are different, is a distinction that has no legal significance. Similarly situated parties should be treated the same. Cheney and Obama are similarly situated to Post and Pierson.

In the second hypothetical, however, most students believe that the factual distinction that Wendel came onto the student's land should make a difference. Why? Most students say, "Because Wendel is trespassing." But only if the court says he is. What if it were a question of first impression? If hunting were really important, *might* a court adopt a rule that a hunter in hot pursuit of a wild animal *is* permitted to go onto private property? Sure. But the court might also adopt a rule that an owner of private property has rights to a wild animal on his or her property that is superior to any claimed right of a trespasser. If the issue were one of first impression, the court is free to adopt whichever rule it thinks best.

The second hypothetical implicitly raises the issue of which rule is better: a rule that permits hunters in hot pursuit of a wild animal to go onto the private property of another or a rule that discourages hunters from going onto the private property of another, even if in hot pursuit of the animal. To analyze that issue, which plane should you focus on? The public policy plane. The issue becomes whether the public policy of maximizing the kill of wild animals outweighs the public policy of protecting private property rights. If the court decides that protecting private property rights is the paramount public policy consideration, what would it do? It would come back down to the rule plane and adopt a new rule of law that promoted that public policy consideration. And that is exactly what the common law courts did when they adopted the rule of *rationi soli*.

The rule of *rationi soli* provides that a wild animal on private property is deemed to be in the constructive possession of the owner of the private property. The owner of the private property *does not have actual* possession of the animal, the owner *does not have certain control* over the wild animal, the owner *does not have occupancy* over the animal, so why should the court give the owner of the land property rights in the wild animal? So as to deter trespass — to promote the public policy of protecting private property rights.

Notice the analysis you implicitly performed if you intuitively concluded that this second hypothetical was a "different case." There was a factual distinction (one party going onto private property in pursuit of the wild animal), but what is different is that this factual distinction introduces a new public policy consideration into the analysis (as a general rule society wants to deter trespass) that justified adopting a new rule of law (*rationi soli* — that owners of private property have constructive possession of all wild animals on their property).

The factual distinction made a difference because it raised a new public policy consideration, in this case one strong enough that the courts adopted a new rule to promote it.

Whether a case is the same case or a different case is not purely a question of fact. Sometimes it will also be a question of public policy. Notice the order of analysis in the second hypothetical. The analysis jumped from the factual plane to the public policy plane, then back down to the rule plane, and then back down again to the factual plane to reach the holding for the hypothetical. The key to legal analysis is the *interaction* between and among the three planes, not just one or two of them. If you intuitively said the second hypothetical was different from *Pierson v. Post*, you probably performed the right legal analysis but without being fully conscious of what you were doing. Now that you are more conscious of it, you should be that much better at it, and at critiquing someone else when they are performing it.

But the professor is not done yet. He or she throws out yet another hypothetical.

3. "What if . . ." — Third Hypothetical

"What if, the same facts as in the case of *Pierson v. Post*, Post and his dogs and hounds are chasing the fox down the beach. Pierson is walking up the beach from the opposite direction, watching all of this unfold before him, only this time, all of a sudden the fox begins to stagger and falls over, completely exhausted. It is lying on the beach, still breathing, but so exhausted it is unable to move. But before Post can get to it, Pierson walks up and grabs it. Who prevails? Same case as the original *Pierson v. Post* or different case?"

What is the purpose of the hypothetical? Think back to the three planes. The rule is like a circle on the rule plane. It casts a shadow down onto the factual plane.

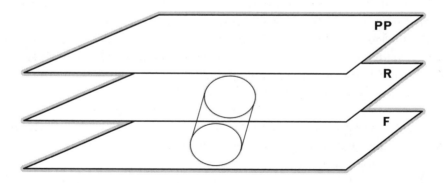

Some fact patterns fall *clearly within* the scope of the shadow and are covered by the rule.

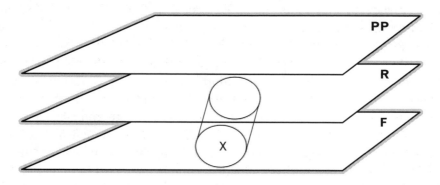

Some fact patterns fall *clearly outside* the scope of the shadow and are not covered by the rule.

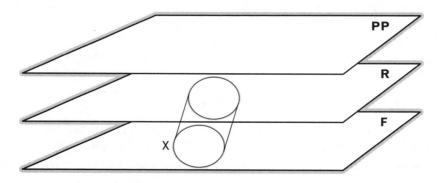

Where did the facts of the actual case of *Pierson v. Post* fall, inside or outside of the shadow? Outside. The court ruled Post's actions did not establish occupancy—they did not establish a property interest in the fox.

With the third hypothetical, the professor has moved the "x" on the factual plane. The issue is whether this new fact pattern falls within the rule or is still outside the rule. Has the professor moved the "x" closer to the rule, possibly even within the circle, or farther from the rule? Does Post have a stronger argument or a weaker argument in this case as compared to the original case?

To establish a property interest in the fox, Post has to prove occupancy. Occupancy requires the party to have the intent to appropriate the animal to one's individual use, the party must deprive the animal of its natural liberty, and the party must bring the animal within his or her certain control. In this third hypothetical, Post can prove the intent to appropriate the animal to his individual use by his actions of chasing after the fox with his dogs and hounds. Post arguably has a stronger argument that he deprived the animal of its natural liberty because the fox was so exhausted that it was unable to move. The issue is whether Post had the fox under his certain control. Post will argue that he did because the fox was unable to move. Pierson will argue that he did not because the fox could have gotten up and run off at any moment. There is still a chance that the fox could have gotten up and escaped. Pierson will argue that certain control was not achieved until he grabbed the fox—only then was certain control assured.

Who prevails? Tough to say—and that is probably why the professor raised the hypothetical. The professor wants to make sure that you realize that there are always fact patterns that fall into the "grey" area where strong arguments can be advanced on both sides of the issue. When it is a close call, how should you analyze it? The ultimate tiebreaker is the relevant public policy considerations. Why did the court in *Pierson v. Post* adopt the rule of occupancy that it did? To promote peace and certainty and to minimize quarrels and litigation. In light of those public policy considerations, should the court stretch the rule of occupancy to cover this fact pattern or construe the rule narrowly so as to exclude this fact pattern? Although Post has a strong argument, Pierson's argument that certain control was not achieved until he, Pierson, grabbed the fox, appears to be the stronger argument because it is more consistent with the court's public policy considerations.

This third hypothetical is a closer call then the original case of *Pierson v. Post*. Visually, the hypothetical moves the fact pattern closer to the edge of the shadow cast by the rule on the factual plane. Around the edge of every rule is some "grey area" where it is difficult to tell if the fact pattern falls within or outside of the rule. Every rule has some grey area. Soft, fact-sensitive rules have more grey area than bright line rules, but even bright line rules have some. While "certain control" appears to be a fairly bright line element, this hypothetical demonstrates that even a bright line element has some grey area where strong arguments can be advanced on both sides. Many law students are surprised at how much uncertainty there is in the law. Get used to it. That is where most law professors like to spend their time, particularly in class, because that is where you must exercise your legal analysis skills the most.

4. "What if . . ." — Fourth Hypothetical

"*What if* Post had been driving down the street in a car when, out of the corner of his eye, he saw the fox dash in front of the car. He swerved to try to avoid it, but he accidentally hit it, killing it. He heard the 'thud' and assumed he had hit the fox, but he was in a rush to get home so he drove on. Pierson, who was out for an evening stroll, saw all of this. Upon inspecting the dead fox, Pierson realized that the fox is a very rare fox and its fur is very valuable. Post later hears the fox is very valuable and that Pierson has it. Post asserts a claim to it. Who prevails?"

Again, what has the professor done? In this fourth hypothetical, the professor has moved the fact pattern yet again to test your knowledge and understanding of the rule—and to test your analytical skills. How is this hypothetical different from the actual case? How is it different from the other hypotheticals? Can Post establish occupancy? Occupancy requires the party to have the intent to appropriate the animal to one's individual use, the party must deprive the animal of its natural liberty, and the party must bring the animal within his or her certain control. Post can prove that he deprived the animal of its natural liberty because he hit and killed the fox.

Has Post brought the fox within his certain control in this fourth hypothetical? Post can argue that he established certain control because the fox is dead; the fox is not going anywhere on its own. Pierson can argue that Post did not bring it within *his* certain control because Post drove off, leaving it for anyone to bring within their certain control. Related to this analysis is the question of whether Post had the intent to appropriate the animal to his individual use. Pierson will argue that Post did not have the intent to appropriate the animal to his individual use. How will Pierson make that argument? Use all of the facts. (Other than on your *Evidence* exam, it is best to assume that all facts in a hypo or on an exam can be proved — *do not worry about how they would be proved*). Pierson will argue that Post did not intend to kill the fox; he *accidentally* killed the fox. He was attempting to avoid the fox when he hit it. He did not have the intent to kill it. Moreover, even though Post heard the "thud" when he hit the fox, he kept on driving. Post had seen the fox out of the corner of his eye, and he heard the impact, so he had reason to believe that he had hit and possibly killed the fox, yet he drove on. Pierson will argue that Post's driving away without stopping is further evidence that Post did not have the intent to appropriate the fox to his individual use. So while Post can establish that he deprived the fox of his natural liberty, and while he has an argument that he brought it within his certain control, he cannot prove that he had the intent to appropriate it to his individual use.

Again, by playing the "what if . . ." game the professor is moving the "x" around the factual plane to test your knowledge and understanding of the rule, of the other elements in particular, and to test your analytical skills, and in this hypothetical, your ability to analyze the relationship between the rule plane and the factual plane. The hypothetical is different from the original case in that Post has a stronger argument with respect to the second and third elements, but he has a tough time proving the first element — that he had the intent to appropriate the animal to his individual use.

C. CONCLUSION

You will be amazed at some of the hypotheticals your professor can create with the "what if . . ." game. *What if* the animal were Post's dog, not a wild fox? *What if* Post had caught the fox, was putting it in a bag, when the fox bit him on the hand and escaped — with Post in hot pursuit? *What if* the fox were an endangered species? You are not necessarily expected to be able to reach the "right" answer, but you are expected to be able to *analyze* the hypotheticals — to be able to think through each hypothetical on all three planes if necessary.

Professors play the "what if . . ." game at different times for different reasons. Sometimes the professor will move the fact pattern around the factual plane primarily to test your knowledge and understanding of the rule that you just learned in the case in question, as well as how the rule plane and the factual plane interact—but there is no real need to use the public policy plane. Sometimes the professor will move the fact pattern around the factual plane to see if you recognize that the new fact pattern has a factual distinction that introduces a new public policy consideration that makes you re-assess whether the prevailing rule is the proper rule or whether the court should adopt a new rule. There are all sorts of reasons a professor may play the "what if . . ." game.

The second hypothetical above—where Wendel came on to your property to shoot and kill the fox—demonstrates why going to class and taking good notes are important. Sometimes your professor will play the "what if . . ." game to teach a new rule and set of public policy considerations through the class' analysis of a hypothetical. The professor will expect you to have the new rule (*rationi soli*) and public policy considerations that support it in your notes. You have the best chance of learning that rule and those public policy considerations by attending class and taking good notes. Anytime a professor asks a hypothetical, be sure to get it down. You will not know until the discussion is over whether it was simply to test your knowledge of the rule you already knew or whether it was to teach you a whole new rule and set of policy considerations.

Different hypotheticals involve different legal analysis. Some hypotheticals will involve primarily just two planes. Some hypotheticals will require you to use all three planes. Be flexible in your legal analysis. Be open to using all three planes, but do not feel compelled to always use all three planes in each hypothetical. Just as different cases can raise and require you to think about the three planes differently, so too can different hypotheticals.

Chapter 8

Introspective Legal Analysis: Russian Dolls

A. INTRODUCTION

As noted before when discussing the evolution of a case, each appellate opinion starts out as a question of law. But there are different *types* of questions of law. That statement, admittedly, is not very helpful, but it is not intended to be. In law school, professors do not *tell* you such information, they expect you to extract that knowledge from the different types of cases you read and analyze. Unfortunately, many students fail to do so. Not all cases are the same analytically. Compare the question of law on appeal in the next case, *Howard v. Kunto*, with the question of law that was on appeal in *Pierson v. Post*.

B. ADVERSE POSSESSION—BACKGROUND

The case of *Howard v. Kunto* involves the rule of adverse possession. Adverse possession is one of the more difficult rules, both conceptually and doctrinally,[1] that you will study in law school. At the conceptual level, adverse possession basically says that if one takes possession of another's land and uses the land in a

---

1. A *conceptual* statement of a rule is basically what the rule is about—what the rule does; what the effect of the rule is. The *doctrinal* statement of the rule is the rule statement itself—the elements that must be satisfied for the rule to apply. At first blush you might think this distinction too abstract to be important, but nothing could be further from the truth. It is critical that you master the difference. You will quickly realize that both courts and professors will make many statements that relate to a rule of law. You need to be able to distinguish when the court/professor is talking *conceptually* about the rule versus when the court/professor is talking *doctrinally* about the rule. The court/professor is talking doctrinally when the words being used are the words that would be applied to the facts of a case to help resolve the dispute.

As you read your casebooks (not just the cases, but the note material before and after them), whenever you come upon a discussion of a rule you should carefully analyze whether each sentence is *about* the rule of law or whether it is a *rule* sentence (this chapter will explain how you can have rule sentences other than the rule statement). Again, that statement is so abstract you probably do not fully appreciate or understand it at this point. By the end of this chapter you will have a greater appreciation and understanding of it. Distinguishing a conceptual statement about a rule from a rule sentence about the rule is a skill learned by practice—like riding a bike. But to master this skill you need to be aware that you should be practicing it. I do not know a single law professor who makes explicit reference to this distinction. It is another one of those methodological skills that law professors assume students will master as part of the "reading and analyzing" analytical process—but there is no express mention of the skill or instruction as to how to master it. Now you have a better understanding of why some students feel that the way law school teaches them how to "think like a lawyer" is by throwing them into the deep end of the pool and telling them to swim!

way that satisfies the requirements of the rule, the law automatically transfers title from the original owner to the adverse possessor.[2] Even at the conceptual level, many students find the doctrine challenging. They believe adverse possession is nothing more than legalized theft: if one party trespasses onto another's property, and if the trespass satisfies the requirements of the rule, the trespasser is rewarded with title to the property![3] The debate over the pros and cons of adverse possession is beyond the scope of this material, but the analytical nature of the question of law on appeal in *Howard v. Kunto* is not.

A couple of quick questions will help set up the analytical points you should take away from the case. First, what does the word "continuous" mean?[4] Second, based on your definition or understanding of "continuous," how would you analyze the following hypothetical? Assume O owns Greenacres. Nevertheless, AP[5] goes into possession of Greenacres, without O's permission, for the summer (AP is trespassing). At the end of the summer AP packs up and moves off Greenacres. AP does not visit Greenacres again during the fall, winter, or spring. When the next summer rolls around, however, AP goes back into possession of Greenacres without O's permission. AP repeats this process for a number of years. Has AP been in continuous possession of Greenacres?[6]

Notice the answer to that question *depends* upon your definition/understanding of the word "continuous." Now you are ready for the case.[7]

C. *HOWARD v. KUNTO*

Howard v. Kunto
COURT OF APPEALS OF THE STATE OF WASHINGTON

Ct. App. Wash. (1970)

PEARSON, J.

[The case is rather complicated factually, more so than is necessary for our purposes. To simplify the case assume the facts are as follows. The Howards

---

2. This sentence is a conceptual statement of the rule of adverse possession because it tells you something about the rule — the legal effect of the rule — but it does not tell you the elements of the rule — what the party must prove to satisfy the rule. Conceptual statements put the rule in context, they help you understand the rule, but they are not the rule or part of the rule.

3. You may be asking yourself "*why* would the law do that?" Notice if you are, you are going to the public policy plane — to the rationale for the rule. The material will touch briefly on the public policy considerations underlying the rule later, but for the most part the public policy considerations are beyond the scope of this coverage.

4. You might want to write down your definition or understanding of the word. Later, it might prove useful to come back and compare your definition or understanding to that which you ultimately take away from the case.

5. Hypotheticals often use a capital letter in lieu of a name for the party to simplify the analysis (students don't need to focus on the name, focus on the generic scenario being presented by the fact pattern). Hypotheticals involving adverse possession often use the abbreviation AP instead of just A or B to make it clear which party is the adverse possessor. O is short for owner.

6. Again, you might want to write out your analysis of the question so that you can come back to it later and critique it in light of the material's analysis.

7. You may not *feel* ready, but that is more set-up than you will get in law school!

owned property in the state of Washington, along the coast. Because of a surveying error, the Howards did not realize they owned the land in dispute — tract B. Instead, the Howards believed they owned tract A. The Howards took possession of tract A. The Kuntos believed in good faith that they owned tract B. Accordingly, the Kuntos entered tract B and took possession of the house on the property. The Kuntos occupied tract B for many years, believing it was their land. Due to the weather in Washington, however, the homes along that part of the coast were used as summer vacation property only. Once the weather turned chilly, the Kuntos and their neighbors packed up and moved back inland. The Kuntos occupied tract B only during the summer.

Many years after the Kuntos first took possession of tract B, the Howards decided to build a dock on tract A. The Howards had the land re-surveyed to ensure the dock was on their property. This new survey revealed the prior surveying error. It showed that the Howards owned tract B (the parcel of land the Kuntos were occupying), not the Kuntos. The Howards asserted their ownership of tract B and sued to eject (remove) the Kuntos. The Kuntos countered by claiming title to tract B based on adverse possession. The trial court ruled that the Kuntos' claim failed. The Kuntos appealed.]

. . .

The trial court's reason for denying their [the Kuntos'] claim of adverse possession is succinctly stated in its memorandum opinion: "In this instance, defendants have failed to prove, by a preponderance of the evidence, a continuity of possession. . . ."

Finding of fact 6, . . . finds defendant's possession not to have been "continuous" because it involved only "summer occupancy."

. . . [One of the issues] presented by this appeal [is] . . . : (l) Is a claim of adverse possession defeated because the physical use of the premises is restricted to summer occupancy?

. . .

We start with the oft-quoted rule that: [T]o constitute adverse possession, there must be actual possession which is *uninterrupted*,[8] open and notorious, hostile and exclusive, and under a *claim of right* made in good faith for the statutory period. (Italics ours.) Butler v. Anderson, 71 Wn.2d 60, 64, 426 P.2d 467 (1967). Also see Fadden v. Purvis, 77 W.D.2d 22, 459 P.2d 385 (1969) and cases cited therein.

We reject the conclusion that summer occupancy only of a summer beach home destroys the continuity of possession required by the statute. It has become firmly established that the requisite possession requires such

---

8. [Notice the rule technically uses the word "uninterrupted" but the court has been talking about whether the possession is continuous. For purposes of adverse possession, these two words are interchangeable and most jurisdictions use the word "continuous," not "uninterrupted." Go back and look at your definition of continuous. You may have even used the word "uninterrupted" in defining it. — Ed.]

possession and dominion "as ordinarily marks the conduct of owners in general, in holding, managing, and caring for property of like nature and condition." Whalen v. Smith, 183 Iowa 949, 953, 167 N.W. 646 (1918). Also see Mesher v. Connolly, 63 Wn.2d 552, 388 P.2d 144 (1964); Skoog v. Seymour, 29 Wn.2d 355, 187 P.2d 304 (1947); Butler v. Anderson, supra; Fadden v. Purvis, supra.

We hold that occupancy of tract B during the summer months for more than the 10-year period by defendant and his predecessors, together with the continued existence of the improvements on the land and beach area, constituted "uninterrupted" possession within this rule. To hold otherwise is to completely ignore the nature and condition of the property. See Fadden v. Purvis, supra.

We find such rule fully consonant with the legal writers on the subject. In F. Clark, Law of Surveying and Boundaries, §561 (3d ed. 1959) at 565: "Continuity of possession may be established although the land is used regularly for only a certain period each year." ... It is not necessary that the occupant should be actually upon the premises continually. If the land is occupied during the period of time during the year it is capable of use, there is sufficient continuity.

. . .

Judgment is reversed with directions to dismiss plaintiffs' action and to enter a decree quieting defendants' title to the disputed tract of land in accordance with the prayer of their cross complaint.

Armstrong, C. J., and Petrie, J., concur.

D. ANALYZING *HOWARD v. KUNTO*

1. The Evolution of the Case

The evolution of *Howard v. Kunto* mirrors that of *Pierson v. Post.* The case started as a dispute between the Howards and the Kuntos that the parties could not resolve on their own. The Howards attorney went to the rule plane and found a rule of law to support the Howards' claim to the property (that rule is not discussed in the case, and it is beyond the scope of this material, but it is based on the fact that they were the original true owners of tract B based on their deed). Faced with the Howards' complaint and claim of title, the Kuntos' attorney went to the rule plane looking for a rule of law to argue in support of the Kuntos' claim to the land. Because the Howards were able to meet the requirements of the rule they were invoking, the Kuntos needed a rule that countered — and trumped — the rule invoked by the Howards. The Kuntos' attorney selected the rule of adverse possession, which if satisfied would trump the rule/claim asserted by the Howards.

At trial the Kuntos lost because the trial court found the Kuntos had not met the requirements of the rule, in particular the requirement that their possession be "continuous/uninterrupted." The Kuntos appealed. The appeal has to be a question of law. What was the question of law on appeal, and how does it compare analytically to the question of law in *Pierson v. Post*?[9]

2. The Question of Law on Appeal

The question of law at issue in *Pierson v. Post* was what constituted the rule of occupancy. Both parties agreed that the rule of occupancy applied to and controlled the case, but the parties disagreed on what *the rule* of occupancy was; the parties disagreed on *the rule statement* for the doctrine. The question of law on appeal was what constituted *the rule statement* for the rule of occupancy.

The rule of law at issue in *Howard v. Kunto* was the rule of adverse possession. Both parties agreed that the rule of adverse possession applied to and controlled the case. In contrast to *Pierson v. Post*, however, in *Howard v. Kunto* both parties also *agreed* on *the rule statement* for adverse possession. The court evidenced this point when it started its analysis of the case with the "oft-quoted rule" of adverse possession: "[T]o constitute adverse possession, there must be actual possession which is uninterrupted, open and notorious, hostile and exclusive, and under a claim of right made in good faith for the statutory period." There was no dispute, no question of law, with respect to what constituted the rule statement for adverse possession.

If the rule statement for adverse possession was not at issue in *Howard v. Kunto*, (1) what *was* the question of law on appeal; and (2) how should the court analyze that question of law?[10] You probably feel more confident about your answer to the first question than you do about your answer to the second question. The first question, "what was the question of law on appeal in *Howard v. Kunto*," goes primarily to your ability to read and analyze the court's opinion. The second question, "how should the court analyze that question of law," goes primarily to the abstract skill of legal analysis—what it means to think like a lawyer. Again, those comments are rather abstract, so much so that you may not fully appreciate them at this point. Putting them in their larger analytical context should help.

3. The Larger Analytical Process

The larger analytical process requires you to think about the big picture from a temporal perspective. In *Pierson v. Post*, the court was called upon to *create* a new rule of law for the rule of occupancy. The court ruled that occupancy was established if the party could prove that he or she had the intent to appropriate the animal to his or her individual use, deprived the animal of its certain liberty, and brought the animal within his or her certain control. Once a rule of law is

---

9. The question "how does it compare analytically" is another way of asking you to compare the question of law in *Howard v. Kunto* to the question of law in *Pierson v. Post*. Are they the same *type* of question of law or different?

10. Again, for analytical purposes, you might want to write down your answers to these questions so that you can critique your analysis later.

adopted, it becomes the test that is applied to *future* fact patterns to determine whether the rule has been established.

Pierson v. Post was a case about how a court sometimes *creates* a new rule statement. After the court created the new rule statement in *Pierson v. Post*, the application of the new rule to the facts of that case was rather straightforward. Once it was clear that *legally* Post had to prove, as part of the rule, that he had certain control of the wild animal, it was fairly clear that *factually* he did not have certain control of the fox while it was still running down the beach. *Pierson v. Post* is primarily about the *creation* of a new rule; *Howard v. Kunto* is *not.* The court made that clear when it set forth the "oft-quoted"—well established—rule statement. Instead, *Howard v. Kunto* is about the *application* of that rule. While the application of the rule in *Pierson v. Post* was rather straightforward, the application of the rule statement in *Howard v. Kunto* is not. *Pierson v. Post* demonstrates the analytical process inherent in *creating* a new rule; *Howard v. Kunto* demonstrates the analytical process involved in *applying* an existing rule to a new and cutting edge fact pattern.

4. Issues Within the Issue

When a court applies a rule of law to a fact pattern, the court starts by breaking the rule into its component parts—its *elements*—and then it applies each element individually to the facts to see if the element is satisfied. The first step is to break the rule in question into its elements.

Thinking back to *Pierson v. Post*, how many elements would you say there are to the rule of occupancy? What are they? Most professors would break the rule of occupancy into three elements. To establish occupancy the plaintiff must prove: (1) the intent to appropriate the animal to his or her individual use; (2) that he or she has deprived the animal of its certain control; and (3) that he or she has brought the animal within his or her certain control.

Now that you have broken the rule of occupancy into its elements, you are in a position to apply each element to a new fact pattern. In applying and analyzing the elements of occupancy, each element becomes its own issue: Is the element satisfied? Each element becomes its own issue within the larger issue of whether the rule applies: Russian dolls.[11]

5. Visualizing the Application Process

Remember you can visualize a rule of law as a circle on the rule plane that casts a shadow down onto the factual plane:

---

11. Russian dolls are figurines within figurines. Traditionally they were either wooden or porcelain. At first blush, there would appear to be only one doll, but the doll can be opened in the middle—much like a plastic Easter egg. When you open the doll, you find yet another doll inside the outer doll. It too can be opened in the middle. When you open it, you find yet another doll inside it. And so on.

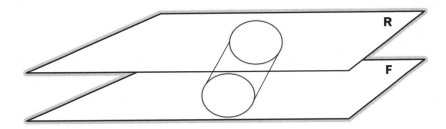

One way to conceptualize the application of the rule to different factual scenarios is to envision different factual scenarios as "x's" on the factual plane. Some cases fall "smack-dab" in the middle of the rule's shadow:

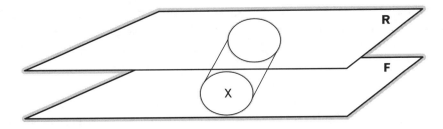

Application of the rule to such a fact pattern is rather straightforward and simple. Application of each element requires you to pair up the element with the fact or facts that satisfy it. Some cases clearly fall "outside" of the rule's shadow:

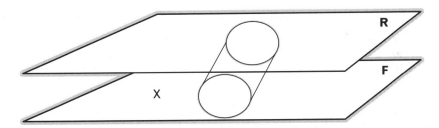

Application of the rule to such a fact pattern is rather straightforward and simple — such as the fox not being under certain control in *Pierson v. Post*. Application of each element requires you to pair up the element with the fact or facts that shows that the element is *not* satisfied.

Some fact patterns, however, fall right along the edge of the rule's shadow:

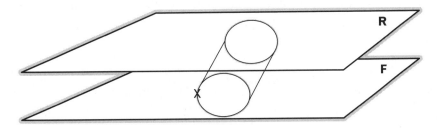

Such fact patterns put pressure on one or more of the elements of the rule. Inherent in the court's analysis of whether the rule applies is the analysis of whether *the element* applies — whether it is satisfied. That is the analytical scenario in *Howard v. Kunto* — was the element of "continuous/uninterrupted" possession satisfied if the Kuntos were in possession of the land during the summers only? The fact pattern fell within what is commonly known as the "gray" area of the rule/element.[12]

6. The Spectrum: Bright Line Rules vs. Soft, Fact-Sensitive Rules

As you get more comfortable applying different rules and elements to different fact patterns, you will come to realize that rules and elements can be placed on a spectrum depending on how much "gray" area there is in the rule/element.

At one end of the spectrum are rules and elements that are rather "bright line." That term may not mean much to you right now, but give it a moment. Bright line rules and/or elements are those that are relatively easy to apply to a typical fact pattern and to determine if the fact pattern falls inside or outside of the rule. This type of rule can be visualized on the rule plane as a circle with the outer edge of the circle being a rather *sharp, bright line.* The circular shadow that bright line rules cast down onto the factual plane are likewise characterized by an outer edge that is also a rather sharp, bright line that facilitates the application and analysis of the rule to most fact patterns.

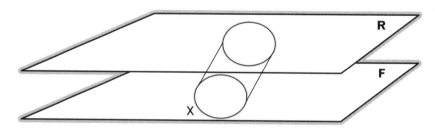

At the other end of the spectrum are rules and/or elements that are more soft and fact-sensitive. The intrinsic nature of such rules and/or elements is that they are more difficult to apply to a typical fact pattern and to determine whether the fact pattern falls inside or outside the rule. This type of rule can be visualized on the rule plane as a circle with a *rather blurred line* for its outer edge. The circular shadow it casts down onto the factual plane are likewise characterized by an

---

12. You might feel like there is no "gray" area in the element of continuous/uninterrupted, but that is based upon *your* definition/understanding of the element. The amount of "gray" area inherent in a rule or element depends upon the *court's* definition/understanding of the element. Why the court's definition/understanding of the element may be different from your understanding will be addressed shortly.

outer edge with a fair amount of "grey" area around the edge of the circle making it more difficult to determine whether fact patterns that fall within this gray area are inside or outside of the rule.

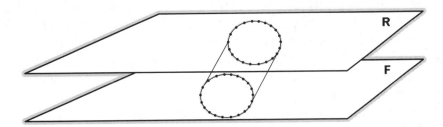

While the discussion of bright line rules vs. soft, fact-sensitive rules may sound very abstract, it is easier to apply than you might think. In fact, you have already read a set of rules that fits neatly into this analytical scheme and constitutes good examples of each type of rule. Reflect back on the different rule statements that were put forth by the court and the dissent in *Pierson v. Post*. The court ruled that the rule of occupancy required the claimant to prove that he or she had the intent to appropriate the wild animal to his or her individual use, that he or she had deprived it of its natural liberty, and that he or she had brought the animal within his or her certain control. The dissent argued that the rule of occupancy should be satisfied as long as the claimant could prove that he or she was in hot pursuit of the wild animal and that he or she had a reasonable prospect of capturing the animal.

Put the two rules on the spectrum. Which rule statement, the majority's or the dissent's, is more bright line? Which rule statement is more soft, fact-sensitive? The dissent's rule statement has more "gray" area. There is more "play" in the wording of the elements, more gray area. What does it mean to say that the party must be in "hot" pursuit? What does it mean to say that the party must have a "reasonable" prospect of capturing the animal? There is much more room for argument and counterargument with respect to whether the elements have been satisfied. Contrast those elements with the majority's requirement that the party must show "certain" control. "Certain" control is more of a bright-line test than "hot pursuit" and "reasonable" prospect of capturing. In a typical fact pattern, it should be easier to tell if "certain control" has been satisfied as opposed to "reasonable prospect to capture."

While it is important to have a sense of how bright line vs. soft, fact-sensitive a rule and/or element is, be careful not to put too much weight on this analytical characteristic. It is intended to help you understand a rule and/or element, to get comfortable with it and what its application and analysis might be like in a typical fact pattern. But each fact pattern is unique, and *every rule and/or element has some gray area*, it is just easier to see the gray area with some rules as opposed to others. The appropriate fact pattern can put pressure on *any* rule/element—as the case of *Howard v. Kunto* demonstrates.

7. *Howard v. Kunto* — Application of Adverse Possession

In contrast to *Pierson v. Post*, in *Howard v. Kunto* the court was *not* called upon to create a rule of law for adverse possession. That rule statement was already well-established and well-accepted. While the exact wording of the rule statement varies from jurisdiction to jurisdiction, a generally accepted statement of the doctrine is that it requires the adverse possessor to show actual entry onto the land in question that gives rise to possession that is open and notorious, exclusive, adverse/hostile, under a claim of right, and continuous/uninterrupted for the statutory period.

Compare the rule statement for adverse possession with the rule statement for occupancy. Most would agree that the rule statement for adverse possession is not as straightforward as (i.e., it is more complicated than) the rule of occupancy. The significance of that statement becomes more apparent when you think about how you would *apply* the rule of adverse possession to a fact pattern. Remember the analytical steps. First, break the rule into its elements. Re-read the rule statement for adverse possession in the last sentence of the prior paragraph. How many elements would you break the rule statement into?

You might be surprised to learn that different professors and authorities disagree on how many elements there are to adverse possession. Some professors break adverse possession into four elements, some five, and some six.[13] You will quickly come to realize that there is more "play" in the law than you might have thought.[14]

Based on the rule statement above, you could have broken the rule into six elements: adverse possession requires (1) actual entry onto the land that gives rise to possession that is (2) open and notorious, (3) exclusive, (4) adverse/hostile, (5) under a claim of right, and (6) continuous for the statutory period.[15] In contrast to the rule of occupancy, however, the elements of adverse possession are not as self-defining. The first element, actual entry, is rather straightforward and self-defining, but some of the others are not. What does it mean to say that the possession must be "adverse/hostile?" What does it mean to say that the possession must be under "a claim of right?"

---

13. Why that is and how they delineate the different elements are beyond the scope of this material.

14. Different courts, and different professors, may construe and interpret a rule differently. Whenever that is the case, take your cues from your professor. He or she will often indicate, through the class discussion, which approach he or she favors and how many elements he or she thinks are inherent in the rule.

15. Do not worry if you came up with a different number of elements. Often words or phrases become a "term of art" that takes on special meaning in the law, a phenomenon that you could not be expected to know. For example, you might have thought that "open" and "notorious" are two separate elements with different meanings. As construed and applied by the courts, however, the phrase "open and notorious" has become a term of art that means the adverse possessor's possession must be such that it gives constructive notice to the true owner. What "constructive notice" means for purposes of adverse possession is best left for your Property class.

When an element is not straightforward and self-defining, it requires the appellate court to provide additional elaboration for the element — *"rule elaboration"* or a "sub-rule." The rule elaboration is necessary to ensure that the lower courts have adequate guidance with respect to how to apply and analyze the element to different fact patterns. Moreover, even when an element appears straightforward and self-defining in the abstract, often there will be fact patterns that will put pressure on the wording of the element — that will make it difficult to tell whether the fact pattern satisfies the element or not. The appellate court will need to provide rule elaboration in such cases to ensure that the element is construed and applied consistent with the relevant public policy considerations. That is what was involved in *Howard v. Kunto*. While the element of continuous/ uninterrupted possession appears straightforward and self-defining enough in the abstract and as applied to the typical fact pattern, the particular fact pattern at issue in the case put pressure on what it means to have "continuous/uninterrupted" possession: What if there is something about the nature of the land such that year round/continuous possession is not the norm?

When the appellate court provides rule elaboration for an element, the court is *creating law*. Granted, it is not a whole new rule, but by clarifying the meaning of *an element* of a rule, the court is clarifying the scope of the rule — the edge of the rule.[16] You will come to learn that almost all rules can be broken down into elements, and most elements have rule elaboration, or sub-rules, within the larger rule: Russian dolls.

Returning to the case of *Howard v. Kunto* again, what was the question of law on appeal? While the larger issue on appeal was whether the Kuntos had satisfied the requirements of adverse possession, the lower court concluded that the Kuntos' possession had not satisfied the continuous possession requirement. This framed the question of law on appeal: What constitutes "continuous possession" for purposes of the adverse possession doctrine? Before the court can decide whether the Kuntos can successfully claim the land based on adverse possession, the court must decide the sub-issue of what constitutes "continuous" possession. The court must provide *rule elaboration* for the element, in essence, *create* a *"sub-rule"* for the element.

Almost every rule of law has elements, and the overwhelming majority of elements have their own rule elaboration. Each element becomes its own sub-issue, most with its own sub-rule. In *Howard v. Kunto*, the larger issue was whether the Kuntos had satisfied the rule of adverse possession. Adverse possession has several elements. Each element is its own sub-issue with its own sub-rule (rule elaboration). The application and analysis of the rule involves breaking the rule into its elements and applying and analyzing each element, each rule elaboration, to the facts: Russian dolls.

---

16. If you visualize a rule as a circle on the rule plane, when the court creates rule elaboration it is clarifying the exact placement of the outer edge of the circle.

Is *Howard v. Kunto* about the rule of adverse possession or is it about the element of continuous possession as required by the rule of adverse possession? It is about both, but if you could pick only one answer, which would you pick? Is the case primarily about the rule or an element within the rule? Which one is *at issue*; which one are the parties really arguing over? First and foremost they are arguing over the element of continuous possession. Analytically, before the court can resolve whether summer-only occupancy can satisfy the requirement of continuous possession, the court must define — or provide *rule elaboration for* — what constitutes continuous/uninterrupted possession. The case of *Howard v. Kunto* is primarily about an element within the rule of adverse possession, the element of continuous/uninterrupted possession.

You will often read cases that are not so much about a *rule of law* as they are about *the rule elaboration* for an element of the rule, a subtle but critical distinction. You should keep the distinction in mind when reading and analyzing cases. You need to be able to distinguish a rule statement from a statement of rule elaboration.

8. Analysis of Typical Student Analysis

Think back to the material above where it asked you to define "continuous" and to think about how you would apply your definition to the issue of whether summer-only occupancy constituted continuous possession. If you are like most first-year law students, you probably used the ordinary dictionary definition of the word "continuous" and concluded that summer-only occupancy is not continuous possession. In *Howard v. Kunto*, however, the court ruled that summer-only occupancy may constitute uninterrupted possession. Why? Why did the court adopt a different meaning, or rule elaboration, for "continuous/uninterrupted"?

A word in a rule statement, an element, may take on a special meaning and become a "term of art." A term of art has a meaning that is different from the ordinary definition of the word or phrase because courts construe and apply the elements in a rule statement with an eye towards *why* we have the rule. Just as courts adopt rules because of certain public policy considerations, courts also define, construe, and apply the elements of the rule because of the public policy considerations underlying the rule. The public policy considerations underlying the rule of adverse possession are, for the most part, beyond the scope of this material. But one major theory of adverse possession is that it is intended to reward adverse possessors who put the land in question to productive use *like an ordinary owner would*. Consistent with that public policy consideration, many courts say that the adverse possessor must act *as an ordinary owner would*.

In *Howard v. Kunto*, when forced to analyze what it means to say that the adverse possessor's possession must be "continuous/uninterrupted," the court went to the public policy considerations underlying the rule: "It has become firmly established that the requisite possession requires such possession and dominion '*as ordinarily marks the conduct of owners in general*, in holding, managing, and caring for property of like nature and condition.'" Based on that public policy consideration, the court created the following rule elaboration for how continuous the possession must be: the possession is continuous as long as "the land is occupied during the period of time during the year it is capable of use. . . ."

How does that compare to the rule elaboration you thought of when the material above asked you to define the word continuous? Do not be too harsh on yourself if you did not come up with anything close to that rule elaboration. You did not know the public policy considerations underlying the rule, and without that knowledge, it is unreasonable to ask you to come up with the accepted rule elaboration for the continuous possession element. But now you should have a better understanding of the analytical process behind creating rules and rule elaboration.

In *Howard v. Kunto*, the court ruled that as applied to coastal property that is only suitable for occupancy during the summer, summer-only occupancy constitutes continuous possession for purposes of adverse possession.

E. LEGAL ANALYSIS – *IT DEPENDS*

Notice the interdependent nature of the analytical process. In *Pierson v. Post*, the issue was what constituted occupancy. Analytically the answer was *it depends*: it depended on what the court decided were the paramount public policy considerations underlying the rule. In *Howard v. Kunto*, the issue was whether summer-only occupancy of the land constituted continuous possession of the land. Again the answer was *it depends*: it depended on the rule elaboration for the element of continuous possession.

Finally, notice the analytical ambiguity inherent in the court's rule elaboration for the continuous possession element. The court defined continuous possession as requiring continuity of possession consistent with the possession of owners in general holding similar property. As applied to the facts in *Howard v. Kunto*, that meant that their summer-only occupancy constituted continuous possession for purposes of adverse possession. Does that mean that summer-only occupancy *always* constitutes continuous possession for purposes of adverse possession? No. Again, the answer is *it depends*. This time it depends on the particular facts of each case. If the nature of land is such that seasonal-only occupancy is how similarly situated owners treat their property, then seasonal-only occupancy would be continuous occupancy. If, however, the nature of the land is such that year round occupancy is how similarly situated owners treat their property, then seasonal-only occupancy would *not* be uninterrupted occupancy.

You will quickly come to realize that the most common answer in law schools is *it depends*; now you have some sense of why that is the case.

F. CONCLUSION

Proper application and analysis of a rule requires you (1) to break the rule into its elements, and then (2) to apply and analyze each element. Applying and analyzing each element implicitly means that each element becomes its own issue, often with its own rule elaboration/sub-rule.

Issues within the larger issue; rule elaboration/sub-rules within the larger rule. Russian dolls.

The Exam Taking Process

Now that you understand what it means to "think like a lawyer," it is time to take that abstract knowledge and turn it into a set of practical ideas and techniques for how to perform better on law school exams.

In particular, Part II will discuss: (1) how law school exams relate to what you do before you take the exam; (2) how to prepare better for law school exams, i.e., how to outline; and (3) how to perform better on law school exams, i.e., how to (a) spot the issues, (b) analyze each issue, and (c) write up your analysis in a clear and effective writing style.

CHAPTER 9

Complete the Circle:
See the Big Picture

There are many steps on the path to success in law school. Each step must be understood in isolation as well as in relation to each other. It helps to visualize the process, to see how each step is related to each other and to the whole. Each step can be depicted as a circle:

First, what do you read before you come to class? You read *cases*. What are cases chock-full of? Most students answer *facts*:

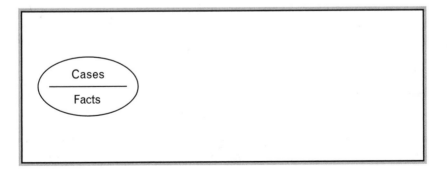

Next, you go to class. What do we — the professor and the students — do to the cases in class? If you had to sum up the process in one word, what do we do to the cases in class? We *analyze* each case. When you analyze a case in class, notice your professor shifts your focus to which parts of the case? The class discussion is chock-full of references to the *rules* (and if there is any validity to the theory developed in the first part of this book, the class analysis of the case should also include some discussion of the *public policy* considerations):

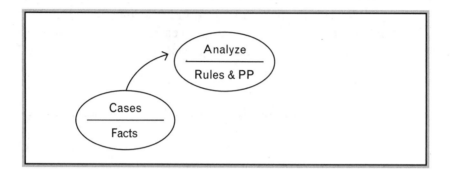

Then, before you take the final, what does conventional law school wisdom say you should create? An *outline*. What is your outline chock-full of? *Rules* (and if there is any validity to the theory developed in the first part of this book, what else should be in your outline? Some *public policy*).

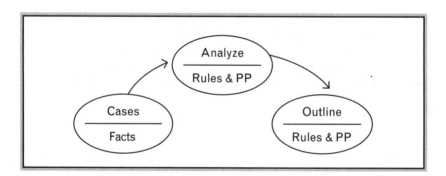

The diagram to this point depicts the semester from the start of classes until the end of classes. As developed so far, the diagram depicts the academic and analytical process leading up to the start of exams. Then the fun really starts.

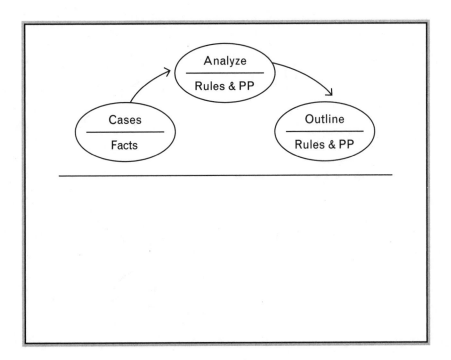

Then you walk into the exam room to take your first exam. What is the format of the typical law school exam? What does the typical exam consist of? *A fact pattern*:

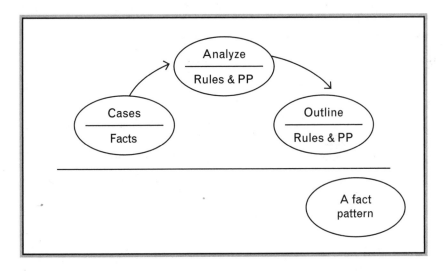

What is the first thing you are supposed to do as you read the fact pattern? *Spot the issues*:

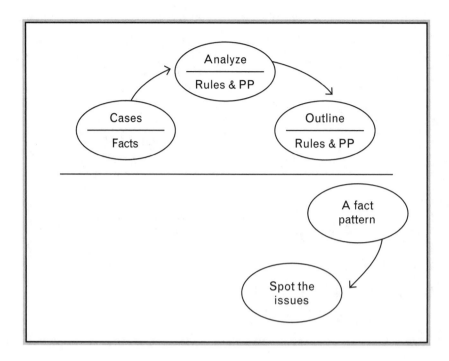

After you spot the issues, what is the next issue, what are you supposed to do to each issue? If you had to sum it up in one word, what are you supposed to do to each issue on the exam? You are supposed to *analyze* it. What does it mean to *analyze* an issue? You apply the relevant *rules and public policy considerations.*

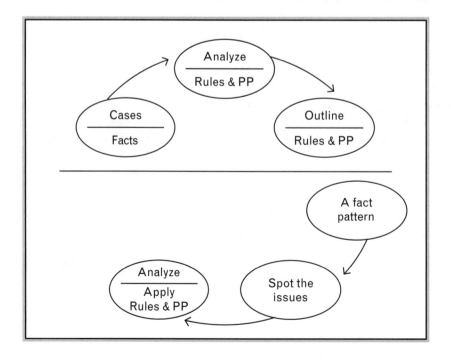

And how should you write up your analysis? Write like a court would *write a well-written judicial opinion.*

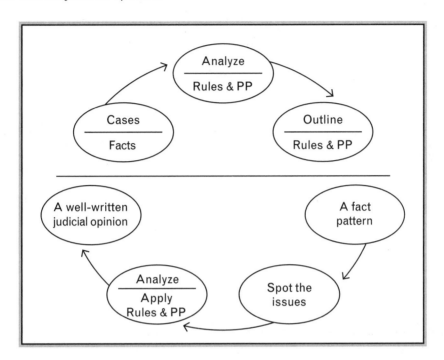

At a conceptual level, that is a law student's circle of life. Each semester you start out reading and analyzing opinions in a certain subject area of the law. By the end of the semester, the professor expects you to be able to write a well written judicial opinion about selected issues in that subject area. You must be able to complete the circle.

The first part of this book focused on the upper half of the diagram — the first half of a law student's circle of life (or at least on the first two bubbles: what it means to read and analyze a case). The second part of this book will focus on the lower half of the diagram — on how to take a law school exam — and on how the other bubbles relate to that task, particularly how outlining relates to it.

CHAPTER 10

Writing Style: Write Like a Judge

The golden rule of *how* to write a law school exam essay is to write something that reads like a well-written judicial opinion.

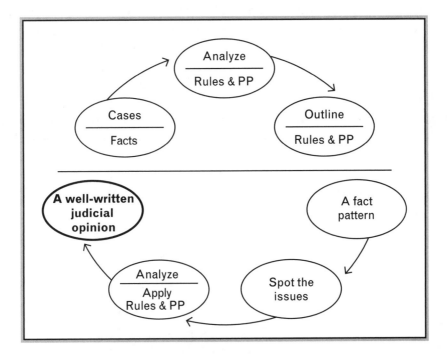

Be professional. Do not make jokes in your essay. Do not vent to the professor about how unfair you think the exam is. Write like you were writing an opinion that would be published and everyone in the class—if not all attorneys and members of the bar—would read it. Be professional.

Notice the goal is to write a *well-written* judicial opinion. You have been reading and analyzing judicial opinions all semester. Subconsciously you have been developing the ability to discern the difference between a well-written judicial opinion and a poorly written judicial opinion. When reading cases, take note of what it is that makes the better-written opinions better. Reading and critically analyzing many judicial opinions during the course of the semester should help you discern what distinguishes a well-written opinion from a poorly written opinion; it should also help you develop the ability to write the former.

But the admonition that you should write like a judge and strive to write a well-written judicial opinion is, admittedly, conclusory and overly broad. *Do not take that advice too literally.* Most judicial opinions start out with a statement of the facts. ***Do not re-write the facts of the exam in your exam essay as an opening statement of the facts.*** Assume that the exam fact pattern *is* the opening part of the judicial opinion you are writing. There is no need to re-write or to paraphrase the facts. In addition, do not worry about the procedural posture of the case (unless the professor has expressly made that a part of the exam by the call of the question). Jump right into the first issue. The first sentence you write literally should start out "*The first issue is . . . .*" Then proceed to analyze and write up your analysis as a judge would. That really is the key — you should analyze and write up your analysis of each issue as a judge would. That is your goal.

While the admonition that you should "write like a judge/write something that looks like a well written judicial opinion" helps to set the proper tone and writing style for your exam, that statement still assumes that you know what it means to analyze an issue — how to do it, and how to write it up. What does it mean "to *analyze* each issue"? How do you do it? How do you write it up structurally? It is time to put the second to last bubble under the analytical microscope.

CHAPTER 11

How to "Analyze" an Issue: IRAC vs. IRRAC

A. INTRODUCTION

What does it mean to *analyze* an issue on an exam?

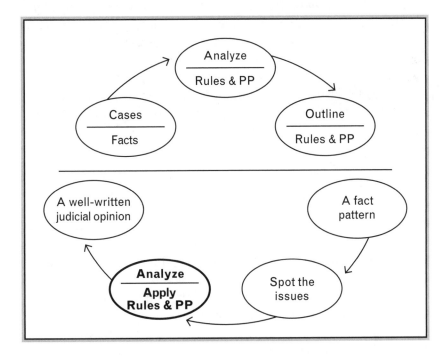

Most students understand it means *to apply the relevant rules and analyze them,* but what does that mean? At a theoretical level that answer is helpful, but at the practical, concrete level it does not really tell you what to write on the page or how to write it. To understand the process we need to break it down even further; we need to put it under the analytical microscope and take it step by step.

First, assuming that analyzing an issue means you need to apply the relevant rule or rules, where do you get those rules? Most students answer "From the cases we read"; some say "from the statutes"; some even say "from the commercial outlines we buy!" While at one level each of those answers has some truth to it, for exam purposes each is wrong. On the exam, you get the rules from *your outline.*[1]

B. SEE THE RELATIONSHIP BETWEEN YOUR OUTLINE AND THE EXAM

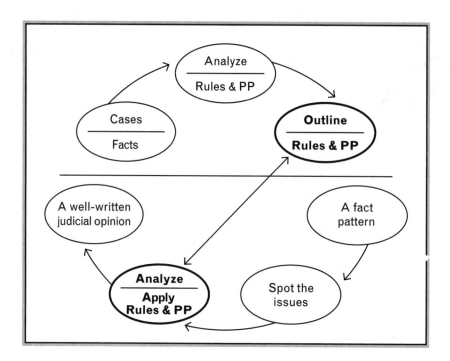

As simple as it sounds, seeing the relationship between your outline and the exam is one of the more important steps to doing well on your exams. The simple fact that you get the rules you use on the exam from *your outline* should help educate you as to how you should write your outline. You want to write your outline with an eye towards to the final. When you are creating your outline, your mindset should be "if this rule were to come up on the exam, what should I write and why?" Every rule that is fair game for the exam should be (1) in your outline and (2) written just the way you would write it on the exam if it were to be tested. *See the relationship between your outline and the exam.*

Notice that the prior paragraph emphasized that you see the relationship between the exam and *your* outline. You have to create *your own outline.*

---

1. If you do not know already, you will learn rather quickly following the start of law school that an outline is a study aid you make for each class that takes the material you have covered in the book, your case briefs, and your class notes, synthesizes it, and condenses it down to the important material you need to know for the final exam.

I write a commercial outline.[2] I make decent money off of it. But if you buy a commercial outline *in lieu* of creating your own outline, while you are helping to put my kids through college, you are hurting yourself. Commercial outlines should be used only to help you create your own outline, not as a substitute for creating your own outline. If you do not create your own outline, you will be writing the rule for the first time on the exam. Even if you understand a rule, it takes time to formulate exactly how you are going to articulate and write the rule — the words you are going to use. Time is of the essence on an exam. You do not want to waste time during the exam thinking about *how* you should word a rule statement. That is one of the reasons it takes so long to create an outline. You have to invest the time to think about the best way to write each rule.

If you have trouble coming up with the right words to use in the rule state-ment, *that* is when a commercial outline can be useful. But you should not consult the commercial outline until *after* you have tried to create your own outline. The struggle to understand a rule — to know it well enough to be able to choose the right words to articulate it — is an important part of the learning process. That struggle will help you *understand* the rule. Your ultimate goal is not just to know a rule statement; it is to understand it — to know when to use it and how to use it. These are just some of the reasons why you should not consult a commercial outline, if at all, until after you have tried to write your own. But when creating your own outline, do not spend too much time on any given rule. If any given rule takes more than ten minutes or so to formulate, you may want to take a peek at how the commercial outline words it. Too much struggle can lead to frustration, which can be counterproductive. Everything in moderation.

Another reason it is important that you create your own outline is that it serves as a check on how well you know each rule. It is easy to understand a rule at the conceptual level. Virtually every law student will tell you he or she understands a given rule. But a conceptual understanding of the rule will not be good enough on the exam. You need to have a detailed understanding of the rule. You need to know the exact parameters of the rule. In creating your outline, for each rule you learned during the semester, *your goal is to write the rule, the whole rule, and nothing but the rule, in one sentence.* If you cannot write the rule in one sentence, that may be a sign that you really do not understand the rule yet. In addition, you want to be able to write each rule in one sentence because time will be of the essence on the exam. You do not want to waste time and words writing three or four sentences on a rule statement if you can write that same rule in one sentence.

But do not take the goal of writing each rule statement in one sentence too literally. *Be flexible*; the *goal* is to write each rule in one sentence, but that is not an absolute rule of outlining. Sometimes it is easier to write, and remember, a rule statement as two short sentences instead of one. When that is the case, go with it. The purpose of outlining is to help you master the material. Whenever modifying

---

2. Wendel, Emmanuel Law Outline: Wills, Trusts, and Estates (2005 Aspen).

the approach suggested herein helps you master the material easier, or faster, or better, feel free to modify. Each student is unique. You want to adopt the approach that works best *for you*. The material is intended to give you a default approach, one that has proven successful for many students, but feel free to modify it where you deem appropriate.

Assuming you adopt the one sentence approach to writing your rule statements, should you paraphrase your rule statements or should you be very careful about how you word your rule statements? Some students argue that you should paraphrase your rule statements because that facilitates your ability to recall them during the exam. But when you paraphrase a rule, you run the risk of changing the rule. If each student in the class paraphrases the rule, the professor may get 30 to 40 different versions of the same rule. But the essence of a legal system is that all similarly situated individuals are subject to the *same* rule. If there are 30 to 40 different versions of the rule, what is the likelihood that all similarly situated persons will be treated the same? There should be only one basic version of each rule (the jurisdictions may be split on what the rule should be, but within each jurisdiction there should be only one version of the rule).

Do not, however, take too literally the admonition that everyone should have the same basic rule statement. Every rule statement has two types of words in it: filler words and operative words. The scope of the rule turns on the operative words, not the filler words. You are free to change and paraphrase the filler words to the extent you do not change the scope of the rule. If, however, you change or paraphrase an operative word, there is a real risk that you are changing the rule. Be very careful about how you word the key operative words in your rule statements. That is another reason why you want to practice writing your rule statements before the exam. If you wait to write a rule statement for the first time on the exam, that significantly increases the risk that the wording you select will not be the best. Practice makes perfect, and the process of creating the outline forces you to think about, and practice writing, your rule statements.

C. IRAC vs. IRRAC

Assuming you have created an outline, and that it contains a perfect one-sentence statement of — each rule you have learned in the class, how do you use that during the exam? Most law students have heard the conventional law school wisdom is that the organizational structure you should use on the exam is IRAC:

> I — Issue,
> R — Rule,
> A — Analysis, and
> C — Conclusion.

Assuming, *arguendo*, for the moment that IRAC is the proper structure to use on the exam, what does that mean? How do you implement it?

Consistent with IRAC, for each issue you spot on the exam, the first sentence you write in your essay about that issue should be the issue statement. Issue statements can come in all different shapes and sizes, but most professors do not give points for an issue statement, so do not spend too much time thinking about them or creating them. Issue statements basically set up your analysis, and most of the points allocated to an issue are for your analysis. So get in and out of your issue statement quickly. As long as the issue is a typical issue (a dispute between only two parties where one party is claiming the other is in the wrong or, conversely, one party is claiming a right), the classic issue statement starts out with a reference to the party invoking the rule in question and ends with a reference to the rule (the name of the rule).

For example, in Property there is a doctrine that some students find strange called adverse possession. Adverse possession provides that where one party enters onto another person's land, without permission, and possesses it for long enough and in compliance with the requirements of the doctrine, the law rewards the party who is trespassing by giving him or her title to the land he or she has possessed. The doctrine of adverse possession has the effect of involuntarily transferring title to land from one party to another. Adverse possession requires the adverse possessor to actually enter the land of another and take possession that is open and notorious, adverse/hostile, exclusive, under a claim of right, and continuous for the statutory period. There are two primary theoretical rationales for the doctrine. One is the statute of limitations approach — that society is punishing the true owner for not bringing his or her cause of action to eject the adverse possessor in a timely manner. The other theoretical explanation for the doctrine is that society is rewarding the adverse possessor for putting the land to productive use. You will study the doctrine in greater detail in your Property class, but for now assume that is the essence of the doctrine.

Assume the first paragraph of the Property exam starts out as follows:

> Pete owns Malibuacres, which is located in California. He currently lives back in Missouri, however, where he is taking care of his mother who is sick. He rarely visits Malibuacres. Dude moves onto Malibuacres, builds a house, farms the land, and lives there for a number of years.

What is the issue? How would you write it? "The issue is whether Dude can claim Malibuacres based on adverse possession." The issue statement starts with a reference to the party invoking the rule (Dude) and ends with a reference to the rule the party is invoking to support his or her claim (adverse possession). The issue statement can be written as a question but it does not need to be. Here, if one wrote the issue in question format, it would be: Can Dude successfully claim the land based on adverse possession? The issue statement, however, can also be written as a declarative sentence: Dude will claim the land based on adverse possession. In the second format, the issue is more implicit: can Dude successfully claim the land? Either type of issue statement should be acceptable to most professors since most do not give points for issue statements.

According to IRAC, after you write your issue statement, what sentence should you write next? Your rule statement for that rule: the one-sentence rule statement you have in your outline that constitutes the rule, the whole rule, and nothing but the rule. Here that rule statement would be: "Adverse possession requires actual entry onto the land that gives rise to possession that is open and notorious, hostile/adverse, exclusive, under a claim of right, and continuous for the statutory period" or something to that effect (keeping the operative terms the same). Adverse possession is one of the more complicated rules in Property. Nevertheless, it can be written as one sentence. Notice also how the one-sentence rule statement contains no reference to the facts. Do not let the facts bleed into your rule statement. The rule statement should be written word for word the way it is in your outline, and obviously your outline rule statement cannot have any references to the facts on the exam because it was created well before the exam. The rule statement on the exam should be the rule, the whole rule, and nothing but the rule (so help you . . .).

According to IRAC, after you have written your rule statement, what do you do next? You apply and analyze the rule. This is where many students start to feel like they have been thrown into the deep end of the pool and told to swim again. What does it mean to analyze a rule? How are students supposed to do that mentally? How are they supposed to write it? That feeling of uncertainty starts to sink back in, and most students begin to struggle. No need for that. If you think about it logically, you will see that there is a method to the madness.

Most students will tell you that applying and analyzing the rule means you apply it to the facts. First, notice the structure—you apply the rule to the facts, not the facts to the rule. More importantly, *how* do you apply the rule to the facts? What do you do mentally? What are the steps in your process? *Break the rule into its parts—its elements—and check to see if each element is satisfied.* Reflect upon that sentence for a moment. If you break the rule statement into its elements and check to see if each element is satisfied, what are you really doing with each element? You are creating *an IRAC for each element.* First you ask, "Is the element satisfied?" Then you ask, "What is the test for the element?" Then you apply the test for the element to the facts to come to your conclusion for the element. Mentally, each element gets its own IRAC.

Return to the adverse possession example above. Assuming that was the first issue on your Property exam, what would your essay look like so far?

> The issue is whether Dude can successfully claim the land based on adverse possession. Adverse possession requires actual entry that gives rise to possession that is open and notorious, adverse/hostile, exclusive, under a claim of right, and continuous for the statutory period.

When you go to apply and analyze the rule, you break the rule into its elements. Depending on your Property professor, you can break the rule statement for adverse possession into four, five, or even six elements (you will come to learn that different professors will teach the same materially differently). One element is open and notorious. Is the element of open and notorious satisfied? In analyzing that question, you instinctively ask, what does it mean to say that the possession must be "open and notorious"? If you have taken Property, you know that there is a test for what constitutes open and notorious possession for purposes of adverse possession. Open and notorious requires that the possession be such that it gives constructive notice to the owner, i.e., if the owner were to walk the property, he or she would notice the adverse possessor. For all practical purposes, the test for the element becomes a sub-rule or *rule elaboration* on the basic rule statement.

In analyzing the element — in applying it to the facts — do you apply the words from the element ("open and notorious") or the words from the rule elaboration for the element ("possession that would give constructive notice to the owner")? You apply the words from the rule elaboration, the sub-rule for the element. *Where do you get that rule elaboration? From your outline! Again, see the relationship between your outline and the exam.* Can you paraphrase the rule elaboration for each element or should you be careful in how you word your rule elaboration? You should be just as careful as you were in writing the base rule statement.

D. WRITING YOUR ANALYSIS

In applying the rule elaboration for open and notorious to the facts of the hypothetical above, is the element satisfied? Most students would not only say "yes," they would say it is a "slam-dunk" — there is no doubt the element is satisfied. If the element is clearly satisfied, do you need to address it at all in your essay? Most law professors would say "yes." Reaching the conclusion that the element is clearly satisfied is legal analysis, and most law professors want to see all of the legal analysis you performed during the exam in your exam essay. There are, however, a minority of law professors who prefer to see you analyze and discuss only those elements that are at dispute. Absent clear instruction from your professor that he or she is of this latter type, you should err on the side of writing your analysis of each element in the rule, even those that are clearly satisfied.[3]

Assuming the element is clearly satisfied, how do you *write* your analysis. One possibility is to write "Open and notorious is clearly satisfied." Some students will write that sentence on the exam. Is that a good idea? No. That is a classic example of a conclusory writing style. It is conclusory because it fails to explain *why* the element is satisfied. All it tells the reader/professor is that the element is satisfied. To the extent you are supposed to perform an IRAC for each element, that sentence only expresses the conclusion. It does not tell the reader/professor the rule elaboration or the facts from the fact pattern that are relevant to the element.

Because many law students think legal analysis means you apply the facts to the law, they will write facts to law. The sentence such a student would typically write would start "Because Dude moved on to the property, built a house, farmed the land, and lived on the land. . . ." How would you finish that sentence?

---

3. If you are comfortable doing so, you might want to ask your professor whether on the exam he or she wants you to analyze only the elements in dispute or all the elements.

"... open and notorious is clearly satisfied." But analyze that sentence. Does that sentence — "Because Dude moved on to the property, built a house, farmed the land, and lived on the land open and notorious is clearly satisfied" — properly express your analysis of the element?

While that sentence is better than the sentence in the prior paragraph, it is still conclusory. While that sentence includes the relevant facts from the fact pattern that go with the element of open and notorious, the sentence fails to make any reference to the rule elaboration. It shows the professor that the student knows that open and notorious is an element of adverse possession, but it does not show the professor that the student knows the pertinent rule elaboration for the element. At best the student is asking the professor to give him or her credit for knowing the right rule elaboration without having written it. That is not a good idea. Most professors will grade only the words on the page; they will not grade what they *think may be* in your head. The sentence as written is conclusory because the sentence fails to include the rule elaboration the student used when analyzing the element in his or her head.

But just as some students over-emphasize the facts, some students over-emphasize the rule/rule elaboration. A student who employ this writing style would write his or her analysis of the element as follows: "Open and notorious, which requires possession that gives constructive notice to the true owner, is clearly satisfied here."[4] How does this sentence compare to the sentences above for the analysis of the element? It has the advantage of including the rule elaboration for the element, but it fails to include the relevant facts from the fact pattern that go with the element. The "A" in IRAC differs from the "R" in that the analysis requires discussion and analysis of the relevant facts from the fact pattern. If there is no discussion and analysis of the facts, the answer is still conclusory. This sentence makes no reference to any of the facts from the fact pattern. Again, the student is asking the professor to give him or her credit for having properly paired up *in his or her head* the rule elaboration with the relevant facts from the fact pattern. That is not a good idea. Most professors will grade only the words on the page and not what they *think may be* in your head. The sentence as written is conclusory because the sentence fails to include the relevant facts the student was thinking of in his or her head.

Proper treatment of a slam dunk element requires two sentences typically: one sentence for the rule elaboration, and one sentence for the application and conclusion. Notice the structure of the writing — it parallels and reflects the structure of proper analysis: lead with the rule elaboration for the element, then apply/analyze and conclude. If the element is clearly satisfied, there is no need to write an issue statement for the element because it is implicit. Proper

---

4. Or another variation on this sentence is: "Open and notorious is satisfied here because Dude's possession clearly gives constructive notice to Pete." Although this sentence blends in some references to the facts (the names of the parties), it fails to explain *why* Dude's possession gives notice; it fails to discuss and analyze the facts that are relevant to the element.

treatment of the open and notorious element as it applies to the hypothetical fact pattern above means that your essay should now read as follows:

> The issue is whether Dude can successfully claim the land based on adverse possession. Adverse possession requires actual entry that gives rise to possession that is open and notorious, adverse/hostile, exclusive, under a claim of right, and continuous for the statutory period. Open and notorious requires possession that would give constructive notice to the true owner. Here, because Dude moved on to the land, built a house, lived in it, and farmed the land, if Wendel had walked the property he would have noticed Dude; the element of open and notorious is satisfied.

Notice how the last two sentences parallel the IRAC structure but at the element level. There is no issue statement for the element — it is implicit. Do not waste time writing one. The analysis leads with the rule elaboration for the element, the "sub-rule" for the element. Then apply the rule elaboration to the facts by raising and discussing the relevant facts from the fact pattern — all of them. Do not paraphrase the facts. Use all of the relevant facts in the fact pattern and use the exact words used in the fact pattern. Do not paraphrase the facts. Then reason to the conclusion for the element.

Lastly, be sure that your application and analysis sentence *connects up* with your rule elaboration sentence by including the key word or test from the rule elaboration sentence. Here, the use of the word "noticed" in the application/conclusion sentence connected the facts/analysis with the rule elaboration in a way that permits the reader to follow, and independently assess, the writer's analysis. A well-written analysis sentence will always be written in such a manner that it provides the reader with a bridge between the facts and the rule elaboration so the connection between the two is obvious, if not explicit.

One minor point should be noted here. Although the structure of the analysis and writing follows IRAC, it need not be in that precise order. The key is that the writing contains the key substantive component parts ("I" — the issue statement — is not essential for slam dunk elements) regardless of the order. For example, the following treatment of the open and notorious element would be equally effective:

> Open and notorious requires possession that would give constructive notice to the true owner. Here, it is satisfied because Dude moved on to the land, built a house, lived in it, and farmed the land, so if Wendel had walked the property he would have noticed Dude.

The key is that the writing expresses the component parts of your analysis, not the order of its presentation per se.

Now you are in a position to understand why the conventional law school wisdom that students should write their exam using IRAC is so misleading. Many students assume that as long as they write the base rule statement in their analysis they have done all they are expected to do. But proper analysis of the rule requires the students to use not just the right rule, but also the right *rule elaboration*. Accordingly, instead of the order of your writing looking like IRAC:

> I — Issue
> R — Rule
> A — Analysis
> C — Conclusion

you might want to structure your writing for each issue on the exam so it follows the IRRAC structure:

> I — Issue
> R — Rule
> RE — Rule Elaboration
> A — Analysis
> C — Conclusion

Or better yet, after the base rule statement, you should have IRACs within the IRAC (for each element an IRAC minus the issue statement):

> I — Issue
> R — Rule
>
> 1. RE for element 1;
> A+C for element 1;
>   2. RE for element 2;
>   A+C for element 2;
>   3. RE for element 3;
>   A+C for element 3; etc.

A question that naturally arises from the above discussion is if the base rule statement has multiple elements, with which element should you start? Some students simply write their analysis the way they memorized the rule, starting with the "first" element and working their way down the list of elements. The problem with that approach arises when the first element is the one in dispute, and you conclude it is not satisfied. Should you still discuss/analyze the other elements, and if so, how do you do that without it sounding very awkward (talking about the other elements after you have concluded the first one is not satisfied)?

Remember the golden rule to exam writing is to write like a judge or court would write it; write something that looks like a well-written judicial opinion. When a court is applying and analyzing a rule that has multiple elements, with which element does the court start? A court usually starts with the elements that are clearly satisfied and works its way to the elements in dispute. Resolution of that last element, the one most in dispute, will also resolve the larger IRAC with respect to the base rule statement. But there are exceptions to every rule. If there is a natural sequence to the elements in a rule, it may make more sense to take the elements in that sequence.

Assuming there is no natural sequence to the rule's elements, you should address the elements that are clearly satisfied first, working your way to the element or elements in dispute. If an element is in dispute, that means it cannot be properly analyzed in two sentences. It will require more analysis. If it is in dispute that typically means there are arguments that can be advanced on both sides of the issue of whether the element is satisfied. Still lead with the rule elaboration, but then write a sentence or two that presents the one party's argument, "Wendel will argue. . . ." Then write a sentence or two that presents the other party's argument, "Dude will argue. . . ." Then step back and play judge and indicate how you think the element should be resolved and why.

If the issue of whether the element has been satisfied is truly a close call, what should your conclusion be? If it is really a close call, what is the ultimate tie-breaker? The public policy justifications behind the rule. You need to bring into the analysis the public policy considerations that gave rise to the rule. What is the conduct the rule is intended to discourage; what is the conduct the rule is intended to encourage? You should bring the public policy considerations into your writing either to support the argument/counterargument of the two parties or to justify your conclusion favoring one party or the other.

Another possible way to handle a truly close call is, unlike a real judicial opinion, to write, "This is a close call that could go either way." If you write that conclusion, you are not writing a true judicial opinion but rather something closer to a bench brief. That probably is the more accurate description of what a well-written exam should look like, but since most law students have never seen a bench brief, it does not make sense to tell you that is what you should write. Just assume that you want to write something that looks like a judicial opinion unless the conclusion is too close to call, in which case you can say that — but then you need to overlap both possible conclusions on all the subsequent issues in the exam. But the material will talk about this more later.

In conclusion, if the rule statement has multiple elements, the structure of your essay will more likely resemble the following:

I — Issue
R — Rule

1. RE
A+C
   2. RE
   A+C
      3. RE
      Argument
      Counterargument
      Public Policy Considerations
      Conclusion

By now you should be starting to realize that IRAC can come in all different shapes and sizes. To help remember this you might want to remember

IRRAC. When you pronounce it, *roll* the R to help you remember that it means Rule and Rule Elaboration, and to help you distinguish it from the traditional IRAC. Be flexible. IRRAC is the basic structure because those are the component parts of your analysis. But how they end up being presented can vary with the issue, the rule, and the public policy considerations.

E. DIFFERENT TYPES OF IRRACs: VARIATIONS ON A THEME

1. Split in the Jurisdictions as to the Rule

As the discussion above demonstrated, it is not uncommon to have IRACs within the base IRAC. In addition, you can have parallel IRACs. How does that arise? What if there is a split in the law? For example, what if some jurisdictions follow the common law rule and some jurisdictions apply the Restatement approach? What do you do then? If the professor does not specify which approach to apply on the exam, you need to apply both (all) approaches in the alternative.

For example, if the call of the question[5] asks you to analyze the issues raised by the fact pattern, and if there is a split in the jurisdictions with respect to the law for a particular issue, analysis of that particular issue will require you to discuss, in the alternative, each of the different approaches. You need to reflect the split in the law in your IRRAC. The classic way to do that is by adding a sentence after the issue statement that basically says "The analysis depends upon which approach the jurisdiction takes." Then bifurcate your IRRAC, typically applying the older approach (the common law approach in the example above) first and working your way to the more modern trend approach (the Restatement approach in the example above). Structurally your IRRAC will look something like the following:

> I — Issue
> "The analysis depends. . . ."

> R — Common Law
> RE — Rule Elaboration
> A — Analysis (including IRACs for each element)
> C — Conclusion

> On the other hand, . . .

> R — Restatement
> RE — Rule Elaboration
> A — Analysis (IRACs)
> C — Conclusion

---

5. The professor's exam instructions at the end of the fact pattern.

You will have parallel IRRACs, but only one issue statement because the issue is the same — it is just the jurisdictional approach to the rule that is split.

2. Split in the Jurisdictions as to the Element

Just as you will have parallel IRRACs when the jurisdictions are split as to the *law* to be applied, sometimes you will have parallel IRRACs within an IRRAC when the jurisdictions are split as to the *rule elaboration* to be applied to an element of a rule. Remember that the test or definition for an element is technically not a rule unto itself; it is rule elaboration for the element. But for all practical purposes, the test or definition for the element is treated like a rule for analytical purposes on the exam. So if there is a split in the jurisdiction with respect to what constitutes the test for the element, you need to reflect that split in your analysis and writing of the element.

For example, the rule of adverse possession requires that the adverse possessor make actual entry onto the land, which gives rise to possession that is open and notorious, exclusive, hostile, under a claim of right, and continuous for the statutory period. The jurisdictions have taken three different approaches to the claim of right element. Some take an objective approach; some a subjective good faith approach; and some a subjective bad faith approach. When writing up one's analysis of adverse possession on an exam, the structure for the writing would be something like the following:

> I — Issue
> R — Adverse possession rule statement

RE for 1st element to be analyzed;
Application and Conclusion for element
   RE for 2nd element to be analyzed;
   Application and Conclusion for element
      RE for 3rd element to be analyzed;
      Application and Conclusion for element
         The analysis for claim of right depends
         on the jurisdictional approach:

| RE for objective approach Application and Conclusion | RE for subjective bad faith Application and Conclusion |

| RE for subjective good faith Application and Conclusion |

Often where you have a split in the jurisdiction with respect to an element, it makes sense to apply it last or close to last because the split often means that your conclusion to the larger IRRAC will be split depending upon the jurisdictional approach to the element.

F. COMPETING RULES

Just as you can have parallel IRRACs, you can have competing IRRACs. In Property, many professors cover the law of wild animals (not so much to teach the rules that govern how to acquire a Property interest in a wild animal but more so for methodological purposes). If T goes on to L's property and shoots and kills a fox, both parties can assert a claim in the fox. T will claim it based on occupancy; L will claim it based on *rationi soli*. Whenever you have competing claims, the issue statement typically will not make a reference to any rule of law but rather will be written in a more fact-sensitive way. For example, in the case of the fox, the issue would be, "Who has a better claim to the fox." Then you would have competing IRRACs with each party invoking the rule of law that supports each party's claim. In this situation you will in essence have "sub-issue" statements because you still need a sentence stating which rule of law each party is invoking:

> I: Who has a better claim to the fox?
>
> Sub-Issue 1: T will claim it based on occupancy.
> Rule: Occupancy requires . . .
> Analysis: Here, . . .
> Conclusion: T can establish occupancy over the fox.
>
> Sub-Issue 2: L will claim the fox based on *rationi soli*.
> Rule: *Rationi Soli* requires . . .
> Analysis: Here, . . .
> Conclusion: L can establish *rationi soli* with respect to the fox.
>
> Wrap-up Conclusion: Because *rationi soli* attached to the fox before T killed it, L should prevail based on first in time, first in right and so as to deter trespass.

1. Affirmative Defenses

You also will have competing IRRACs where one party is asserting a claim and the other party is asserting an affirmative defense. Typically the affirmative defense is its own rule of law that deserves its own IRRAC. Where you have competing IRRACs, if both parties can meet the requirements of the rule they are invoking, you will need a wrap-up conclusion that analyzes and explains which claim trumps and why. The "why" often requires you to use the relevant public policy considerations with respect to each of the competing rules.

In the end, IRAC is not a rigid structure but rather it should be viewed as a flexible template. Moreover, IRAC is rather misleading because most rules of law have elements and most elements have their own rule elaboration. The key to a good exam is the quality of the rule statements and the quality of the rule elaboration statements because the rule statements set up the rule elaboration, and the rule elaboration sets up and greatly affects the quality of the analysis. The mental template that you take into the exam should be IRRAC, not IRAC:

> I — Issue
> R — Rule
> RE — Rule Elaboration
> A — Application/analysis
> C — Conclusion

And where should you get your one-sentence rule statements and your rule elaboration? From your outline — *see the relationship between your outline and the exam.*

G. WRITING YOUR OUTLINE

If you are working on your Property outline, and you are outlining the doctrine of adverse possession, how would you do it? There is no absolute formula for how to outline, but you want to make sure you include the basic elements that you would use if the rule in question comes up on the exam. First, start with your heading, typically the name of the rule in question:

> I. Adverse Possession

What might you want to consider putting right underneath the heading (or pretty close to right underneath it)? The one sentence rule statement for adverse possession:

> I. Adverse Possession
> Adverse possession requires actual entry that gives rise to possession that is open and notorious, exclusive, adverse/hostile, under a claim of right, and continuous for the statutory period.

Then what should come next? Your rule elaboration. Break the rule statement into its elements and next to each element write its rule elaboration.

If you followed that format in your outline, notice the basic structure for each rule in your outline:

> H — Heading
> R — Rule statement
> R — Rule elaboration

Just to help you see the relationship between your outline and the final a little better, could you turn your heading into a generic issue statement? (I'm not necessarily recommending it, but just to make an analytical point, could you turn your heading into a generic issue statement?) The classic issue statement starts with a reference to the party invoking the rule and ends with a reference to the rule being invoked. Obviously, when you are writing your outline, there is no way you will know the name of the party in the exam fact pattern who will be invoking the rule. So just call that party "X." Assuming the party's name is X, in your outline can you write a generic issue statement instead of a heading? Sure you can: "Can X claim the land based on adverse possession?" If you did that, notice what that would do to the format of your outline:

I — Generic issue statement
R — Rule statement
R — Rule elaboration

Compare that to the writing structure you are going to use on the final:

Exam format	Outline format
I — Issue	I — Generic issue statement
R — Rule statement	R — Rule statement
R — Rule elaboration	R — Rule elaboration
A — Application/analysis	
C — Conclusion	

If you see the relationship between the final and your outline, and if you outline with an eye towards the final, how much of the final is done before you even enter the exam room? If you were to weight each part of the IRRAC equally, 60 percent of the exam is already done before you even enter the exam room. Most of the exam should be done before you enter the exam room.

Proper outlining takes a lot of time. But when done properly and viewed properly, it should pay big dividends on the final. The only part of the exam you should be sweating during the test is the application/analysis and conclusion. Once you spot an issue, the issue statement, rule statement, and rule elaboration should be easy. You have already practiced those sentences and you should have the rule and rule elaboration memorized well enough that those sentences should just roll off your tongue.

One of the easiest rule statements in law school is the rule statement for what is necessary for a valid contract. When asked that question, most students answer without hesitation "offer, acceptance, and consideration." Your goal is to be able to recall and recite every rule statement and every rule elaboration with the same ease, comfort, and speed that you can recall the rule for what is necessary to have an enforceable contract. Ideally, the day before each exam, you should have a single sheet of paper that lists only the names of every rule you learned in that course, and you should be able to go down the list and recite the rule statement for each rule and then the rule elaboration for each rule with same ease, comfort, and speed that you recited the rule for what is necessary for an enforceable contract.

Remember not to take the exam writing format and the outline format too literally. The material above says that the structure should be:

Exam format	Outline format
I — Issue	I — Generic issue statement
R — Rule statement	R — Rule statement
R — Rule elaboration	R — Rule elaboration
A — Application/analysis	
C — Conclusion	

But you would not literally follow that structure because assuming that the rule has more than one element, you should apply the rule elaboration for one element before raising the rule elaboration for the next element. For example, assuming adverse possession has six elements, your rule statement and rule elaboration in your outline should run seven sentences. But on the exam, if adverse possession is the first issue, after writing the issue statement can you just download the seven sentences from your outline that constitute the rule and rule elaboration? No. You should raise and apply each rule elaboration one at a time, as a general rule completing one element *before* raising and analyzing the next. So your actual exam format should be:

```
            I — Issue
            R — Rule
        RE
        A+C
            RE
            A+C
                RE
                A+C
                    RE
                    A+C
                        RE
                        A+C
                            RE
                            A+C
```

And remember, you cannot just download the rule elaboration sentences as they are in your outline because you should lead with the elements that are clearly satisfied and work your way to the element or elements in dispute. So you need to show judgment and analysis not just in the way you apply the elements but in the order that you present them.

H. THE QUALITY OF YOUR ANALYSIS vs. THE QUALITY OF YOUR WRITING

There is one last point that needs to be noted about analyzing an issue on the exam. It can be made easiest by returning to the diagram at the start of the chapter that depicted the big picture:

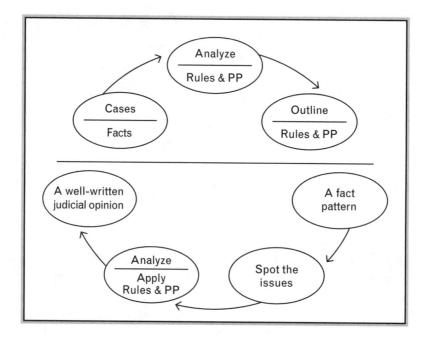

The material has been focusing on the second to last step in the process, the "analyze each issue" step.

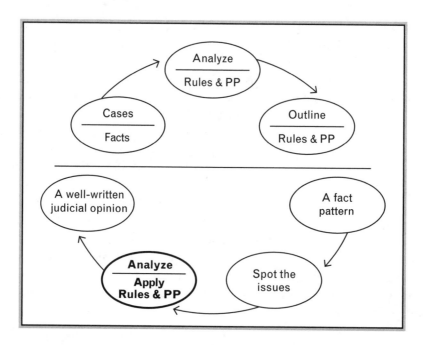

But really, the second to last step in the process and the last step are one and the same for grading purposes:

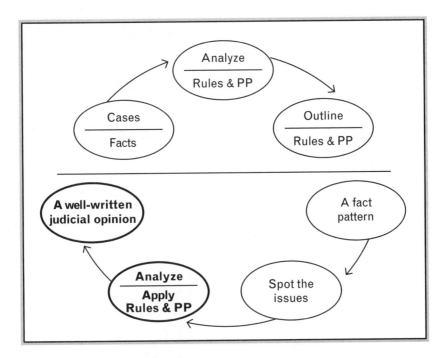

The only way a professor can assess the quality of your analysis is by how you express it — how you write it. If the quality of your analysis in your head is an "A" exam, but the quality of your writing is a "C" exam, your final grade will be a "C." Professors cannot read your mind.

The quality of your writing has to reflect the quality of your analysis for you to get full credit for the quality of your analysis. That is one of the primary reasons law students get so frustrated with their exams. They believe — and may even be right — that the quality of the analysis in their head was an "A" exam. But if the quality of your writing — your issue statements, your rule statements, your rule elaboration statements, your application and analysis statements, and your conclusion statements — does not match the quality of your analysis in your head, the former will control, not the latter.

Practice your exam writing before your first set of exams. Most law schools have old exams on file somewhere in the library or on electronic reserve. Make sure you take one or two before the final exam. Get comfortable with your exam writing style so during the exam you are not *thinking* about your exam writing style — you are just doing it. During the exam, you should be focused on *what* you are writing, not *how* you are writing it. Practice your exam writing style until the basic format and structure becomes second nature.

The other skill you need to master to do well on your exams is the ability to spot issues.

CHAPTER 12

The Circuitry Behind
Issue Spotting

A. ISSUE SPOTTING — WHY?

The key to developing your issue spotting ability is to remember what makes law school exams unique. Unlike undergraduate exams, where the professor typically asks you to tell him or her about a particular topic, a law school exam is a fact pattern where your first task is to "spot the issues." Part of the reason many law students struggle with law school exams is they fail to see the logic behind this method of testing. Why a fact pattern?

The logic behind the fact pattern approach to testing is that the professor is asking you to act as an attorney. One way to conceptualize a fact pattern is to think about it as if a new client has just walked into an attorney's office — your office — and told you, the attorney, the facts of a problem or dispute. You are being asked to act like an attorney: spot the issues raised by the fact pattern and write up an analysis of the issues based on the facts given. In particular, you are being asked to think along the following lines of analysis: (1) what are the issues; (2) what is your analysis, i.e., what causes of actions could the parties assert and what is your analysis of each cause of action; and (3) what additional facts would you like to know and why are they relevant?

B. ISSUE SPOTTING — HOW?

Understanding the logic behind the fact pattern method of testing is helpful, but to really understand what it means to spot an issue and to improve your ability to do so, you need to put yourself into the shoes of the professor when he or she is drafting the exam. Because the classic law school exam is a fact pattern, the way a professor tests a rule is by creating a fact pattern that raises an issue where proper analysis of the issue requires the student to raise and discuss the rule the professor wants to test. That is a tough sentence; you might want to read it again because it is also an important sentence. How does a professor create his or her fact patterns? The method behind the madness can be visualized by returning to the three planes.

When you read a case, either consciously or subconsciously, you are reading it on three planes: the factual plane, the rule plane, and the public policy plane.

The particular dispute involved in the case can be depicted as an "x" on the factual plane. The rule you learned in that case can be depicted as a circle on the rule plane:

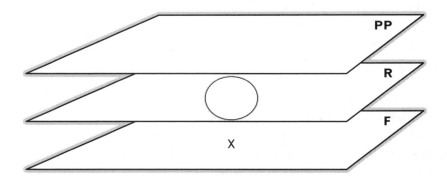

Consciously or unconsciously, you have associated the rule with the facts of that case. The problem with that association is you are not going to see that exact fact pattern again. Even if the professor wants to test that rule on the final, you are not going to see that exact fact pattern again. That would be too easy. Instead, on the exam you will see a different fact pattern that the professor believes is similar enough in nature that it should trigger your association with the rule if you know the rule well enough.

The last clause of the prior paragraph — the reference to "if you know the rule well enough" — is the first reason so many students have trouble issue spotting. They think that as long as they know the rule well enough, they should be able to spot the issue. Actually over-focusing on the rule can *create* issue spotting problems, not solve them. The rule is written on the *rule* plane, but the fact pattern is written on the *factual* plane. You need to build a bridge mentally between the rule on the rule plane and the factual plane. That bridge is known as the triggering fact: the fact the professor must include in the fact pattern to trigger your association with the rule.

C. THE TRIGGERING FACT

There are several keys to developing your issue spotting ability. First, remember that every rule of law is written for a *generic* fact pattern, not just for the particular fact pattern in the case you read. The case you read is just a particular example of a fact pattern that raises the rule in question. You want to take away from the case the generic fact pattern that goes with the rule of law, not the particular fact pattern in the case.[1] You want to "step back" from the particular

---

1. The particular fact pattern in the case you read may or may not be representative of the more generic fact pattern. You will develop a feel for when the particular fact pattern is representative of the generic fact pattern and when it is not as you develop your analytical skills.

facts of the case and say to yourself "those may be the particular facts of this case, but what are the generic facts that go with this rule"? Notice how that step in your analysis shifts your focus from looking backwards at the facts of the case in question to looking forward to the generic facts that will include other similar disputes that may occur in the future (i.e., the dispute on the exam). Moreover, you want to word your generic fact pattern using factual terms, not the terms of the rule. If you use the terms from the rule, that is going back to the rule plane too much and is counter to the purpose of focusing on the generic *fact* pattern.

One way to think about the generic fact pattern is that every rule of law has a classic fact pattern that goes with it. The classic fact pattern is the fact pattern where the rule makes the most sense. The classic fact pattern can be depicted on the three planes as an "x" right in the middle of the shadow the rule casts down on the factual plane. The classic fact pattern is the most obvious example of the generic fact pattern that goes with the rule.

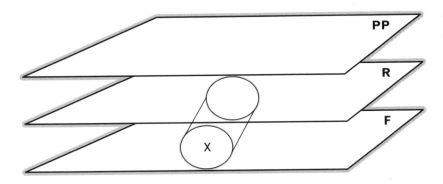

On the other hand, the generic fact pattern can be visualized on the factual plane as a small circle that often corresponds to the size of the scope of the rule on the rule plane, but it is slightly smaller than the shadow cast by the rule. It includes the "typical" fact patterns that come within the scope of the rule, but not necessarily all the fact patterns:

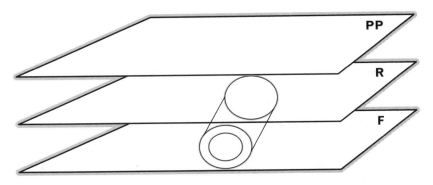

The particular case that you read to learn the rule is *just one example* of a particular fact pattern that comes within the scope of the rule.[2] There are countless variations of the particular fact pattern that come within the scope of the rule (or close enough to raise the issue). If the professor wants to test that rule on the exam, he or she will create another fact pattern that comes within the scope of the generic fact pattern or close enough to raise the issue associated with the generic fact pattern. The circuitry of "spotting the issue" is that the professor assumes that you will see enough similarity between the fact pattern on the exam and the fact pattern from the case you read (or a hypothetical you discussed in class) to realize that you should raise and analyze the rule in question. The first step in building the analytical bridge between the two particular fact patterns is the generic fact pattern.

Another technique that can help you develop your issue spotting abilities is to put yourself in the shoes of the professor. If a professor wants to test a particular rule of law on the exam, how does he or she go about it? What is the thought process he or she goes through? While each professor is unique, the logical process is that first the professor thinks of the rule he or she wants to test. Then the professor thinks of the generic fact pattern that goes with that particular rule. Within that generic fact pattern is an indispensable fact, or a "triggering" fact that must be present to trigger the students' association with the rule. Each rule of law not only has a generic fact pattern, but within the generic fact pattern is a triggering fact (or combination of facts). The professor thinks of the generic triggering fact, then he or she thinks of a particular example or version of the triggering fact, and then the professor builds a storyline around that particular example or version of the triggering fact.

Some triggering facts are rather obvious and straightforward. Assume you are the Criminal Law professor and you want to test the homicide doctrine. What has to happen in your fact pattern? Someone has to die. If no one dies, you cannot expect the students to discuss homicide — maybe attempted homicide, but not homicide if no one dies. And notice, just because someone dies, that does not automatically mean you will need to discuss homicide in your exam answer. The person may have died of natural causes and there is no good faith argument under the facts that it was homicide. But the triggering fact that should trigger you to at least *think* about the rule — to spot the *potential* issue — is that someone dies.

If you see someone die during a Criminal Law exam, the "homicide" light bulb in your head should go off and you should analyze it to see if a *good faith argument* can be raised that it is homicide. Notice the test for spotting an issue is *not* whether the rule is satisfied; it is *not* whether a court would conclude that the

---

2. For purposes of this discussion, the phrase "comes within the scope" does not necessarily mean that the fact pattern met the requirements of the rule, only that if it did not, a good faith argument could be advanced that the facts did meet the requirements of the rule. In other words, that proper analysis of the issue included analysis of the rule because one or more of the parties could assert it in good faith even if it was unlikely that in the end a court would hold that the rule had been satisfied.

death is a homicide, the test for spotting an issue is *whether it can be argued in good faith* to a court that the rule applies (in this example that it is a homicide). Do not play judge when analyzing what constitutes an issue, play the role of an attorney, of a zealous advocate. Can an argument be asserted in good faith to a court of law that the rule applies?

That begs the question: what constitutes an argument in good faith? From a legal and ethical perspective, that is a difficult, technical point that is beyond that scope of this material. For academic purposes, however, understand that the typical first-year law student is too quick to play judge, too quick to dismiss an argument that can be asserted in good faith. One approach to what constitutes good faith is "if you can say it — or write it — without laughing out loud, it constitutes a good faith argument." That test might be a bit extreme, but for purposes of whether you should raise and assert an argument on an exam, it probably is a good standard. Too many law students leave too many good faith arguments in their head because they think the argument is not a winner — and that applies not only to issue spotting, but also to the argument/counter-argument analysis of an element within a rule. Only after playing the role of zealous advocate should you then step back and play judge. Only then should you give your conclusion with respect to how you think a court would most likely rule and why.

Triggering facts run the gamut from very obvious to very subtle. The triggering fact for homicide on a Criminal Law exam is very obvious: someone has to die. That constitutes a "freight train" issue. If someone dies during the Criminal Law exam, that fact is so "loud" it is like a freight train coming through the room during the exam: every student should "spot" it. But other triggering facts are much more subtle. The professor will expect only a handful of students to "spot" the more subtle triggering facts. You can maximize your chances of spotting even the subtle issues by being more sensitive to the triggering fact(s) that go with each rule. You can develop your sensitivity by putting yourself into the shoes of the professor who is drafting the exam.

For example, assume you are the Property professor and you want to test adverse possession on the exam. How would you do it? Remember adverse possession is a doctrine that involuntarily transfers title from one party to another when the one party has met the requirements of the rule. The rule statement for adverse possession is that there must be actual entry onto the land that gives rise to possession that is open and notorious, adverse/hostile, exclusive, under a claim of right, and continuous for the statutory period. Remember, the Property exam is going to be a fact pattern, so if you were the Property professor who wanted to test adverse possession you would need to think of the generic fact pattern that goes with the rule of adverse possession (not the rule per se), and then, within that generic fact pattern, the trigger fact that must be present to trigger the students' association with the rule. Then you need to create a particular example of that trigger fact and build a storyline around it so the fact pattern makes sense. What is the triggering fact(s) for adverse possession?

Most students, when asked that question for the first time, respond, "Someone goes onto someone else's land." If that was your answer, are you living at home right now? Most students answer "no," they are living in an apartment. Does that mean you adversely possess the land where you live? No, most students are tenants. But notice then your statement of the triggering facts for adverse possession — "someone goes onto someone else's land" — is too broad. It does not distinguish the tenant from the adverse possessor. What is the difference between the two? That difference helps to clarify the triggering fact for adverse possession.

Given a second chance to identify the triggering fact for adverse possession, some students answer, "Someone goes onto someone else's land *adversely*." That is better but notice the last word in that triggering fact statement, "adversely," is a word that comes more from the rule statement for adverse possession than from the factual plane. You want to write your triggering fact as much as possible on the factual plane, not the rule plane. You are writing the triggering fact to sensitize yourself to a *fact* pattern that may appear on the final exam. Try to avoid using legal terms in your triggering fact. If possible, re-word the legal term in a more factual way.

Try re-wording the triggering fact for adverse possession one more time: "Someone goes onto someone else's property without permission." That is better. Notice there are an infinite ways that a professor could create a particular fact pattern in which that happens, but no matter the particular facts, now that you have identified the triggering facts you should spot the issue.

Every rule of law has a generic fact pattern and a triggering fact or set of facts. In your outline, at the end of the section for the rule in question, consider dropping in a new heading called "Triggering Fact." Next to it, write what you believe is the triggering fact for that particular rule of law. For some rules, this will be easy; for others, it will be very difficult. Do not worry. You do not need to state the perfect triggering fact. As long as you think about it and give it a good faith effort you will increase your sensitivity to the generic fact pattern that goes with rule, thereby improving your issue spotting skills.

D. TRIGGERING FACTS vs. SET-UP FACTS

Lastly, notice that a corollary to the triggering facts concept is that there are only two types of facts in an exam fact pattern: triggering facts and set-up facts. Triggering facts are those words in the fact pattern that are intended to trigger your association with the rule — that make you spot the issue. All the rest of the facts in the fact pattern are just set-up fact. They are there to set-up the triggering facts and to transition out of the one issue into another. Think back to the hypothetical Property exam fact pattern in the prior chapter:

> Pete owns Malibuacres, which is located in California. He currently lives back in Missouri, however, where he is taking care of his mother who is sick. He rarely visits the property. Dude moves onto Malibuacres, builds a house, farms the land, and lives there for a number of years.

As you read each sentence in the above fact pattern, ask yourself whether the sentence contains any triggering facts or whether it contains just set-up facts. "Pete owns Malibuacres, which is located in California." Set-up or triggering facts? Set-up. "He currently lives back in Missouri, however, where he is taking care of his mother who is sick." Set-up or triggering facts? Set-up. "He rarely visits the property." Set-up or triggering facts? Set-up. "Dude moves onto Malibuacres, builds a house, farms the land, and lives there for a number of years." Set-up or triggering facts? Triggering facts — that sentence should have made you think of adverse possession. You might want to circle the triggering facts and in the margin next to them write the abbreviation for the rule ("AP") that it made you think of. That indicates you have spotted the issue and where at least some of the relevant facts are with respect to the issue. You should read the exam fact pattern twice to maximize your chances of spotting all the triggering facts, but after you do so, you are ready to start writing.

The material so far has addressed how you go about spotting an issue and how you should organize and write your analysis of the issue: IRRAC. But on virtually every exam fact pattern, you will spot more than one issue. Which issue should you start with? What should be the macro organization of your exam essay? The macro organization of your exam essay is also important to your issue spotting ability because it can affect your ability to spot the "latent issues" on the exam: the issues raised not by the fact pattern per se, but by your analysis of the issues raised by the fact pattern.

CHAPTER 13

The Macro Organization of Your Exam Essay

A. INTRODUCTION

The exam proctor says you may begin the exam. You read the exam instruction cover page and then open the exam to the fact pattern. You read the fact pattern. You circle or underline the triggering facts—the facts that make you think of a rule of law—and you write the name of the rule (in abbreviated form) in the margin next to each triggering fact. You read the fact pattern a second time, just to make sure you have spotted all the issues (the "freight train" issues jump out the first time, you may spot some of the more subtle issues the second time through). You are ready to start writing. Where should you begin?

Some students argue you should start "with the most important issue"; others argue for "the issue with the most points allocated to it"; others argue for "the issue that is the easiest to do, the most clearly satisfied." While all of these answers have some merit to them, they also have some problems associated with them, not the least of which is they show that the students do not fully understand the structure of an exam.

B. "SLIDERS"—THE PARALLEL "LEGAL" WORLD

On an exam, each issue arises in the *legal* environment that exists at the time the issue arises. That sentence sounds very circular. You may even have had to read it twice (if not three times). What does it mean to say that an issue arises in a "*legal* environment" when all you have on the exam is a fact pattern—a factual environment? *As you resolve each issue on an exam, you allocate legal rights to one or more of the parties to the issue.* When I first started teaching, the students who received the lowest grade in both of my classes that first semester started their exam answers by raising and trying to analyze the last issue in the fact pattern. I was surprised and did not understand at first the apparent correlation between where the students began their exams and how they performed. But then it dawned on me—the last issue in the fact pattern arises in a very different *legal* environment than the first issue.

Virtually every fact pattern in law school is written in chronological order. It starts at some point in time and moves forward in time from there. That is not an accident. Law professors think long and hard not only about *which* issues are on the exam but also *the order* in which the issues arise because as you resolve each issue you are allocating legal rights to one or more of the parties to the issue. You are building a parallel universe that mirrors the fact pattern; only this parallel universe has an overlapping legal environment based upon the legal rights that proper analysis of the issues has allocated to the respective parties. To properly analyze an issue, you have to analyze it in the *legal* environment that exists at the time the issue arises. As a general rule, to know what the proper legal environment is you have to analyze the issues in the order that they appear in the fact pattern so that you have set the table for the issue that you are analyzing.

A simple example will demonstrate the importance of taking the issues in the order in which they appear in the fact pattern. Most Property professors cover the law of finders. Without going into all the nuances of the law of finders, two of the more important rules of the law of finders are that (1) a finder has superior rights to a found item over all but the true owner; and (2) when an item is found on private property, the owner of the private property where the item is found has superior rights to the found item over all but the true owner. Another important part of the Property course is the law of adverse possession. The material has already discussed the law of adverse possession, but just to refresh your recollection, adverse possession is a way of involuntarily transferring title from one party to another. Pursuant to the law of adverse possession, if one party actually enters the property of another, giving rise to possession that is open and notorious, exclusive, adverse/hostile, under a claim of right, and continuous for the statutory period, the adverse possessor acquires title to the land that he or she has actually possessed.

Now assume the first two paragraphs of the Property exam are as follows:

> Wendel owns Malibuacres, which is located in California. One day Anne wanders onto Malibuacres while out for a walk and finds a half-buried box of old gold coins.
>
> Thereafter Wendel moves back to Missouri. He moves in with his ailing mother to help care for her. He is so concerned with his mother's health that he rarely visits Malibuacres. Dude moves onto Malibuacres, builds a house, lives in the house, and farms the land for a number of years.

If those are the first two paragraphs of the Property final exam, what are the issues? The first issue is one of finders. Who has a superior claim to the gold coins, Wendel or Anne? The second issue is one of adverse possession. Can the Dude successfully claim Malibuacres based on adverse possession? Are these two freestanding, independent issues or is there an overlap that affects the analysis of each? They are two freestanding, independent issues. Resolution of the first issue does not affect the second issue, nor does resolution of the second issue affect the first issue.

Now reverse the order of the paragraphs on the Property exam:

> Wendel owns Malibuacres, which is located in California. Nevertheless he moves back to Missouri and moves in with his ailing mother to help care for her. He is so concerned with his mother's health that he rarely visits Malibuacres. Dude moves onto Malibuacres, builds a house, farms the land, and lives there for a number of years.
>
> Thereafter, one day Anne wanders onto Malibuacres while out for a walk and finds a half-buried box of old gold coins.

If those are the first two paragraphs of the Property exam, what are the issues? The first issue is one of adverse possession, and the second issue is one of the law of finders. Are these two issues the same as they were in the first exam above? No. This time, because the adverse possession issue comes first, the party who can assert the claim of the landowner in the second issue depends on proper analysis of the first issue. If Dude meets the requirements of adverse possession, he will assert the landowner's claim to the found item. If Dude cannot meet the requirements of adverse possession, Wendel will assert the landowner's claim to the found item.

If you take the issues out of order — if you analyze the finder's issue first — you either would miss the overlap and run the risk of incorrectly analyzing the issue, or halfway through it you might realize that who may assert the landowner's claim depends on how the first issue comes out and you might start analyzing the first issue in the middle of the second issue. All of a sudden to you the exam starts to look like this awful exam full of interwoven issues, while really it is not. But if you take the issues out of order and then halfway through them start raising other issues because of their overlaps, your exam answer will take a turn for the worse.

C. GENERAL RULE – TAKE THE ISSUES IN CHRONOLOGICAL ORDER

With respect to the macro organization of your exam essay, keep it simple. After you have spotted all the issues and you are ready to start writing, as a general rule *start with the first issue*. Start at the top of the fact pattern and walk your way down the fact pattern. Break the exam into five, six, seven — however many there are — bite-size issues. Assume each issue is its own freestanding independent issue and let your analysis of the prior issues wash down over the subsequent issues.

And keep your wits about you for any "latent" issues that may arise as a result of the overlapping legal analysis. Many students assume that an issue can arise only from a triggering fact. Not so. An issue can also arise from proper legal analysis of the issues that do arise from the triggering facts. As you work your way through the analysis of the fact pattern, new insights, new issues, and new analysis may come to you. Keep your mind open to these news issues and new insights into the analysis.

Remember that while taking the issues in the order they appear in the fact pattern is the general rule, there are exceptions to every rule. Sometimes it will make sense to re-arrange the issues, to take them in an order other than the order in which they appear in the fact pattern. There are two common scenarios in which you will want to re-order the issues.

The first scenario where you probably will want to re-organize the issues on an exam is when you have an affirmative defense. Remember that an affirmative defense is a rule of law that can be asserted in defense to a claim/rule of law. On an exam, often the triggering fact for the affirmative defense will appear earlier in the fact pattern than the triggering fact for the cause of action to which it is an affirmative defense. Does it make sense to raise and analyze an affirmative defense before the cause of action to which it is a defense? No. Move the affirmative defense analysis down, raising and discussing it *after* the cause of action to which it is an affirmative defense.

The other exception to the general rule of taking the issues in the order that they appear in the fact pattern is for "add-on" rules. What is an "add-on" rule? The best way to understand what is an "add-on" rule is to think about your outline. Most students study their outline "vertically": when they come to a rule heading in their outline, they read down vertically, focusing on the material under that heading, doing their best to understand and memorize everything they can about that rule. Once they have studied that rule, they move on to the next rule and repeat the process. Most students never study the material in their outline "horizontally": they usually do not analytically turn the outline on its side and ask "what is the relationship between this rule and the next rule; what is the relationship between this rule and the rule before it?" If you turn your outline horizontally, what you will realize is that some rules are "entry" rules and some rules are "add-on" rules. Add-on rules are rules that can only be tested in connection with, and typically as an add-on to, another rule.

An example would be helpful. In Property, there is the doctrine of adverse possession. Adverse possession says that if an adverse possessor enters the property of another and possesses it in a way that satisfies the requirements of the rule, the adverse possessor gets title to the land in question. A natural follow-up issue is to how much land does the adverse possessor get title? The answer is only as much land as the adverse possessor actually possessed unless he or she is claiming adverse possession under *color of title*. If the party is able to claim adverse possession under color of title, he or she gets not only the land he or she actually possessed, but also the land he or she constructively possessed under the terms of a defectively written instrument (typically a defective deed) that he or she thought was valid.

Color of title is its own rule with its own requirements, but it is an add-on rule. It is not an independent, freestanding rule that can be tested on its own. It can be tested only as an add-on to adverse possession. Adverse possession is the entry rule for color of title. Adverse possession, however, can be tested on its own as an independent, freestanding rule. Adverse possession can be tested without testing color of title, but color of title cannot be tested without adverse possession being tested. If you study adverse possession in some depth, and if you think about the material horizontally, you will come to realize that adverse possession has a number of add-on doctrines (color of title, tacking, and the disability doctrine, to name a few).

On an exam, often the triggering fact for an add-on rule appears earlier in the fact pattern than the triggering fact for the entry rule. But it does not make sense to raise and analyze the add-on rule before the entry rule. Move the analysis of the add-on rule down to after the analysis of the entry rule.

As a general rule, take the issues in the order in which they appear in the fact pattern, but if it makes sense to vary from that order (affirmative defenses, add-on rules), feel free to do so. But make sure you have thought it through and there is a good analytical rule to do so, not just that you think the issue is "more important" or "easier to analyze."

D. CALL OF THE QUESTION: "WOULD" vs. "SHOULD" vs. "STATE OF NIRVANA"

The call of the question is extremely important on a law school exam. The call of the question is the sentence or short paragraph at the bottom of the question where the professor indicates how he or she wants you to analyze the question.

If the call of the question instructs you to "analyze how the issues raised by the fact pattern *would* be resolved," your job is to spot the issues and analyze how a court would mostly likely rule on the issue, and why, under the rule you are applying. If there is a split in the jurisdictions as to the applicable rule, apply each rule in the alternative and indicate how a court applying *each rule* would likely rule on the issue, and why. If, when you apply the rule to the facts, it is a close call whether the rule should apply, you need to raise and apply the relevant public policy considerations that support the rule.

If the call of the question instructs you to "analyze how the issues raised by the fact pattern *should* be resolved," your job is not only to spot and analyze each issue raised by the fact pattern, but, more importantly, where there is a split in the jurisdictions, first and foremost, you need to raise and address the split. You need to indicate the different legal approaches, and then, *before* you apply the rule to the facts, you need to analyze which rule the court *should* adopt, and why. The analysis of which rule the court *should* adopt and why will occur on the public policy plane. What are the public policy arguments that support rule A; what are the public policy arguments that support rule B; which set of public policy arguments is better, and why? Then, after you have resolved which rule the court *should* adopt, and why, you come back down to the factual plane and apply the rule the court should adopt to the facts. A professor who wants you to address on the exam which rule the court should adopt and why can also send you that instruction by telling you the fact pattern occurred in some newly formed jurisdiction, such as the "State of Nirvana." How so? If the jurisdiction is a newly formed jurisdiction, each issue that arises on the exam is a question of first impression. As to any issue where there is a possible split in the rule, a court in that newly formed jurisdiction would have to address which rule should apply, and why, before the court could apply it. If that is what a court in that jurisdiction would have to do, so too should you.

Lastly, there is the pure policy question. The typical pure policy question reads something like the following:

> Congratulations. You have been hired as a legislative assistant to Senator Boxer. Senator Feinstein has proposed the following statute: [text of proposed statute]. Please advise Senator Boxer whether she should vote for or against the proposed statue, and why.

This type of exam question has no fact pattern. How are you supposed to analyze it? Notice what the professor is asking you to do. He or she has given you a proposed new rule. Asking you to analyze whether the Senator should vote for or against it is analogous to asking you to analyze whether the proposed rule *should* be adopted. Proper analysis of that issue would require you to indicate what is the prevailing approach (or approaches) to that rule of law, comparing and contrasting how the new proposed statute differs from the prevailing approach. Then, you need to go to the public policy plane. What are the public policy arguments that support that prevailing approach; what are the public policy arguments that support the new proposed statute; which set of public policy arguments is better, and why? There is no application of the rule to the facts, just analysis of which rule is better, and why.

Be sure to pay close attention to the call of the question on the exam.

CHAPTER 14

Multiple Choice Questions: Mini-Essays

Although the classic law school exam format is a one-hour fact pattern, at most law schools some professors will also have some multiple choice questions on their exam. This is particularly true for subjects that are tested on the multiple choice portion of the bar exam. The logic is to help prepare you for the bar exam. If the bar examiners are going to test you on that material using multiple choice questions you should get used to being tested on the material in that testing format. So you should expect to take some multiple choice questions during your law school career, and if not in school, you will have a full day's worth on the bar exam.

There are two common ways students analyze multiple choice questions. Visualize a standard multiple choice question:

> 1. A finds a ring, but she loses it on her way home. Thereafter B finds the ring, but on her way home C robs her of the ring. C takes it to the jeweler, D, to have it appraised. D suspects that it is not really C's, so D takes it from C and refuses to give it back.
>
> Assess each party's claim to the ring and rank the claims from strongest to weakest:
>
> A. The order is D, A, B, C.
> B. The order is A, B, C, D.
> C. The order is A, B, D, C.
> D. The order is C, A, B, D.

The classic multiple choice question consists of a mini-fact pattern, the "call of the question" (the question you are being asked to analyze), and then typically four possible answers: A, B, C, and D. You are to select the "correct/best" answer.

A. THE ANALYTICAL OPTIONS

There are two ways students tend to analyze multiple choice questions. Under both approaches, the students read the mini-fact pattern and the call of the question first. The difference is in how they treat the answers. Some students assume the information in the answers will help them analyze the problem and reach their conclusion, and thus they read the answers *before* they have reached their own conclusion. Other students read the answers *only after* they have reached their conclusion. Analytically, the issue is should you read the answers *before* you have reached your conclusion to help you analyze the question or should you read the answers *only after* you have reached your conclusion? The answer is the latter.

B. ANALYZE AS IF IT WERE AN ESSAY

You should read the answers to a multiple choice question *only after* you have reached your own conclusion. The reason why is because if you read the answers too soon, your analysis becomes "which answer is the best" and there is no logical way to analyze that question. You have lost your IRRAC analytical approach and are basically "winging it" analytically. Students who tend to peek at the answers before they have reached their own conclusion tend to score significantly below their essay scores. At first, it was difficult to figure out why these students did better when they did not have the answers (the essay questions) and why they did worse when they had the answers (the multiple choice questions). At first blush, it seems counterintuitive. You would think having the possible answers in front of you would provide an advantage. The reason why these students did significantly poorer on the multiple choice portions of their exam than they did on their essays is they all peeked at the answers before they had reached their own conclusion. Once they did, they had no logical way to analyze which answer was the best.

Treat the multiple choice question the same way you would an essay question. First, read the fact pattern looking to spot the issues. Notice the careful wording in the prior sentence—issues. While some multiple choice questions will have only one issue, most multiple choice questions will have several inter-related issues. Some students assume that a multiple choice question can have only one issue in it and once they spot the first issue, they shut down their issue-spotting skills. Not a wise approach to taking multiple choice questions. Keep your issue spotting skills on alert throughout the whole fact pattern.

When you spot an issue, mentally you perform the same IRRAC analysis for the multiple choice issue that you would if it were an essay question. The only difference is you do not have to write out your analysis. Then read the call of the question, paying close attention to the particular question you are being asked to answer. Determine what you think is the best answer to the call of the question *before* you start reading the possible answers.

C. USE THE "OTHER" ANSWERS TO CHECK YOUR ANALYSIS

That does not mean you should not use the answers to help you finalize your conclusion, but use them more as a check on your answer, not to help you analyze to your conclusion. That may sound like a subtle distinction, but it is an important one. After you reach your conclusion, when you read the answers looking for your conclusion, try to say to yourself affirmatively why each of the "other" answers that do not match your conclusion is wrong. If you *can* affirmatively say to yourself why each of the other answers is wrong, it should give you more confidence that when you find your answer, it is the correct answer.

Sometimes you will find that while you can affirmatively say why some of the other answers are wrong, there will be one that you cannot think of a reason why it is wrong. In fact, it looks pretty good, and that answer starts to plant that seed of doubt in your head that your answer, which is there, is wrong. The best way to handle that situation is as follows. Unless that "other" answer makes you think of something that you have overlooked so that now you have an affirmative reason to say your answer is wrong, stick with your answer and move on to the next question. You need to have confidence in your analytical abilities, and unless the other answer gives you a reason to affirmatively say your answer is wrong, stick with your answer.

D. WATCH YOUR TIME

There is one last minor point with respect to multiple choice questions. Remember that the standard time allocation is two minutes a question. You should always calculate how much time you have per question. You cannot spend too much time per question. If you spend too much time on the early questions, you will not get to the later questions. You should move through the questions at a nice pace, averaging whatever the appropriate time is per question (depending on how many questions there are and how much time has been allocated to this portion of the exam) to ensure that you have time to answer all of the questions.

CHAPTER 15

Post-Exam Blues: How to Self-Diagnose Your Exam Performance

A. INTRODUCTION

At many law schools the typical law school exam is a three-hour, closed-book exam. The first hour typically is a set of multiple choice questions (approximately 30), and then the rest of the exam typically is a set of essay questions. The classic structure for the essay questions is two one-hour questions. The logic behind the classic law school exam format is that it best prepares you for the bar exam because it matches the conditions under which you will take the bar exam. In most states the bar exam is one day of multiple choice questions (the bar exam allocates two minutes per question which translates into 30 questions an hour). And the bar exam typically is also one day of essay questions (but some states, notably California, have two days of essays), with each essay typically sixty minutes long. Academic freedom permits most law professors to give whatever type of exam they want, but the norm is some mixture of multiple choice and essay questions.

B. TYPICAL PROFESSORIAL FEEDBACK

Law professors are notorious for providing minimal feedback on exams. At some schools, all the student receives is the final grade. If the professor uses multiple choice questions on the exam, rarely will you get those back. Because it is difficult and time consuming to develop a good set of multiple choice questions, most professors are reluctant either to release them or let students see them after the exam. (Some professors will let you look at them but under tightly controlled conditions.) The best you can probably hope for with respect to the multiple choice portion of the exam is a separate grade for how you did on that portion of the exam. As for the essay questions, some professors are good at providing feedback and will write meaningful comments on your exam. But the norm is probably the opposite. There may be a few check marks in the margin of the essay, or a few cryptic comments, but little that will help you identify why you received the grade you did or what you can do to improve your performance. Whatever feedback you do receive on your essay questions, it is important to develop your own ability to self-diagnose your performance to help improve your performance on future exams.

Keep your grades in perspective, particularly your first semester grades. Your first semester grades may be the poorest assessment of your academic abilities in law school. It is the first time you have taken a set of law school exams. Throughout the first semester you have made assumptions about what the academic process is like and how each step in the process relates to the other steps. It is only *after* you have completed that first semester and received your grades that you are in a position to assess which assumptions served you well and which assumptions served you poorly. Make the necessary adjustments and commit to working just as hard, if not harder, the second semester. The key is to identify where you went wrong and to make the proper adjustments. Your second semester grades are much more indicative of your true academic abilities because they reflect the changes you will make after getting your first semester grades to improve your performance. While it is nice to have a good first semester academically, your second semester is probably more indicative of your true abilities.

C. THERE ARE ONLY TWO WAYS YOU CAN LOSE POINTS ON AN EXAM

In developing your self-diagnostic skills, keep in mind the law student's "circle of life." You start the semester reading and analyzing cases in a particular area of the law, and by the end of the semester you are expected to be able to write what basically amounts to a well-written judicial opinion on selected issues in that area of the law.

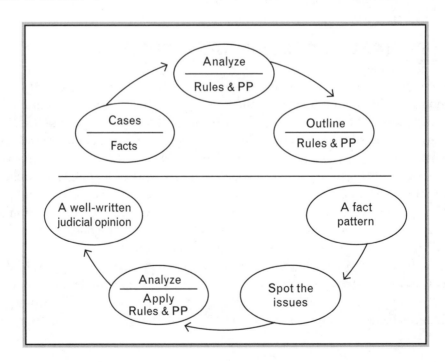

The lower half of the diagram represents the exam process. From a diagnostic perspective, there are only two ways you can lose points on a final. You either did not spot all the issues, or you did not properly write up your analysis.[1] The first bubble in the lower half of the diagram — a fact pattern — is a given. The third bubble in the lower half of the diagram — analyze the issues — is subsumed into the fourth bubble. The professor can only assess the quality of your analysis by the quality of your writing. So if you are unhappy with your grades, figure out your problem: Do you have an issue spotting problem? Do you have an exam writing problem? Or do you have a little of both? And then work on your weakness.

Even assuming there are only two things you can do wrong on an exam — miss issues or not write the proper analysis — how do you diagnose which problem you have? Often you can determine your problem based on the feedback you get even if the feedback is minimal. If you have lots of positive comments in the margin of your essay ("good," "very good," etc.), but you did not receive a good grade, that is usually a sign that you have an issue spotting problem. The professor apparently liked everything you wrote, you just did not write enough. You did not write anything about the issues you missed and lost all the points associated with those issues. On the other hand, if you have lots of critical comments in the margin of your essay ("conclusory," "rule statement?," etc.) you probably have an exam writing problem.

D. DIAGNOSING YOUR EXAM WRITING STYLE

Another way to assess your exam writing performance is to critique your exam after you get it back. During the exam it is natural *not* to think about whether you are writing up your analysis properly. You should be focusing on *what* you are writing, not *how* you are writing it. But many students fool themselves. Just as they think they know a rule, but cannot state it in one sentence because their understanding is too vague and conceptual, many students think their exam writing embodies the proper exam writing structure. With the start of the exam, however, they are hit with an adrenaline rush and they just start writing whatever comes into their heads. After the exam is over, their mind plays tricks on them. They are convinced they wrote in the classic IRRAC exam structure.

One way to check to see if you are writing in the proper exam writing format is after you get your exam back, re-read your exam answer and classify each sentence you wrote on the exam. Based on the game plan developed in this book, there basically are only five types of sentences you should write on an

---

1. This latter clause admittedly assumes that you properly analyzed the issue in your head, but you failed to write it up properly. If you think you have a problem with your analysis during the exam, you need to go back and review the material in the first part of the book. There is no doubt that the key to clear and effective exam writing is clear and effective legal analysis, but what it means to properly analyze an issue is the subject of the first part of the book.

exam: (1) an issue sentence; (2) a rule sentence; (3) a rule elaboration sentence;[2] (4) an analysis sentence; and (5) a conclusion sentence. Every sentence you write should fit into one of these five categories. If it does not, why are you writing it? What purpose is the sentence supposed to serve? Go through your exam and classify each sentence you wrote. Put the appropriate abbreviation (I, R, RE, A, C) in the margin next to the sentence. If it is easy to put a letter next to almost all your sentences, and the structure basically corresponds to IRRAC (or better yet IR–RAC, RAC, RAC . . .), then you probably do not have an exam writing problem. If, on the other hand, you have difficulty deciding which type of sentence it is, and/or if the sequencing of your sentences does *not* resemble IRRAC/IR–RAC, RAC, RAC, then you probably have some exam writing issues.

If you have some exam writing problems, the best way to work on those problems is to practice writing more exams. But first take them under ideal *student* conditions. Most professors have a collection of old exams on reserve (or available electronically). Get an old exam and take it under ideal student conditions: open outline and no time constraints. Be very conscious about each sentence you write and about the structure of your analysis — that you are following the IRRAC/IR-RAC, RAC, RAC writing structure. Be conscious of what each sentence should look like and what the structure of each paragraph should look like. Create the perfect model in your head.

Then, start to make the transition to exam conditions. Take another exam open outline but under time constraints. Do your best to still write in the same style and structure. Finally, take another exam under exam conditions: closed-book and with time constraints. Again, do your best to still write in that ideal writing style and structure with which you should now be more conscious and comfortable. If you have an exam writing weakness, that is the best way to turn your exam writing style into a strength.

E. ISSUE SPOTTING EXERCISES — TRIGGERING FACTS

If you have an issue spotting problem, the best way to correct it is to work on your "triggering facts." Every rule of law has a generic fact pattern that goes with it, and within every generic fact pattern is a triggering fact or set of facts that must be present to trigger your association with the rule. Many students spend so much time creating and memorizing their outlines, they forget that their outlines are primarily on the rule plane but the fact pattern is on the factual plane. You need a bridge to help you see the connection between the rules in your

---

2. Remember that rule elaboration includes mandatory rule elaboration — the test or definition for the element that you must apply to the fact pattern to properly analyze the facts — as well as optional rule elaboration — sentence about the rule that describe the rule and/or help you understand the rule, and the public policy considerations behind the rule.

outline and the fact pattern. That bridge is the triggering fact or facts for each rule.

You can also work on your issue spotting skills by *mentally* taking as many old exams as you can. You will quickly come to realize that taking old exams — actually writing out a practice answer to each of them — is very time consuming. Once you are comfortable with your exam writing skills, writing out old exams is inefficient. Once you know how you should write an exam, do not write a practice answer for each of the old exams but instead just "issue spot" them. Read each exam twice, noting all of the issues that you spot. Many professors will tell you that for all practical purposes there are only so many ways some rules can be raised. The more old exams you read and issue spot, the more likely you will be prepared for whatever fact pattern the professor throws at you.

Lastly, taking multiple choice questions is a great way to help you develop your issue spotting ability. One way to think about a multiple choice fact pattern is that it is nothing more than a paragraph or two from the essay fact pattern. Reading as many multiple choice problems as you can will help sensitize you to the different ways the rules in the course can be tested. The more fact patterns you can read and issue spot — be they old essay fact patterns or multiple choice fact patterns — the better prepared you will be for whatever fact pattern you see on the exam.

F. COMPARE YOUR MULTIPLE CHOICE vs. ESSAY GRADES

If your professor gives you separate grades for the multiple choice portion of your exam and for the essay portion of the exam, you can also use that information to help you diagnose your exam performance. Do not overreact to the difference between the two scores on any one exam but rather look for patterns across a number of exams. If your multiple choice scores are consistently and meaningfully higher than your essay scores, that is usually a sign that you have an exam writing problem. The key difference between the multiple choice portion of the exam and the essay portion of the exam is you do not have to write out your analysis on the former and you do on the latter. If you are consistently scoring better on the multiple choice portion of the exams that means that you are spotting and analyzing the issues well, but when you have to write up your analysis on the essay portion of the exam, you do not do as well — that is a classic sign of an exam writing problem.

On the other hand, if you consistently score higher on the essay portion of the exam than you do on the multiple choice portion, that often is a sign that you are peeking too early at the answers on the multiple question portion of the exam. If you consistently score better on the essay portion of the exam, notice what that means: you score higher when you do *not* have the answer. If that is true, then on the multiple choice portion of the exam, take the answers away. Keep your hand over the answers until you have reached your own conclusion and only then should you look at the answers to find your answer.

G. DON'T KILL THE MESSENGER, INSTEAD SPEND SOME TIME WITH HIM OR HER

Lastly, but in many respects most importantly, do not be afraid to use your professors to help you diagnose your exam taking problems. Go see one or more of your professors and ask him or her to explain why you received the grade you did. Do not be belligerent or combative. Make sure the professor knows that you accept the grade but that you are interested in doing better in the future and would like some help in identifying what you did wrong. Almost all professors will be happy to meet with a student and go over the exam under those conditions. The professor probably will not use the terms and concepts developed in this book per se, but he or she will probably use terms and concepts that you should be able to interpret from the perspective of the terms and concepts developed in this book. Your professor's feedback will be invaluable to helping you improve your performance on your next set of exams.

And if your law school has an academic support program, be sure to spend some time with the professors in that program. They, more than anyone, can help you identify your weaknesses and help you develop strategies to overcome them.

Time to Take Off the Training Wheels: Variations on the Legal Analysis Theme

Part I of this book introduced you to a conceptual and analytical model of what it means to "think like a lawyer." While that model is important in that it gave you a working approach to what it means to think like a lawyer, legal analysis is much more complex than the simple model introduced in Part I.

While it often makes sense from a learning perspective to start with the simple — the paradigm — the book would be remiss if it did not introduce you to more complex forms and examples of legal analysis. Part III does just that. It exposes you to the more advanced forms of legal analysis that probably will be more applicable to your legal research and writing class, but which may also have relevance and application to your exams, particularly if you have a take-home final.

CHAPTER 16

Extrospective Legal Analysis: Case Synthesis

A. CONCEPTUAL OVERVIEW

The law is constantly changing. Some students have a hard time understanding why that is so. Like legal analysis, the law depends upon the interaction of the rule plane, the public policy plane, and the factual plane. The public policy and factual planes are not static; they are constantly changing. Public policy considerations change over time. Such changes put pressure on the law to change. New factual scenarios arise over time. For example, computers and the Internet did not exist just a few decades ago. The development of new technology has created new factual scenarios that have put pressure on existing rules. The courts have struggled with whether the same law should apply to the Internet or new rules — rules created by the courts typically. The law has to evolve constantly to stay up with changing public policy considerations and newly evolving factual scenarios.

The evolutionary nature of the law is at the heart of the analytical skill commonly referred to as case synthesis. Case synthesis is the process of synthesizing cases to create a new rule. That statement is so obtuse it is admittedly of limited analytical value. The task of mastering case synthesis is even more confusing because the term "case synthesis" is a misnomer for several reasons. Those reasons will become apparent as this material breaks down the case synthesis process.

Conceptually, case synthesis is the opposite of rule elaboration. Rule elaboration is *introspective*. A court takes a single rule and *breaks down* the rule into its elements, creating rule elaboration for one or more elements of the rule. On the other hand, case synthesis is *extrospective*. A court takes several cases/rules that individually do not apply to the case before the court, but the court analyzes the cases collectively, in relation to each other, to see if there is an *overarching* public policy consideration and new legal standard that connects the cases and which supports adopting a new rule of law for the case pending before the court. With rule elaboration, the court looks *inward* on the rule, creating rule elaboration for an element of the rule — a new sub-rule within the larger rule. With case synthesis, the court looks *outward* from each case/rule to see if there is an overarching interest that connects them to create a new legal standard that applies to the prior cases and the pending case. Conceptually, one way to think about case synthesis is that it is the inverse of rule elaboration.

There are many different reasons why a court's opinion may raise and discuss a prior case. A brief discussion of some of the principal reasons will help your overall analytical skills as well as your mastering the skill of case synthesis.

B. REFERENCING A PRIOR CASE

1. Citing to a Case

You will see, if you have not already noticed, that judicial opinions typically refer to one or more prior cases.[1] Analytically, the first point you should note is whether the opinion is "citing" to the prior case or "discussing" the prior case. A judicial opinion typically refers to a prior case to support the court's reasoning, giving weight to its legal analysis. Usually the court will just "cite" to the prior case, it will not discuss the case.[2] When the court merely cites to a prior case, the court is implicitly asserting that the relevance and applicability of the prior case to the pending case is so obvious and direct that there is no need to discuss its relevance or applicability.[3] Students typically skim over such citations in an opinion.[4]

2. Discussing a Case: Binding vs. Persuasive Authority

On the other hand, if the court *raises and discusses* a prior case in its opinion, the court is signaling that this case *potentially* has special relevance to the pending case.[5] The typical reason why the court raises and discusses a prior case is if there

---

1. Although the court typically refers to many prior cases, it need not do so and could refer to just a single case. The discussion here will use the singular because it applies to each and every reference a court makes to an earlier opinion.

2. A cite (or citation) to a prior opinion often takes the form of a reference to the name and official cite form of the case, but it does not discuss the case — it does not include a discussion of the facts, the rule, or the rationale of the opinion. Often you will see "string" cites — the opinion citing to several cases at once — at the end of a sentence.

3. While the following is a generalization and should be treated as such, if the court merely cites to a prior case, that often means that the parties to the case did not dispute the relevance and applicability of the case in question.

4. A mere citation typically tells you so little about the case you have to assume the court is properly citing to it. The only way you can analyze whether the court is properly citing to a case is to read and analyze the full opinion of the cited case. For your typical substantive classes (Property, Contracts, Torts, etc.), that would entail too much reading. Unless the note material in the casebook elaborates on a case cited within an opinion, such citations within an opinion usually play no role in your analytical process. If, however, the note material or the casebook provides additional information about a case that is being cited, that usually is a sign you should analyze more critically the court's citation to the prior case. When you are practicing law, however, checking cites to make sure that the underlying case supports the point for which the court is citing it, is a much more common practice. Because of that, you may be asked to do so as part of a legal research and writing assignment, but typically not as part of your substantive classes.

5. While the following is a generalization and should be treated as such, if the court discusses a prior case that often means that the parties to the case did not agree on the relevance and applicability of the case in question.

is an issue with respect to whether the prior case constitutes "binding" authority versus "persuasive" authority.[6] A full discussion of what constitutes "binding" versus "persuasive" authority is beyond the scope of this material, but a basic understanding of the difference is important to understanding case synthesis.

Binding authority is legal authority that a court *must* follow. Persuasive authority is legal authority that a court is *not required* to follow, but will follow if it deems the authority persuasive — if the court is persuaded the prior opinion *should be* followed. Classic examples of binding authority are (1) statutory rules that have been adopted by a legislative body in that jurisdiction that apply to the case pending before the court, and/or (2) prior judicial opinions from higher courts within that jurisdiction that apply to the case pending before the court.[7] If the statute or judicial precedent is from a different jurisdiction, however, the court is not *bound* to follow it. At best such authority may be persuasive authority — the court may follow it if the court finds the reasoning behind the authority *persuasive*. At the macro level, the initial difference between binding authority and persuasive authority is fairly simple. It is jurisdictionally based.

But within a particular jurisdiction, there is much more to the subtle distinction between binding authority and persuasive authority. Within a jurisdiction, lower courts are *bound* to follow the rules of law established by the higher courts and the legislature in that jurisdiction *only* if the rule *applies* to the case before the court. With respect to case law, a prior case constitutes binding precedent only if the subsequent court finds that the case pending before it is the *same case* as the prior case. If the facts are *"the same,"* the case is the same and the prior opinion from the higher court within that jurisdiction is binding authority. If the facts are sufficiently different, however, the case is not the same so the court need not follow the prior opinion. The court *may* follow the prior opinion, but if it does, it is at best *persuasive* authority. The issue becomes whether the two cases are the same. What does it mean to say the cases are the same?

3. Same Case vs. Different Case

Understandably, the parties to a subsequent case will have different vested interests concerning the relevance of a prior opinion that may constitute binding authority. The party who would benefit from application of the prior case will argue that the prior case is *the same* case and therefore it constitutes

---

6. Binding versus persuasive authority is unrelated to case synthesis, but giving you the bigger analytical picture should help you appreciate the different ways prior cases can be used analytically.

7. Professors often use the terms binding *precedent* and binding *authority* interchangeably. While there is substantial overlap between the two terms, technically they are not identical — but the difference has relevance only in certain situations. Binding *authority* also includes statutory authority within the jurisdiction. A court within a jurisdiction is required to follow and apply the statutory rules in that jurisdiction as long as the statutory rule applies and it is not unconstitutional. Binding *precedent* refers only to a prior case within the same jurisdiction that is binding on a subsequent case. The term binding authority is broader than the term binding precedent. Binding precedent is also binding authority, but binding authority need not be binding precedent.

binding precedent. The party who would be harmed by application of the case will argue that the cases are *distinguishable* and the prior case does *not* constitute binding authority. Often the arguments advanced by the respective parties will end up in the court's discussion of the relevance of the prior case.

When there is an issue as to whether a prior opinion constitutes binding precedent, typically the court will raise and discuss the prior case and its applicability. Pay close attention to such discussions. The skill of analyzing whether a subsequent case is the same case or a different case is an important skill that you will need to master. Analytically, you will come to realize that whether two cases are the same is not only a question of fact, it is also a question of public policy. If the facts are so similar that the relevant public policy considerations are the same, the cases arguably are the same case and the prior case should constitute binding authority. If, however, the facts are similar but the public policy considerations are not the same (either because a new public policy consideration applies or not all of the public policy considerations that applied to the prior case apply to the subsequent case), the cases may be different and the prior case will not constitute binding authority.

Even if a prior case does not constitute binding authority, however, it may constitute persuasive authority. Persuasive authority is when the cases are sufficiently similar that the court is persuaded that the reasoning and logic of the prior case should apply and control the subsequent case. The court is not bound to follow the prior case, but it thinks it contains the better analysis. The most obvious example of persuasive authority is when the same case factually has arisen and been decided by a higher court, but in a different jurisdiction. The court hearing the subsequent case is not bound to follow the opinion in the prior case because it is from a different jurisdiction. But if the court is persuaded by the prior court's reasoning, the court hearing the subsequent case will adopt the rule created in the prior opinion and follow it as persuasive authority.

Just as with binding authority, where there is a prior case that may constitute *persuasive* authority, you can understand why one of the parties to the subsequent case would want to raise and argue its applicability, and why the other party would argue against it. While there may be factual differences between the cases, one party will want to argue that for legal purposes the cases are essentially *the same case* and therefore should be treated the same; the other party will argue that the cases are distinguishable both factually and legally. The issue of whether the cases are the same or different is not just a question of the facts; often it is also a question of the relevant public policy considerations. Again, such discussion and analysis often ends up in the court's opinion.

Where a prior case may constitute binding or persuasive authority, you should have a better understanding now of why the court in the subsequent opinion may raise and discuss the case as opposed to merely citing to it. Often the outcome of the case will turn on the issue, and the parties will disagree on the issue. Analytically, understanding the difference between binding and persuasive authority is important in its own right.

C. CASE SYNTHESIS

Understanding the difference between binding and persuasive authority is also important because it will help you understand the analytical process involved in case synthesis. First, typically the issue of binding authority or persuasive authority involves only one prior case. The issue is the relevance of *that particular case* to the current case. It is a one-on-one analysis.[8] In contrast, case synthesis typically involves a court raising and analyzing the potential relevance of *several* prior cases. In case synthesis, no one case individually constitutes direct binding authority, and no one case standing alone constitutes direct persuasive authority. The issue is whether *collectively* the cases reflect an overarching public policy consideration and legal principle that support creating and applying a new rule of law to the case pending before the court.

The court analyzes the potential relevance of the cases to see (1) if the court can discern an overarching public policy and legal principle; and (2) if so, whether that overarching public policy and legal principle should apply to the case before it. Where the court finds an overarching public policy and legal principle, the court "synthesizes" the cases: it discerns and articulates the new overarching public policy and legal standard that connects the cases, including typically the case pending before the court.

While that discussion of case synthesis is helpful conceptually, it is not that helpful analytically. Analytically — mechanically — how does one synthesize a case? Interestingly, one of the reasons "case synthesis" is so confusing is because of its name. The term "case synthesis" confuses some students because when they hear the word "*case*," they think about the facts of a case. Accordingly, some students think case synthesis occurs *primarily* on the *factual* plane. Nothing could be further from the truth. While the facts are relevant to the process, first and foremost cases are synthesized on the public policy and rule/legal[9] planes.

When a court analyzes a series of cases to see if there is an overarching interest that unites the cases, first and foremost that overarching interest is a public policy consideration. It may be a newly evolving public policy consideration or an "under-articulated" public policy consideration — an old public policy consideration, the applicability of which to the pending issue has not been fully appreciated. Either way, the public policy consideration will be reflected in the different rules of law adopted in each of the different cases that are being synthesized. Typically the rule in each case will be worded such that it fits the factual scenario in *that* case.

When the court analyzes the cases to see if they can be synthesized, the court is looking for a common thread that unites the cases on both the public policy plane and on the legal plane. Typically the cases will evidence a pattern — an evolving line of cases — that reflects this new public policy consideration. And if

---

8. In some cases, there might be more than one possible binding precedent, but each one is analyzed separately.

9. The legal plane is just another way of referring to the rule plane. They are one in the same.

the court can synthesize the cases, the court will discern and articulate a new *legal* standard that is consistent with the newly evolving public policy consideration and that overarches and connects the cases.

So what previously appeared to be a number of disparate, independent cases now can be characterized as a group of cases and rules that reflect the larger, newly adopted legal standard and public policy consideration. Typically the overarching public policy consideration and new legal standard will also apply to the case pending before the court, leading to yet another *new* rule in that case as well that connects up with — and maybe even extends — the evolving public policy consideration and legal standard. The analytical process of synthesizing cases involves the interaction of the three planes, the public policy plane, the legal plane, and the factual plane — yet most students overfocus on the factual plane when trying to synthesize cases.

While case synthesis is unrelated to binding authority, it arguably is a subset of persuasive authority, only "the authority" is not a single case but rather an evolving line of cases. The argument is that the opinion*s*, when viewed together, reflect an emerging public policy consideration and legal standard that should be articulated and applied to the pending case to control it as well.

Admittedly case synthesis is a very abstract process. Any discussion of it is inherently abstract as well. An example of case synthesis should be helpful. Please read and analyze the following case, *Kelly v. Gwinnell*.[10] Pay close attention to the "cases within the case" and how the court uses them. Once you understand how the court is using the cases you will be in a position to critically analyze the court's synthesis. Do you think the court got it right in adopting the rule of law it did, or do you agree with the dissent? *Kelly v. Gwinnell* is an interesting case both substantively (for the rule it adopts) and analytically (for how it justifies adopting the rule). This material will leave the substantive analysis for your Torts class. Instead, focus on the court's analytical process — on its case synthesis.

D. EXAMPLE OF CASE SYNTHESIS: *KELLY v. GWINNELL*

Kelly v. Gwinnell
SUPREME COURT OF NEW JERSEY

476 A.2d 1219 (1984)

WILENTZ, C.J.

This case raises the issue of whether a social host who enables an adult guest at his home to become drunk is liable to the victim of an automobile accident

---

10. Both the majority opinion and the dissent have been heavily edited for purposes of this material.

caused by the drunken driving of the guest. Here the host served liquor to the guest beyond the point at which the guest was visibly intoxicated. We hold the host may be liable under the circumstances of this case.

At the trial level, the case was disposed of . . . by summary judgment in favor of the social host. The record . . . discloses that defendant Donald Gwinnell, after driving defendant Joseph Zak home, spent an hour or two at Zak's home before leaving to return to his own home. During that time, according to Gwinnell, Zak, and Zak's wife, Gwinnell consumed two or three drinks of scotch on the rocks. Zak accompanied Gwinnell outside to his car, chatted with him, and watched as Gwinnell then drove off to go home. About twenty-five minutes later Zak telephoned Gwinnell's home to make sure Gwinnell had arrived there safely. The phone was answered by Mrs. Gwinnell, who advised Zak that Gwinnell had been involved in a head-on collision. The collision was with an automobile operated by plaintiff, Marie Kelly, who was seriously injured as a result.

After the accident Gwinnell was subjected to a blood test, which indicated a blood alcohol concentration of 0.286 percent.[11] Kelly's expert concluded from that reading that Gwinnell had consumed not two or three scotches but the equivalent of thirteen drinks; that while at Zak's home Gwinnell must have been showing unmistakable signs of intoxication; and that in fact he was severely intoxicated while at Zak's residence and at the time of the accident.

Kelly sued Gwinnell . . . [who] sued the Zaks in a third party action; and thereafter plaintiff amended her complaint to include Mr. and Mrs. Zak as direct defendants. The Zaks moved for summary judgment, contending that as a matter of law a host is not liable for the negligence of an adult social guest who has become intoxicated while at the host's home. The trial court granted the motion on that basis. . . . The Appellate Division affirmed, Kelly v. Gwinnell, 190 N.J. Super. 320, 463 A.2d 387 (1983). It noted, correctly, that New Jersey has no Dram Shop Act imposing liability on the provider of alcoholic beverages, and that while our decisional law had imposed such liability on licensees, common-law liability had been extended to a social host only where the guest was a minor. Id. at 322-23, 463 A.2d 387. . . . It explicitly declined to expand that liability where, as here, the social guest was an adult. Id. at 325-26, 463 A.2d 387.

The Appellate Division's determination was based on the apparent absence of decisions in this country imposing such liability (except for those that were promptly overruled by the Legislature).[12] Id. at 324-25, 463 A.2d 367. The absence of such determinations is said to reflect a broad consensus that the

---

11. Under . . . [the law that applied at that time], a person who drives with a blood alcohol concentration of 0.10 percent or more violates N.J.S.A. 39:4-50 as amended by *L.* 1983, *c.* 129, the statute concerning driving while under the influence of intoxicating liquor.

12. The Appellate Division noted that several state court decisions imposing liability against social hosts under circumstances similar to those in this case were abrogated by later legislative action. We note that legislation enacted in Oregon did not abrogate the state court's holding in Wiener v. Gamma Phi Chapter of Alpha Tau Omega Fraternity, 258 Or. 632, 485 P.2d 18 (1971). The court found that a host directly serving liquor to a guest has a duty to refuse to serve the guest when it would be unreasonable under the circumstances to permit the guest to drink.

imposition of liability arising from these social relations is unwise. Certainly this immunization of hosts is not the inevitable result of the law of negligence, for conventional negligence analysis points strongly in exactly the opposite direction. "Negligence is tested by whether the reasonably prudent person at the time and place should recognize and foresee an unreasonable risk or likelihood of harm or danger to others." Rappaport v. Nichols, 31 N.J. 188, 201, 156 A.2d 1 (1959); see also Butler v. Acme Mkts., Inc., 89 N.J. 270, 445 A.2d 1141 (1982) (supermarket operator liable for failure to provide shoppers with parking lot security). When negligent conduct creates such a risk, setting off foreseeable consequences that lead to plaintiff's injury, the conduct is deemed the proximate cause of the injury. "[A] tortfeasor is generally held answerable for the injuries which result in the ordinary course of events from his negligence and it is generally sufficient if his negligent conduct was a substantial factor in bringing about the injuries." Rappaport, supra, 31 N.J. at 203, 156 A.2d 1; see Ettin v. Ava Truck Leasing Inc., 53 N.J. 463, 483, 251 A.2d 278 (1969) (parking tractor-trailer across street is substantial factor in cause of accident when truck with failed brakes collides into trailer).

Under the facts here defendant provided his guest with liquor, knowing that thereafter the guest would have to drive in order to get home. Viewing the facts most favorably to plaintiff (as we must, since the complaint was dismissed on a motion for summary judgment), one could reasonably conclude that the Zaks must have known that their provision of liquor was causing Gwinnell to become drunk, yet they continued to serve him even after he was visibly intoxicated. By the time he left, Gwinnell was in fact severely intoxicated. A reasonable person in Zak's position could foresee quite clearly that this continued provision of alcohol to Gwinnell was making it more and more likely that Gwinnell would not be able to operate his car carefully. Zak could foresee that unless he stopped providing drinks to Gwinnell, Gwinnell was likely to injure someone as a result of the negligent operation of his car. The usual elements of a cause of action for negligence are clearly present: an action by defendant creating an unreasonable risk of harm to plaintiff, a risk that was clearly foreseeable, and a risk that resulted in an injury equally foreseeable. Under those circumstances the only question remaining is whether a duty exists to prevent such risk or, realistically, whether this Court should impose such a duty.

In most cases the justice of imposing such a duty is so clear that the cause of action in negligence is assumed to exist simply on the basis of the actor's creation of an unreasonable risk of foreseeable harm resulting in injury. In fact, however, more is needed, "more" being the value judgment, based on an

---

Eight years later the legislature enacted Or. Rev. Stat. § 30.955, limiting a cause of action against a private host for damages incurred or caused by an intoxicated social guest to when the host "has served or provided alcoholic beverages to a social guest when such guest was visibly intoxicated." The legislature did not, therefore, preclude liability of private hosts under a negligence theory but instead decided that the social guest must be visibly intoxicated before the host will be held accountable for injuries caused by the guest's intoxicated conduct.

analysis of public policy, that the actor owed the injured party a duty of reasonable care. Palsgraf v. Long Island R.R. Co., 248 N.Y. 339, 162 N.E. 99 (1928). In Goldberg v. Housing Auth. of Newark, 38 N.J. 578, 583, 186 A.2d 291 (1962), this Court explained that "whether a duty exists is ultimately a question of fairness. The inquiry involves a weighing of the relationship of the parties, the nature of the risk, and the public interest in the proposed solution." See also Portee v. Jaffee, 84 N.J. 88, 101, 417 A.2d 521 (1980) (whether liability for negligently inflicted emotional harm should be expanded depends "ultimately" on balancing of conflicting interests involved).

When the court determines that a duty exists and liability will be extended, it draws judicial lines based on fairness and policy. In a society where thousands of deaths are caused each year by drunken drivers, where the damage caused by such deaths is regarded increasingly as intolerable, where liquor licensees are prohibited from serving intoxicated adults, and where long-standing criminal sanctions against drunken driving have recently been significantly strengthened to the point where the Governor notes that they are regarded as the toughest in the nation, . . . the imposition of such a duty by the judiciary seems both fair and fully in accord with the State's policy. Unlike those cases in which the definition of desirable policy is the subject of intense controversy, here the imposition of a duty is both consistent with and supportive of a social goal — the reduction of drunken driving — that is practically unanimously accepted by society.

While the imposition of a duty here would go beyond our prior decisions, those decisions not only point clearly in that direction but do so despite the presence of social considerations similar to those involved in this case — considerations that are claimed to invest the host with immunity. In our first case on the subject, Rappaport, supra, 31 N.J. 188, 156 A.2d 1, we held a licensee liable for the consequences of a customer's negligent operation of his automobile. The customer was a minor who had become intoxicated as a result of the consumption of liquor at various premises including the licensee's. While observing that a standard of conduct was contained in the statute prohibiting licensees from serving liquor to minors and in the regulation further prohibiting service to any person actually or apparently intoxicated, our decision that the licensee owed a duty to members of the general public was based on principles of common-law negligence.

We later made it clear that the licensee's duty is owed to the customer as well, by holding in Soronen v. Olde Milford Inn, Inc., 46 N.J. 582, 218 A.2d 630 (1966), that the licensee who served liquor to an intoxicated customer was liable to that customer for the death that resulted when the customer fell in the licensed premises while leaving the bar. While the situation of a licensee differs in some respects from that of a social host, some of the same underlying considerations relied on here in disputing liability are present in both: the notion that the real fault is that of the drunk, not the licensee, especially where the drinker is an adult (as he was in *Soronen*); and the belief — not as strong when applied to licensed premises as when applied to one's home — that when people get together for a friendly drink or more, the social relationships should not be intruded upon by possibilities of litigation.

The Appellate Division moved our decisional law one step further, a significant step, when it ruled in Linn v. Rand, 140 N.J. Super. 212, 356 A.2d 15 (1976), that a social host who serves liquor to a visibly intoxicated minor, knowing the minor will thereafter drive, may be held liable for the injuries inflicted on a third party as a result of the subsequent drunken driving of the minor. There, practically all of the considerations urged here against liability were present: it was a social setting at someone's home, not at a tavern; the one who provided the liquor to the intoxicated minor was a host, not a licensee; and all of the notions of fault and causation pinning sole responsibility on the drinker were present. The only difference was that the guest was a minor—but whether obviously so or whether known to the host is not disclosed in the opinion.[13]

In *Rappaport*, we explicitly noted that the matter did not involve any claim against "persons not engaged in the liquor business." 31 N.J. at 205, 156 A.2d 1. We now approve *Linn* with its extension of this liability to social hosts. In expanding liability, *Linn* followed the rationale of *Rappaport* that the duty involved is a common law duty, not one arising from the statute and regulation prohibiting sales of liquor to a minor, neither of which applies to a social host. Cf. Congini v. Portersville Valve Co., — Pa. —, —, 470 A.2d 515, 517-18 (1983) (in which the Pennsylvania Supreme Court relied exclusively on statutes criminalizing the provision of alcohol to minors as the basis for extending liability to a social host). The fair implication of *Rappaport* and *Soronen*, that the duty exists independent of the statutory prohibition, was thus made explicit in Linn. As the court there noted: "It makes little sense to say that the licensee in *Rappaport* is under a duty to exercise care, but give immunity to a social host who may be guilty of the same wrongful conduct merely because he is unlicensed." 140 N.J. Super. at 217, 356 A.2d 15.[14]

The argument is made that the rule imposing liability on licensees is justified because licensees, unlike social hosts, derive a profit from serving liquor. We reject this analysis of the liability's foundation and emphasize that the liability proceeds from the duty of care that accompanies control of the liquor supply. Whatever the motive behind making alcohol available to those who will subsequently drive, the provider has a duty to the public not to create foreseeable, unreasonable risks by this activity.

We therefore hold that a host who serves liquor to an adult social guest, knowing both that the guest is intoxicated and will thereafter be operating a motor vehicle, is liable for injuries inflicted on a third party as a result of the

---

13. The case was decided on a motion for summary judgment. The court noted that the record did not indicate the minor's age. The opinion does not rely at all on the host's ability easily to determine the fact that the guest was a minor, a factor relied on to some extent in the arguments seeking to distinguish the present case from *Linn*.

14. While *Linn*'s statement of the legal rule does not explicitly go beyond the situation in which the social guest was a minor (140 N.J. Super. at 217, 219, 220, 356 A.2d 15), its reasoning would apply equally to an adult guest.

negligent operation of a motor vehicle by the adult guest when such negligence is caused by the intoxication. We impose this duty on the host to the third party because we believe that the policy considerations served by its imposition far outweigh those asserted in opposition. While we recognize the concern that our ruling will interfere with accepted standards of social behavior; will intrude on and somewhat diminish the enjoyment, relaxation, and camaraderie that accompany social gatherings at which alcohol is served; and that such gatherings and social relationships are not simply tangential benefits of a civilized society but are regarded by many as important, we believe that the added assurance of just compensation to the victims of drunken driving as well as the added deterrent effect of the rule on such driving outweigh the importance of those other values. Indeed, we believe that given society's extreme concern about drunken driving, any change in social behavior resulting from the rule will be regarded ultimately as neutral at the very least, and not as a change for the worse; but that in any event if there be a loss, it is well worth the gain.

. . .

This Court senses that there may be a substantial change occurring in social attitudes and customs concerning drinking, whether at home or in taverns. We believe that this change may be taking place right now in New Jersey and perhaps elsewhere. It is the upheaval of prior norms by a society that has finally recognized that it must change its habits and do whatever is required, whether it means but a small change or a significant one, in order to stop the senseless loss inflicted by drunken drivers. We did not cause that movement, but we believe this decision is in step with it.

We are well aware of the many possible implications and contentions that may arise from our decision. We express no opinion whatsoever on any of these matters but confine ourselves strictly to the facts before us. We hold only that where a host provides liquor directly to a social guest and continues to do so even beyond the point at which the host knows the guest is intoxicated, and does this knowing that the guest will shortly thereafter be operating a motor vehicle, that host is liable for the foreseeable consequences to third parties that result from the guest's drunken driving. We hold further that the host and guest are liable to the third party as joint tortfeasors, Malone v. Jersey Central Power & Light Co., 18 N.J. 163, 171, 113 A.2d 13 (1955); Ristan v. Frantzen, 14 N.J. 455, 460, 102 A.2d 614 (1954); Matthews v. Delaware, L. & W. R.R., 56 N.J. L. 34, 27 A. 919 (Sup. Ct. 1893), without implying anything about the rights of the one to contribution or indemnification from the other. . . .

Our ruling today will not cause a deluge of lawsuits or spawn an abundance of fraudulent and frivolous claims. Not only do we limit our holding to the situation in which a host directly serves a guest, but we impose liability solely for injuries resulting from the guest's drunken driving. *Cf.* Immer, 56 N.J. at 482, 267 A.2d 481 (interspousal immunity abandoned only in actions arising out of negligent operation of automobiles). Automobile accidents are thoroughly investigated by law enforcement officers; careful inquiries are routinely made as to whether the drivers and occupants are intoxicated. The availability of clear objective evidence establishing intoxication will act to weed out baseless claims and to prevent this cause of action from being used as a tool for harassment.

We therefore reverse the judgment in favor of the defendants Zak and remand the case to the Law Division for proceedings consistent with this opinion.

GARIBALDI J., dissenting.

. . . [T]he Legislature is better equipped to effectuate the goals of reducing injuries from drunken driving and protecting the interests of the injured party, without placing such a grave burden on the average citizen of this state.

Prior to today's decision, this Court had imposed liability only on those providers of alcoholic beverages who were licensed by the State. *See* Rappaport v. Nichols, 31 N.J. 188, 156 A.2d 201 (1959). The Appellate Division also had expanded the liability to a social host who served liquor to a minor. Lind v. Rand, 140 N.J. Super. 212, 356 A.2d 15 (App. Div. 1976).[15] Although both of these cases were based on common-law negligence, the courts deemed the regulations restricting the service of alcohol to minors significant enough evidence of legislative policy to impart knowledge of foreseeable risk on the provider of the alcohol and to fashion a civil remedy for negligently creating that risk."

. . .

As stated earlier in this dissent, this Court has, in the past, imposed civil liability on commercial licensees who serve alcoholic beverages to intoxicated patrons. Commercial licensees are subject to regulation by both the Alcoholic Beverage Commission (ABC) and the Legislature. It is reasonable to impose tort liability on licensees based on their violation of explicit statutes and regulations.

I have no quarrel with the imposition of such liability because of the peculiar position occupied by the licensee. A social host, however, is in a different position. . . .

A significant difference between an average citizen and a commercial licensee is the average citizen's lack of knowledge and expertise in determining levels and degrees of intoxication. Licensed commercial providers, unlike the average citizen, deal with the alcohol-consuming public every day. This experience gives

---

15. If this case involved service of alcohol by a social host to a minor guest, I would vote with the majority in approving Lind v. Rand, supra, 140 N.J. Super. 212, 356 A.2d 15, to the extent it has been interpreted as applying only to social hosts who serve liquor to minors. The distinction I draw is based on the clearly and frequently expressed legislative policy that minors should not drink alcoholic beverages, see, e.g., N.J.S.A. 33:1-77, and on the fact that minors occupy a special place in our society and traditionally have been protected by state regulation from the consequences of their own immaturity. Although the majority sees no basis for this distinction, I am not alone in making it. Compare Klein v. Raysinger, — Pa. —, 470 A.2d 507 (1983) (in which the Supreme Court of Pennsylvania refused to extend liability to a social host who serves an adult guest) with Congini v. Porterville Valve Co., — Pa. —, 470 A.2d 515 (1983) (decided on the same day as Klein by the same court but extending liability to a social host who served liquor to a minor guest); see also Senate Bill S-1054 (recently passed by the Senate and Assembly imposing criminal liability on social hosts who serve liquor to minors but not mentioning hosts who serve liquor to adults).

them some expertise with respect to intoxication that social hosts lack. A social host will find it more difficult to determine levels and degrees of intoxication.

The majority holds that a host will be liable only if he serves alcohol to a guest knowing both that the guest is intoxicated and that the guest will drive. . . . Although this standard calls for a subjective determination of the extent of the host's knowledge, a close reading of the opinion makes clear that the majority actually is relying on objective evidence. The majority takes the results of Gwinnell's blood alcohol concentration test and concludes from that test that "the Zaks must have known that their provision of liquor was causing Gwinnell to become drunk . . .".

Whether a guest is or is not intoxicated is not a simple issue. Alcohol affects everyone differently. . . .

The nature of home entertaining compounds the social host's difficulty in determining whether a guest is obviously intoxicated before serving the next drink. In a commercial establishment, there is greater control over the liquor; a bartender or waitress must serve the patron a drink. Not so in a home when entertaining a guest. At a social gathering, for example, guests frequently serve themselves or guests may serve other guests. . . . Furthermore, the commercial bartender usually does not drink on the job. The social host often drinks with the guest, as the Zaks did here. The more the host drinks, the less able he will be to determine when a guest is intoxicated. It would be anomalous to create a rule of liability that social hosts can deliberately avoid by becoming drunk themselves.

. . .

A more pressing distinction between the social host and commercial licensees is the host's inability to fulfill the duty the majority has imposed even if the host knows that a particular guest is intoxicated. It is easy to say that a social host can just refuse to serve the intoxicated person. However, due to a desire to avoid confrontation in a social environment, this may become a very difficult task. It is much easier in a detached business relationship for a bartender to flag a patron and either refuse to serve him or ask him to leave. We should not ignore the social pressures of requiring a social host to tell a boss, client, friend, neighbor, or family member that he is not going to serve him another drink. Moreover, a social host does not have a bouncer or other enforcer to prevent difficulties that may arise when requesting a drunk to stop drinking or not to drive home. We have all heard of belligerent drunks.

III

The most significant difference between a social host and a commercial licensee, however, is the social host's inability to spread the cost of liability. The commercial establishment spreads the cost of insurance against liability among its customers. The social host must bear the entire cost alone. . . .

. . .

IV

In conclusion, in trivializing these objections as "cocktail party customs" . . . and "inconvenience" . . . the majority misses the point. I believe that an indepth review of this problem by the Legislature will result in a solution that will further the goals of reducing injuries related to drunk driving and adequately compensating the injured party, while imposing a more limited liability on the social host. Imaginative legislative drafting could include: funding a remedy for the injured party by contributions from the parties most responsible for the harm caused, the intoxicated motorists; making the social host secondarily liable by requiring a judgment against the drunken driver as a prerequisite to suit against the host; limiting the amount that could be recovered from a social host; and requiring a finding of wanton and reckless conduct before holding the social host liable.

I do not propose to fashion a legislative solution. That is for the Legislature. I merely wish to point out that the Legislature has a variety of alternatives to this Court's imposition of unlimited liability on every New Jersey adult. Perhaps, after investigating all the options, the Legislature will determine that the most effective course is to impose the same civil liability on social hosts that the majority has imposed today. I would have no qualms about that legislative decision so long as it was reached after a thorough investigation of its impact on average citizens of New Jersey.

E. ANALYZING THE COURT'S OPINION

1. *How* It Is Written

Whether you agree or disagree with the New Jersey Supreme Court's opinion in *Kelly v. Gwinnell*, it is an excellent example of a well-written judicial opinion — one that you should study not only for its insights into the case synthesis process, but also for its insights into how to express legal analysis.[16]

a. Issue Statement

The court clearly identifies the issue in the very first sentence of the opinion.[17] Notice *how* the court phrases the issue. The issue is not stated on the factual plane. It does not include any express reference to the particular facts of the case. All references to the factual scenario before the court are *generic* references: "a social host," not the Zaks; "an adult guest," not Gwinnell; "the victim," not Kelly. The generic statement of the issue on appeal places the issue more on the rule plane than on the factual plane. As a general rule, that is how you should write the issue statements in your case briefs. Whether you should use the more

---

16. To get a full sense of the beauty of the opinion, you might want to read the full majority and dissenting opinions to see the analytical structure of each. Each opinion has been heavily edited down for purposes of this coverage.

17. "This case raises the issue of whether a social host who enables an adult guest at his home to become drunk is liable to the victim of an automobile accident caused by the drunken driving of the guest."

generic approach or a more fact-specific approach when you are writing your memorandums and briefs in legal research and writing will depend on the nature of the issue you are analyzing (whether it involves a question of law or simply a question of application).

b. "Question of First Impression"

After the opening paragraph, the court's opinion sets forth the facts and the procedural posture of the case. In discussing the procedural posture, the court notes that "[t]he Appellate Division's determination was based on the apparent absence of decisions in this country imposing such liability. . . ." This is a variation on a theme you have seen before. In essence, what is the court saying here? If the court were to impose liability, what would the court be doing? It would be *making law*. The analytical decision — the decision-making process of *whether* to make new law — is analogous to the analytical decision-making process of *what* the law should be. Before doing either, what should the court take into consideration? *Public policy: what type of society do we want, and why*. Notice how little of the court's opinion is taken up discussing the facts of the case. The issue is a legal issue, a point the court expressly notes.[18] The question of law, whether the court should make *new law* and impose a duty on a social host under these circumstances, is a question of public policy. The public policy considerations and legal discussion take up the bulk of the court's opinion. The court is well aware of what it is doing, and it addresses the process head-on on the appropriate planes: the public policy and legal planes.

2. *How* the Court Analyzed the Issue — Case Synthesis

a. Overview

Although the court realized it was making new law, and breaking with the traditional and overwhelmingly majority approach to the issue, the court also wanted to minimize the appearance of what it was doing. Generally, courts do not want to look like they are acting like a legislature. In *Kelly v. Gwinnel*, the court employed case synthesis to assert that what it was doing was not *really* that new or that radical of a departure from existing case law. Using case synthesis, the court implicitly argued[19] that its holding was but a natural and logical

---

18. "The Zaks moved for summary judgment, contending that *as a matter of law* a host is not liable for the negligence of an adult social guest who has become intoxicated while at the host's home. The trial court granted the motion on that basis." (Emphasis added.)

19. Technically, when writing memorandums and briefs, it is not appropriate to say that the court "argued. . . ." The attorneys argue to the court, and the dissent may argue in opposition to the court, but the proper terminology is to say that the court held, or the court ruled, or the court stated. Technically, the court does not argue. Here, however, the comment is about the effect of the court's action and how it tried to convince the legal community that its holding was appropriate, so the phrasing is characterizing the court's opinion, not really describing the court's opinion.

extension of prevailing authority within the jurisdiction, that the underlying cases constituted persuasive authority.[20]

The court synthesizes the cases first by identifying an overarching public policy consideration it concludes run through the cases (the newly evolving public policy against drunk driving). And then, second, after the court re-analyzes each case from the perspective of the newly identified public policy consideration, the court articulates a new legal standard that connects the cases in a way that has not been previously articulated. A careful reading of the opinion reveals each step in the case synthesis process. The process involves the three planes, with the key being the interaction between the public policy plane and the legal plane.

b. The Backdrop

The court's opinion starts off by adopting the classic structure of a well-written opinion. First, the court sets forth the facts of the case, showing how the dispute arose on the factual plane. Then the court goes to the rule plane, looking for a rule that might apply. The rule it found (as brought to its attention by the attorneys no doubt) was the common law rule of negligence. But the court notes that its applicability is subject to debate:

> The usual elements of a cause of action for negligence[21] are clearly present: an action by defendant creating an unreasonable risk of harm to plaintiff, a risk that was clearly foreseeable, and a risk that resulted in an injury equally foreseeable.[22] Under those circumstances the only question remaining is whether a duty exists to prevent such risk or, realistically, whether this Court should impose such a duty.

The question the court ends with, whether such a duty *should* be imposed, requires the analysis to move to which plane? The public policy plane.

c. Articulating the Public Policy Consideration

Over the course of the next five sentences the court makes *three* different express references to the fact that whether to impose a duty in such cases is a question of public policy.[23] After stating that the threshold question of whether to impose

---

20. Conceptually, one way to think about case synthesis is that it is analogous to "spin control." Anyone familiar with our political process is familiar with the post-debate process where after two candidates engage in a lively debate, each politician's handlers attempt to "spin" the interpretation of the debate so that the re-characterization of the debate favors his or her candidate. Case synthesis is analogous in many respects. Notice how the majority, in discussing each of the cases it is synthesizing, re-characterizes what the case stands for — the scope of the case.

21. The rule of law the court selects is negligence.

22. Notice *how* the court applies the rule. It breaks it into its elements, making express reference to the word elements, and applies each one to the facts of the case. The court does not pair up each element with the appropriate fact because at this point in the opinion the court wants to focus on the legal issue in the case — whether a duty exists.

23. "In most cases the justice of imposing such a duty is so clear that the cause of action in negligence is assumed to exist simply on the basis of the actor's creation of an unreasonable risk of foreseeable harm resulting in injury. In fact, however, more is needed, 'more' being the value

such a duty is a public policy issue, the court identifies the particular public policy interest that applies to the issue: *"the reduction of drunk driving."*[24] The court spends the next paragraph articulating and discussing the "new" public policy consideration that may justify changing the law and imposing a duty on a social host.

d. Transitioning Back to the Legal Plane

Having set the public policy framework, the court then comes back down to the rule plane, presenting each case in retrospect so that it fits within, and supports, this new public policy framework. The court's transition sentence from identifying the overarching public policy consideration to synthesizing the cases on the legal plane is very insightful. It goes to the core of the synthesis process: "While the imposition of a duty here would go beyond our prior decisions, those decisions not only point clearly in that direction but do so despite the presence of social considerations similar to those involved in this case—considerations that are claimed to invest the host with immunity."

Reflect upon that sentence for a moment—it states the essence of case synthesis. The first clause of the sentence implicitly acknowledges that at one level the prior cases are different from the pending case: "imposition of a duty here would *go beyond* our prior decisions. . . ." (Emphasis added.)[25] Nevertheless, in the second half of the sentence the court asserts that at another level the cases are the same: "those decisions [the prior cases being synthesized] not only point clearly in that direction [the direction of imposing a duty] but do so despite the presence of social considerations similar to those involved in this case-considerations that are claimed to invest the host with immunity." Yes, there are differences between and among the cases, but there are also similarities. In the end, if the cases can be synthesized that means the court concluded that the similarities outweigh the differences, leading to the articulation of a new legal standard that explains the connection between the cases and supports the new legal rule in the pending case.

---

judgment, based on an analysis of *public policy*, that the actor owed the injured party a duty of reasonable care. Palsgraf v. Long Island R.R. Co., 248 N.Y. 339, 162 N.E. 99 (1928). In Goldberg v. Housing Auth. of Newark, 38 N.J. 578, 583, 186 A.2d 291 (1962), this Court explained that 'whether a duty exists is ultimately a question of fairness. The inquiry involves a weighing of the relationship of the parties, the nature of the risk, and the *public interest* in the proposed solution.' See also Portee v. Jaffee, 84 N.J. 88, 101, 417 A.2d 521 (1980) (whether liability for negligently inflicted emotional harm should be expanded depends 'ultimately' on balancing of conflicting interests involved).

When the court determines that a duty exists and liability will be extended, it draws judicial lines based on fairness and *policy*." (Emphasis added.)

24. Remember that one way to conceptualize what public policy is, is to ask, "What is the socially desirable conduct; what conduct should be encouraged, what conduct should be discouraged, and why?" The court expressly refers to the reduction of drunk driving as "a social goal." The court is very conscious that it is asserting a "newly" evolving public policy consideration that constitutes the overarching interest that connects the cases it is about to synthesize.

25. The court is also acknowledging that none of the prior cases, individually, constitute either binding or persuasive authority.

e. The Analytical Steps Inherent in Case Synthesis

When synthesizing cases, the norm is to start with the oldest opinion, presenting it in a way that lays the foundation for the synthesis of the other cases. In *Kelly v. Gwinnell*, the court starts with *Rappaport*,[26] the oldest case in the line.[27] The court's discussion of *Rappaport* makes no reference to any of the other cases. The court is *not synthesizing* cases yet, it is just laying the foundation. In describing the case, the court goes out of its way to emphasize that the rationale was based not only on statutory grounds, but also on principles of common-law negligence. The court is emphasizing the aspect of the case that will serve as the basis for synthesizing the other cases. The *Rappaport* case could be construed from either a statutory perspective or from a judicial, common-law negligence perspective. The court is, in essence, "spinning" what the case stands for to support its current analysis and case synthesis.[28] Doctrinally, the *Rappoport* case stands for the rule that under a negligence analysis, a licensee owes a duty to a minor who was served by the licensee and who later is in an automobile accident.

Next the court raises and discusses the *Soronen* case. The court implicitly acknowledges that doctrinally, the *Sorenen* opinion *extends* the scope of a licensee's duty: "We later made it clear that the licensee's *duty is owed to the customer as well ...*"). The court has begun the case synthesis process. It is *lining up* the cases, showing how even though at one level the cases are different, at another level the cases are "the same"[29] — that they can be synthesized.[30] Here, the

---

26. To facilitate the analysis of the court's analysis, the relevant part of the opinion will be set forth in a footnote below the analysis: "In our first case on the subject, *Rappaport*, supra, 31 N.J. 188, 156 A.2d 1, we held a licensee liable for the consequences of a customer's negligent operation of his automobile. The customer was a minor who had become intoxicated as a result of the consumption of liquor at various premises including the licensee's. While observing that a standard of conduct was contained in the statute prohibiting licensees from serving liquor to minors and in the regulation further prohibiting service to any person actually or apparently intoxicated, our decision that the licensee owed a duty to members of the general public was based on principles of common-law negligence."

27. In legal research and writing, you will often have to "present" a case — to raise and discuss it as part of your memorandum or brief. Notice *how* the court presents the case. The opening sentence about the case is on the rule plane. Next the court tells you the facts of the case. Then the court gives you the rationale for the court's decision — the public policy considerations that justified the rule and holding. The court covers all three planes in an order that makes it easy for the reader to understand the case. You might want consider using the New Jersey Court's example as a model for how to raise and discuss a case in your legal writing — absent contrary guidance from your legal research and writing professor.

28. Inasmuch as case synthesis depends upon how the underlying cases are "spun," you should be able to see why case synthesis is at best a form of *persuasive* authority. The attorneys for Kelly first make this argument to the court — that the cases can be spun this way. The attorneys for Zaks (the social hosts) will challenge this depiction of the cases and argue that the other party is mischaracterizing what the cases stand for. Ultimately it is up to the court to decide if it thinks the cases can be synthesized or if the characterization — the spinning — is inappropriate.

29. Technically the cases are not the same obviously. Factually they are not the same. But legally they were treated the same — a duty was imposed on the licensee. To say that the cases are legally the same is to say that the factual differences do not make any legal difference because at the public policy level the cases are the same and therefore legally should be treated the same — a duty and liability should be imposed.

30. Conceptually, one way to visualize case synthesis is it involves lining up the cases like stepping stones across a creek. Analytically the question is whether the cases can be positioned so that the distance from one stone to the next is analytically manageable. If the gap between two cases is too

connection between the cases is that both involve a licensee's duty, the difference in the cases is to whom the duty is owed.[31] Depending on why you are discussing the cases, you can spin them as essentially the same case, or as different cases. For purposes of the issue in *Kelly v. Gwinnell*, the court concluded that these two cases constituted stepping stones that were so close together the "analytical" step from one to the next was easy. Synthesizing these two cases was easy. The problem is the next step. *Kelly v. Gwinnell* involves a social host, not a licensee. Can that case be positioned so that analytically imposing the duty on a social host is a manageable leap in the evolving law?

At first blush the analytical gap between the scope of the duty a licensee owes versus the scope of the duty a social host owes appears more daunting. But notice how the court portrays the gap. The court has already decided that it is going to synthesize the cases — that it is going to make this leap — so it wants to downplay the gap — the differences — and emphasize the similarities:[32] "While the situation of a licensee differs *in some respects* from that of a social host, some of the *same underlying considerations* relied on here in disputing liability are *present in both*: the notion that the real fault is that of the drunk, not the licensee, especially where the drinker is an adult (as he was in *Soronen*); and the belief — not as strong when applied to licensed premises as when applied to one's home — that when people get together for a friendly drink or more, the social relationships should not be intruded upon by possibilities of litigation."

From a case synthesis perspective, there are several points to note about the above sentence. The court has begun to discuss the cases *collectively*. That is a natural step in the case synthesis process. The court minimizes the references to particular cases and instead talks in more general, generic terms, using overarching references and phrasing that tend to connect the cases. In addition, the differences the court acknowledges are primarily on the factual plane, while the underlying shared considerations are primarily on the public policy plane.[33] The court is laying the foundation for its ultimate position that the

great, case synthesis arguably is inappropriate. The challenge is to portray the cases as similar enough that the reader thinks the "analytical" difference from one case to the next is short enough that the cases can be synthesized into a manageable line of cases — of stepping stones from one case to the next.

31. Strategically, notice how the court has started with two cases that arguably are very easy to synthesize. The court has the reader leaning in favor of synthesizing the cases — at least the cases presented so far.

32. Judicial opinions are a form of *persuasive* writing. The court is trying to persuade other courts, the practicing bar, academics, and the public in general that the court got it "right" — that its opinion is defensible. If the court had decided against synthesizing the cases, it would be downplaying the similarities and emphasizing the differences.

33. Notice also *structurally* how the court is presenting each case. The court ends each case presentation with the key point it wants the reader to remember. In discussing the *Rappaport* case, the court ended by emphasizing the common law basis of the opinion — the foundation it would use to help synthesize the cases. In discussing the *Soronen* case, the court ends by pointing out that some of the same social considerations present in the *Rappaport* and *Soronen* cases also present the in the *Kelly* case — a key argument in the case synthesis process: that the cases really are more similar than dissimilar.

differences are meaningless legally because the same paramount public policy considerations apply.

Because the court realizes that the analytical jump from *Rappaport*/*Soronen* to *Kelly*—the leap from imposing a duty on a licensee to imposing a duty on a social host who served an adult—is substantial, the court points out that there is another potential stepping stone in between that may make the leap more manageable—the appellate court decision in *Linn* where a social host served a minor. The court begins by acknowledging that *Linn* is different from the other cases and that *Linn* "moved our decisional law one step further, a significant step. . . ." Again, the court is lining up the cases, but this time the court acknowledges that the step from *Rappaport*/*Soronen* to a social host is a significant step. The implicit issue is whether that was an appropriate step, because in many respects that is the key step. If the step is manageable as applied to a social host and a minor, the step from there to a social host and an adult is not that great. As the court said, "all of the considerations urged here [in *Kelly v. Gwinnell*] against liability were present [in *Linn*]."[34] If *Linn* can be synthesized, the step to *Kelly v. Gwinnell* is but another small step.

The court synthesizes the *Linn* opinion with the court's prior opinions by emphasizing the common rationale underlying the cases: "In expanding liability, *Linn* followed the rationale of *Rappaport* that the duty involved is a common law duty, not one arising from the statute and regulation prohibiting sales of liquor to a minor, neither of which applies to a social host." By asserting that the duty is based on common law, not purely statutory grounds, the court is returning to the point it emphasized when it first raised and discussed *Rappaport* earlier in the opinion. The court is synthesizing *Linn* with *Rappaport* by asserting that the duty being imposed in each case stems from the same "common law" source. The court further supports this connection by invoking Soronen as well: "The fair implication of *Rappaport* and *Soronen*, that the duty exists independent of the statutory prohibition, was thus made explicit in *Linn*." But notice how *Rappaport* and *Soronen* have been re-characterized (the "*fair implication*" of the cases, not their express reasoning) to support and be consistent with the reasoning in *Linn*. Synthesizing the cases often requires re-characterizing what an opinion stands for so that all of the cases now stand for and support the same principle and rule.

Notice also the subtle but critical point at this stage of the synthesis: the court knows it also has to synthesize *Kelly v. Gwinnell* with these cases. The prior three cases—*Rappaport*, *Soronen*, and *Linn*—could have been synthesized on purely statutory grounds. In *Rappaport* and *Linn*, a minor was served alcohol. There are

---

34. Conceptually you could argue that the court has put the cases on a spectrum, with the licensee cases (*Rappaport* and *Sorenen*) at one end of the spectrum and *Kelly v. Gwinnell* at the other end of the spectrum. In putting *Linn* on the spectrum, the court notes that *Linn* is much, much closer to the *Kelly v. Gwinnell* end of the spectrum (the only difference being that the guest was a minor in *Linn*, like in *Rappaport*), yet the appellate court imposed liability. The implicit issue is whether the appellate court's decision to impose liability on the social host is defensible: can it be synthesized with the court's prior opinions?

strict statutory prohibitions against serving alcohol to a minor. The court has gone out of its way to argue that these cases were also based on common law negligence principles because if the cases were based solely on statutory grounds they should not apply to *Kelly v. Gwinnell* because the person served was an adult, not a minor. That is where *Soronen* comes into play. In *Soronen*, the person served was an adult, not a minor, but the party who served the alcohol was a licensee. But in *Kelly v. Gwinnell*, the party who served the alcohol is a social host, not a licensee. There are plenty of statutory rules regulating licensees who serve alcohol. The underlying three cases can all be synthesized fairly easily on statutory grounds. The court has gone out of its was to "spin" each case as being defensible from a common law negligence perspective as well because that is the only basis the court can use to synthesize the cases with *Kelly v. Gwinnell*.

Kelly v. Gwinnell involves a social host, not a licensee, who served alcohol to an adult, not a minor. There is no direct statutory support for imposing liability in *Kelly v. Gwinnell* based on the party who provided the alcohol — a social host. There is no direct statutory support for imposing liability in *Kelly v. Gwinnell* based on the party who consumed the alcohol — an adult. If a duty is to be imposed, it must be imposed on common law negligence principles, hence the "spinning" of the prior cases to emphasize that aspect of each of them.[35]

At this point in the case synthesizing process, the court has connected up the cases, but if the court had stopped there, its opinion would have been conclusory. Saying that a social host should be treated the same legally as a licensee is conclusory without an explanation for *why*. Up to this point in the opinion, the court has merely hinted at why the two should be treated the same, but historically the courts have thought the differences sufficient to justify drawing the line here — between the licensee and the social host. To complete the synthesis the court needs to put forth a new line in the sand, a new legal standard for distinguishing when a duty should be imposed that is consistent with the case synthesis the court is performing. And the court does so: "The argument is made that the rule imposing liability on licensees is justified because licensees, unlike social hosts, derive a profit from serving liquor. We reject this analysis of the liability's foundation and emphasize that the liability proceeds from the duty of care that accompanies control of the liquor supply. Whatever the motive behind making alcohol available to those who will subsequently drive, the provider has a duty to the public not to create foreseeable, unreasonable risks by this activity."

By articulating that "liability proceeds from the duty of care that accompanies control of the liquor supply," the court broadens the scope of liability in a way that permits the cases to be properly synthesized. The new legal standard

---

35. Case synthesis is a bit like reverse engineering. Analytically, the court had to think through what would work as the basis for connecting up the cases, and then it went back and wrote the opinion and presented each case so as to emphasize the aspects of each case that supported the connection and de-emphasize the parts of the opinion that undermined the connection. Case synthesis is an example of persuasive writing.

obliterates any distinction between a social host and a licensee — the traditional distinguishing fact for duty purposes. The new legal standard "synthesizes" the cases, providing a new explanation for how the cases are the same, not different. Based on that new legal standard, *Kelly v. Gwinnell* is no different from *Rappaport* and *Soronen* because it does not matter whether the party who serves the alcohol is a social host or a licensee; based on the new legal standard, *Kelly v. Gwinnell* is also no different from *Linn* because it does not matter if the party served is a minor or an adult. *The party who controls the supply of liquor owes a duty of care not to create foreseeable, unreasonable risks of harm associated with the supply of alcohol.*

Having synthesized the cases, and articulated a new legal standard, the court then articulates the new rule of law for *Kelly v. Gwinnell*, the next case in the line: "We therefore hold that a host who serves liquor to an adult social guest, knowing both that the guest is intoxicated and will thereafter be operating a motor vehicle, is liable for injuries inflicted on a third party as a result of the negligent operation of a motor vehicle by the adult guest when such negligence is caused by the intoxication."[36] Having articulated a new rule of law, a well-written opinion should set forth the public policy considerations that explain *why* that should be the rule. In *Kelly v. Gwinnell*, the court does not disappoint. One may not agree with the public policy explanation, but structurally and analytically the court completes the case synthesis process:

> We impose this duty on the host to the third party because we believe that *the policy considerations* served by its imposition far outweigh those asserted in opposition. While we recognize the concern that our ruling will interfere with accepted standards of social behavior; will intrude on and somewhat diminish the enjoyment, relaxation, and camaraderie that accompany social gatherings at which alcohol is served; and that such gatherings and social relationships are not simply tangential benefits of a civilized society but are regarded by many as important, we believe that the added assurance of just compensation to the victims of drunken driving as well as the added deterrent effect of the rule on such driving outweigh the importance of those other values. Indeed, we believe that given society's extreme concern about drunken driving, any change in social behavior resulting from the rule will be regarded ultimately as neutral at the very least, and not as a change for the worse; but that in any event if there be a loss, it is well worth the gain. (Emphasis added.)

---

36. Why does not the court simply articulate a new rule of law based on the new legal standard — that control of the liquor supply creates a duty? Courts tend not to want to articulate a rule that is any broader than necessary to resolve the dispute before it. A rule that is broader runs several risks. The broader the wording in the rule statement, the more likely it may encompass factual scenarios that the court did not anticipate. The pros and cons of imposing the rule on that particular fact pattern were not argued to the court. So when articulating a new rule, courts prefer to word the rule only as broadly as necessary to resolve the particular dispute before it that caused the court to create the rule. It leaves the true scope of the rule to be hashed out in subsequent cases. Hence another reason the law is constantly evolving — there are always issues with respect to the scope of a rule relative to new fact patterns.

In the end case synthesis is driven, first and foremost, by the policy considerations underlying and connecting up the dots in the line. Proper synthesis requires the court to identify not only the public policy consideration, but also to articulate a defensible legal standard that goes hand in hand with the public policy considerations and which connects and explains the otherwise disparate underlying cases. Typically the new public policy considerations and legal standard are then applied to the pending case to see if it fits in the line, to see if it too should be synthesized.

3. Recap of Case Synthesis in the context of *Kelly v. Gwinnell*

Case synthesis constitutes an analytical process by which a court steps back and reassess a series of cases that it thinks might be connected, identifying and articulating a new public policy consideration and legal standard that runs between them. In reassessing each case, the court often "spins" each case to emphasize what the court now, in retrospect, believes each case stands for so that it fits into the new vision of the cases — the case synthesis process. The final issue then is whether the same public policy considerations and legal standard also apply to the case pending before the court.

In *Kelly v. Gwinnell*, the court stated that the "new" public policy underlying the cases being synthesized was the social goal of reducing drunk driving. Having identified the relevant public policy consideration, the issue on the rule plane was whether that public policy consideration justified extending liability to social hosts. Prior cases had distinguished social hosts from licensees for a variety of reasons, but in *Kelly v. Gwinnell*, the court repudiated that distinction and set forth the new legal standard — that the controlling variable was whether the party in question had control over the supply of alcohol. Accordingly, the new rule and decision in *Kelly v. Gwinnell* is just a natural extension of the evolving line of cases. The court effectively employed case synthesis to reason that the underlying cases constituted persuasive authority for its ruling that "a host who serves liquor to an adult social guest, knowing both that the guest is intoxicated and will thereafter be operating a motor vehicle, is liable for injuries inflicted on a third party as a result of the negligent operation of a motor vehicle by the adult guest when such negligence is caused by the intoxication."

4. Case Synthesis: Skill or Art?

Case synthesis is one of the more difficult skills to master in law school because it is so loose and "case" specific. Whether a group of cases can be synthesized depends on the grouping of the cases: whether there is a unifying public policy consideration; whether the rules adopted in each case can be synthesized by articulating a new legal standard that encompasses, explains, and unites them;

and whether the public policy consideration and newly articulated legal standard apply to the pending case. Each grouping of cases is unique. Admittedly, case synthesis is a very difficult task. It may be more appropriate to describe it as an *art* as opposed to a skill. Either way, the following hypotheticals will test your understanding of the art of synthesizing cases.

F. WHAT IF...

1. First Hypothetical

What if, after the opinion in *Kelly v. Gwinnell* is published, you had the same facts as *Kelly v. Gwinnell*, only this time Gwinnell, after being served all that alcohol by the Zaks, made it all the way home to his apartment without being in an automobile accident. After reaching his apartment safely, however, Gwinnell laid down on his couch, lit up a cigarette, and promptly passed out. The lit cigarette started a fire that destroyed the apartment building, seriously injuring Kelly, the tenant who lived upstairs. Kelly sued not only Gwinnell for causing the fire, but also Zak under negligence and the social host liability doctrine. Should Kelly be able to recover from Zak? Why or why not?[37]

2. Analysis of First Hypothetical

How should you go about analyzing the hypothetical? The facts present a dispute that arises on the factual plane — can Kelly successfully sue Zak? What is the first step in your analysis? The first step in analyzing a new fact pattern is to identify all rules of law that may apply to it. Here the hypothetical has told you the rules of law you are to apply. Kelly sued Zak "under negligence and the social host liability doctrine."[38] Once you have identified the rules of law at issue, what is the next step involved in applying the rule to a new fact pattern?

The starting point for applying a rule of law to a new fact pattern is to state the rule. That is a bit unfair here because although the court invoked the rule of negligence in *Kelly v. Gwinnell*, negligence was not really the focus of the court's opinion. The social host liability doctrine was the focus. The law of negligence is one of the more complicated rules you will study in law school. This material will leave the details of the rule of negligence for your Torts class. So if your analysis is

---

37. Again, for analytical purposes, you might want to write down your answers to these questions so that you can critique your analysis later.

38. The hypothetical has given you the rule of law that you are to apply. That is more than you will be told, typically, on an exam. On a traditional law school exam, you would have been given only the fact pattern and it would have been up to you to "spot the issue" — to see the similarities between the fact pattern in the hypothetical and the fact pattern in the case you read to realize that the rule you learned in the case applied to the fact pattern. Issue spotting is covered in greater detail in Part II of the book.

a bit fuzzy, that is understandable since you are being asked to apply a rule that you do not really know or understand yet.

What is the rule of law for negligence that you take away from *Kelly v. Gwinnell*? That is a tough question because the court makes several statements that go to the rule of negligence. The court stated: "Negligence is tested by whether the reasonably prudent person at the time and place should recognize and foresee an unreasonable risk or likelihood of harm or danger to others. . . . When negligent conduct creates such a risk, setting off foreseeable consequences that lead to plaintiff's injury, the conduct is deemed the proximate cause of the injury." But later on, the court stated: "The usual elements of a cause of action for negligence are clearly present: an action by defendant creating an unreasonable risk of harm to plaintiff, a risk that was clearly foreseeable, and a risk that resulted in an injury equally foreseeable. Under those circumstances the only question remaining is whether a duty exists to prevent such risk or, realistically, whether this Court should impose such a duty."

A rule of negligence that you might have extracted from the court's opinion is that the plaintiff must prove that the defendant owed the plaintiff a duty of care, that the defendant breached that duty by creating an unreasonable risk of foreseeable harm, that the plaintiff was harmed, and that the defendant's conduct caused the harm (duty, breach, causation and harm). Notice the social host liability doctrine is rule elaboration for when a duty should be imposed on a social host to create liability when a third party is injured by a party whom the social host served. What is the rule elaboration; what is the rule of law you take away from *Kelly v. Gwinnell* for what constitutes the social host liability doctrine?

While reasonable minds may disagree on the exact wording of the rule statement in *Kelly v. Gwinnell*, a good sentence to start with is the following: "We hold only that where a host provides liquor directly to a social guest and continues to do so even beyond the point at which the host knows the guest is intoxicated, and does this knowing that the guest will shortly thereafter be operating a motor vehicle, that host is liable for the foreseeable consequences to third parties that result from the guest's drunken driving." Although the court says that this is the court's holding, it is worded so generically it is more a rule statement than an application of the rule to the facts of the case. Drop the first four words in the sentence and you arguably have a good rule statement for the social host liability doctrine: "[W]here a host provides liquor directly to a social guest and continues to do so even beyond the point at which the host knows the guest is intoxicated, and does this knowing that the guest will shortly thereafter be operating a motor vehicle, that host is liable for the foreseeable consequences to third parties that result from the guest's drunken driving."

Do the facts of the first hypothetical come within the scope of the social host liability doctrine as articulated by the court in *Kelly v. Gwinnell*? Break the rule/rule elaboration into its elements and apply each element, going element by element. Strictly applying the social host liability doctrine as articulated in *Kelly v. Gwinnell*, it is pretty clear that the rule does not apply. The last clause provides that the "host is liable for the foreseeable consequences to third parties that result *from the drunken driving."* Here, in the first hypothetical, the harm did not result from the guest's drunken driving. The guest made it home to his apartment safely, but then he passed out on the couch starting a fire. The first hypothetical is distinguishable from *Kelly v. Gwinnell* and it does not come within the scope of the rule as stated in the case.

But that should not have been the end of your analysis. Can you argue, in good faith, that *Kelly v. Gwinnell* is yet another case in the evolving line of cases and that it can be synthesized with the other cases to impose liability whenever "a host provides liquor directly to a social guest and continues to do so even beyond the point at which the host knows the guest is intoxicated, that host is liable for the foreseeable consequences to third parties that result from the guest's drunken behavior"? Should the social host liability doctrine be limited to injuries caused by the guest's drunken driving behavior or should it be extended to apply to any and all harm inflicted on third parties as a result of the guest's drunken behavior?

Notice this is a question of first impression. It is an issue on which good faith arguments can be advanced on both sides of the issue. A full-blown development of both sides is beyond the scope of this material, but the issue will be discussed briefly.

The threshold question is did you think of this line of argument? You cannot learn and interpret rules of law as if they are static, fixed in time. Admittedly some rules are more fixed than others, but the law is constantly evolving. Public policy considerations change; new factual scenarios arise. You should be open to that possibility with respect to almost any law. To the extent an opinion synthesizes a new line of cases, how far should that line of cases extend? Assuming a new fact pattern arises, the threshold issue was whether the new case falls *within* that line of cases, in which case the rules articulated should apply, or whether the new case falls outside the new line of cases? Assuming the new case falls *outside* the line of cases, that should not be the end of your analysis. If the new case falls *beyond* the current line of cases, the follow-up issue is whether the current line of cases should be extended to include the new case, thereby extending the line further. Can the new case be *synthesized* with the current line of cases?

As applied to the first hypothetical and the line of cases in *Kelly v. Gwinnell*, as noted above, this new fact pattern falls outside the holding of *Kelly v. Gwinnell*. It is *beyond* the rule of law as established in *Kelly v. Gwinnell* because the court there extended liability only for injuries that are "the foreseeable consequences to third parties that result from the guest's drunken driving." Follow up issue: *should* the holding in *Kelly v. Gwinnell* be extended to include the facts present in the first hypothetical? If you did not think about that issue in your initial analysis, take a moment to consider it. Should the line of cases discussed in *Kelly v. Gwinnell* be extended to include this hypothetical?[39]

---

39. Again, for analytical purposes, you might want to write down your answers to these questions so that you can critique your analysis later.

A full-blown analysis of that issue is beyond the scope of this material, but it should include a proper analysis of the public policy considerations and legal principles discussed in *Kelly v. Gwinnell*. The overarching public policy consideration was the reduction of drunk driving — as evidenced by the statutory activity aggressively attacking the problem. That public policy consideration does *not* apply to the hypothetical under consideration. Imposing liability in the hypothetical would have no effect on the rate of drunk driving. Is there an equally strong public policy consideration against the underlying conduct that created the immediate risk of harm — smoking? Interestingly, at the time of the *Kelly v. Gwinnell* opinion, there was not a strong public policy against smoking — but today there is a newly evolving public policy consideration against smoking. Is that a strong enough public policy consideration to impose liability here on the social host?

Even assuming, arguendo, a sufficiently strong public policy consideration, the court's discussion of negligence also pointed out that the elements of negligence require that the injury must be "clearly foreseeable": Negligence requires "an action by defendant creating an *unreasonable* risk of harm to plaintiff, a risk that was *clearly foreseeable*, and a risk that resulted in *an injury equally foreseeable*." It is reasonably foreseeable that a drunk guest who is going to drive himself or herself home might be involved in an accident. Is it equally foreseeable that the guest may get all the way home to their apartment safely, light up a cigarette, and pass out while smoking the cigarette, starting a fire that injures a neighbor? Most reasonable minds would conclude that the latter risk of injury is not nearly as foreseeable as that caused by a drunk driver.

If you concluded that the court's holding in *Kelly v. Gwinnell* should *not* be extended to the facts of the first hypothetical, your developing case synthesis skills are correct. The facts of the first hypothetical are basically the facts of Griesenbeck v. Walker, 199 N.J. Super. 132, 488 A.2d 1038 (N.J. Super. A.D., 1985). *Griesenbeck* was the next case that came along in New Jersey. The court was asked to extend social host liability doctrine to cover the case. You are free to read the full opinion, but in a nutshell the court declined to extend the duty to the facts presented on the grounds that (1) the pubic policy considerations for doing so were not as strong, and (2) the risk of harm and the foreseeability of the harm presented by the fact pattern were not as strong as that presented by the drunk driver. The court declined to extend the social host liability doctrine to include this scenario.

3. Second Hypothetical

What if, after the opinion in *Kelly v. Gwinnell* is published, Zak decides to host a party. Zak invites a number of guests, including Kelly and Gwinnell. Zak acts as the bartender during the party, serving the alcohol to all of his guests. Zak serves Gwinnell the same number of drinks as alleged in the original case. Gwinnell gets drunk, and unfortunately, it turns out he is a belligerent drunk. Gwinnell gets into a fight and ends up punching Kelly in the face, breaking several bones in her jaw and cheek. Kelly sues Gwinnell, but she also sues Zak alleging negligence and social host liability. Should Kelly be able to recover from Zak? Why or why not?[40]

4. Analysis of Second Hypothetical

Does the second hypothetical come within the scope of the holding and rule of law in *Kelly v. Gwinnell*? This threshold issue should be pretty easy based on the above analysis of the first hypothetical. In *Kelly v. Gwinnell* the court imposed social host liability only if the injures were the result of a drunk driver being in an automobile accident. The injuries in the second hypothetical are not the result of a drunk driver being in an automobile accident; they are the result of a drunk being in a fight. The second hypothetical does not come within the scope of the social host liability doctrine as articulated in *Kelly v. Gwinnell*.

Should the line of cases synthesized in *Kelly v. Gwinnell*, and the rule of law articulated in it, be extended to include the fact pattern set forth in the second hypothetical? This time you should have raised and analyzed that issue. Once again, good faith arguments can be raised on both sides of the issue. More importantly analytically, do you think this variation is a *stronger* or *weaker* case for extending the line of cases and rule of law as set forth in *Kelly v. Gwinnell*?[41]

The second hypothetical arguably is a stronger case for extending the social host liability doctrine. Although it does not involve the overarching public policy consideration that was present in *Kelly v. Gwinnell*, the reduction of drunk driving, there is a strong public policy interest against fighting. There are plenty of statutory rules, both criminal and civil, that arguably reflect the strong public policy interest against fighting. The public policy consideration may not be as strong as the interest against drunk driving, but it is not insignificant.

Moreover, the risk that a drunk guest will get into a fight and punch someone is a more foreseeable risk. The risk that a drunk guest may get into a fight and hurt someone is a clearly foreseeable risk, and the injury — being hurt from a punch thrown by a drunk — is equally foreseeable.

The second hypothetical presents a stronger argument for extending the social host liability doctrine to impose liability on the social host.

So did the court do so? Did the court extend the social host liability doctrine and impose liability in the second hypothetical? Inasmuch as there is a court opinion, *Griesenbeck v. Walker*, that provides insights into the analysis of the first hypothetical, most students automatically assume there must also be a court opinion that tells them the "right" answer to the second hypothetical as

---

40. Again, for analytical purposes, you might want to write down your answers to these questions so that you can critique your analysis later.
41. Again, for analytical purposes, you might want to write down your answers to these questions so that you can critique your analysis later.

well. The students assume the facts of the second hypothetical must also be based upon a subsequent case, but it is not. The fact pattern is purely hypothetical, but it is easy to see how it *could* be a new case—either in the real world or on an exam!

That is one way professors draft exams to test their students' understanding of the law *and to test their analytical abilities.*

CHAPTER 17

Legal Analysis and Statutory Construction

A. INTRODUCTION

The discussion of legal analysis and what it means to think like a lawyer has assumed that the focus has been on the common law — judge made law. That is the traditional focus of legal analysis in law school, at least in the first year of law school. Most first-year courses (Property, Torts, Contracts, Criminal Law) are heavily common law oriented, and they are typically taught from the case method approach. But that is by no means the only type of law. The issue that naturally arises is to what extent, if any, is legal analysis different with respect to statutory law. While complete analysis of legal analysis and statutory construction is beyond the scope of this book,[1] the material would be incomplete without at least an introduction to the issues.

B. THEORETICAL PERSPECTIVE

From a purely abstract perspective, the process of *creating* statutory law follows the same basic analytical model as the creation of common law, at least at the macro level. In creating statutory law, the legislature strives to adopt the best law that it can create. In thinking about what the law *should* be, the legislature should identify and take into consideration the competing public policy considerations. After deciding which ones are the most important and why, the legislature comes back down to the rule plane and attempts to draft statutory language that does the best job of promoting the public policy considerations that it deems most important. That law is then applied by the courts to disputes to resolve them.

---

1. For a more thorough treatment of the issues inherent in statutory construction, two excellent resources are Antonin Scalia, A Matter of Interpretation: Federal Courts and the Law (1997); and William N., Jr. Eskridge, Philip P. Frickey, and Elizabeth Garrett, Legislation and Statutory Interpretation (2000).

C. MORE PRACTICAL PERSPECTIVE

That abstract view, however, is overly simplistic from a number of perspectives. First, the political process is much more partisan and open to special interest groups and lobbyists than is the judicial process. Accordingly, some have argued that the risk that the statutory language ultimately adopted does *not* reflect the "best" possible law is greater with respect to statutory law than common law (judge made law). The counterargument is that the legislative process has greater investigatory ability. The legislature can hold committee hearings. Before adopting the law, the legislature can seek input from a greater number of parties who will be affected by the law. The debate over whether statutory law or common law is "better" is beyond the scope of this material.

The above description of legal analysis with respect to statutory law is also overly simplistic because it glosses over the challenges inherent in applying statutory law. While the legislature drafts and creates statutory law, the judiciary construes and applies it. There is a latent tension in that model. In a democratic system, it is generally accepted that when the duly elected legislative branch has spoken (by adopting a statute), it is the role of the judiciary to apply that law. Assuming the statute is constitutional, the courts are not free to second-guess the legislature. Once the legislature has spoken, the court's job is to follow and apply the statute whether the court agrees with the law or not. The problem that arises is what is the role of the court when the statutory law is ambiguous? What role, if any, should the courts play in construing ambiguous statutory language? If you subscribe to the view that whenever a court is *construing* ambiguous language the court is *making* law, you can see the tension. If the legislature has spoken, the courts are not supposed to, yet if the statutory language is ambiguous, the courts must construe the ambiguity before they can apply it. In construing the ambiguous language, are the courts really making law, and if so, does that violate the principle that where the legislature has spoken the courts are not supposed to?

D. THE LEGISLATIVE INTENT APPROACH

Now that you have a sense of the issue, it should come as no surprise that the authorities are split over the role of the courts in construing statutory language — and that split runs the gamut. The traditional and widely accepted view is that the court's role is to ascertain and follow the legislative intent behind the statute. The court is *not* free to do what it wants — to construe the ambiguous language as it deems best — but rather the court is, in essence, charged with the duty to act as an agent for the legislature. The court has a duty to determine the legislative intent behind the statute and to construe the ambiguity consistent with the legislative intent. In determining the legislative intent, the court should take into consideration the legislative history behind the statute.

At the theoretical level, the legislative intent approach to statutory construction makes sense and is consistent with the three planes of legal analysis. Where the statutory language is ambiguous on the rule plane, the court should go back to the purpose of the statute — to the public policy plane and the public policy considerations identified and analyzed in the statute's legislative history. Because the democratically elected legislature has spoken, however, the court is not free to engage in the legal analysis process as it would like, or as it deems best. Rather, the court must undertake the task from the perspective of the legislature so as not to violate the separation of powers inherent in the democratic process. Theoretically the court is supposed to step into the shoes of the legislature and construe the ambiguity as it thinks the legislature would have.

At the practical level, however, there are several problems with the legislative intent approach to statutory construction. Saying that it is the court's job to step into the shoes and construe the ambiguity as the legislature would implies that the legislature is a monolithic entity. Typically, it is not. Typically the legislature entity is made up of two bodies, the House of Representatives and the Senate. Moreover, each of those bodies is made up of dozens of individuals, each with his or her own intent with respect to the statute. Critics of the legislative intent approach scoff at the idea that there is single legislative intent that the court can ascertain and utilize in construing the ambiguous statutory language. The critics argue that when a court adopts and attempts to implement the legislative intent approach that at best the court is employing the average reasonable legislator model. Some commentators question whether it is appropriate to speak of "the average reasonable legislator" given the political and partisan nature of the legislative process.

Moreover, even assuming, arguendo, that it is appropriate for the court to seek the legislative intent behind a statute, there is disagreement over *what evidence* of legislative intent it is appropriate for the court to consider. It is fairly easy to manipulate the legislative history behind a statute. Individual legislators can insert whole speeches into the record that were not really given, which after the fact color the apparent legislative history behind the statute. In light of such concerns, some argue that only committee reports are reliable when seeking legislative intent. Others, however, argue that everything in the legislative record is relevant but it is up to the court to decide how much weight to give the particular part of the statute's legislative record. And lastly, even assuming there is no dispute as to what evidence of legislative intent is appropriate, which "intent" is the appropriate intent: the specific intent behind the statutory language or the more general public policy considerations behind the statute? Intent can be spun narrowly or broadly depending on how one wants to use it.

E. THE TEXTUALIST APPROACH

Because of the concerns over the legislative intent approach, some commentators argue for the textualist approach. Under the textualist approach, if there is an ambiguity in the statutory language the court should *not* attempt to resort to legislative history to help it construe the ambiguity but rather it should limit its efforts to the text and structure of the statute. The court should focus on the text of the statute and on the overall structure of the statute. The court may also use well-established rules of statutory construction in reading and analyzing the statutory language, but the court is not free to resort to legislative history or public policy considerations generally. The textualist approach assumes that the statutory language itself is the best evidence — and only appropriate evidence — of the legislature's intent. Any attempt at going beyond the language and structure of the statute constitutes judicial law-making which is inconsistent with the principle that where the duly elected legislature has spoken it is inappropriate for the courts to do so.

In essence, the textualists believe that the court's efforts at construing statutory language should be limited to the rule plane. The court should not go to the public policy plane at all, either under the guise of trying to ascertain legislative intent or in trying to determine the public policy considerations behind the rule more generally. Under the textualist approach, once the legislature has spoken the court should limit itself to the words and structure of the statute. By structure of the statute, the textualists mean the court should strive to construe the ambiguity so it is consistent with other parts of the statute: all parts of the statute should be construed consistent with the principles (1) that each part of the statute is presumed to have its own meaning and purpose or the legislature would not have adopted it; (2) that the different parts of the statute should be construed individually so the whole makes sense; and (3) if the ambiguous word or phrase is used elsewhere in the statute it should be assumed the legislature used the word or phrase to mean the same thing in this context absent evidence to the contrary.

The argument against the textualist approach is that it is too formalistic. Words do not have meaning in isolation, or even in the context of the statute, without reference to the purpose of the statute. Reference to the purpose of the statute requires at a minimum reference to the legislative history. Too often a fact pattern may arise that falls within the letter of the statute but not the spirit of the statute. Under a textualist approach, the court should apply the statute regardless of the absurdity of the result. The absurdity of such an approach has led some to adopt the realist, or pragmatic, approach to statutory construction.

F. THE REALIST/PRAGMATIC APPROACH

Under the realist or pragmatic approach to statutory construction, courts should accept that law making is a dynamic process and that each player in the process has a duty to act in a way that maximizes social utility. The realists recognize that the court has a more limited role in creating law when the legislature has spoken — the court cannot adopt a rule that contradicts the legislature — but the court should feel free to construe the ambiguity in a way that does the most good under the circumstances. Under the realist approach, courts are not limited to legislative intent and legislative history in determining what is best of society. In determining how to construe and apply a statute, the court is free to identify what *it* thinks was the purpose behind the statute from the totality of the circumstances: the legislative history, the nature of the law, and the nature of the interests affected by the law. Under the realist or pragmatic approach to statutory construction, the statute is judged just as much by the spirit of the law — as determined by the court — as it is the text of the law. Needless to say, the realists and the textualists do not see eye to eye on the issue of statutory construction.

G. THE THREE PLANES

Notice the different schools of statutory construction run the gamut. The textualists try to limit the court's inquiry to the rule plane, while both the legislative intent approach and the realist approach permit the court to go the public policy plane, but for different purposes. There are other points along the spectrum,[2] but these are primary approaches to legal analysis with respect to statutory construction. Yet each of these approaches can be explained from the perspective of the interaction of the three planes — the legal plane, the public policy plane, and the factual plane — with respect to the role of courts and legal analysis when faced with statutory construction. It all comes back to the three planes. It is just a question of how the fact that the law was adopted by the legislature, but is to be construed by the courts, should affect the use of the three planes. There is no clear answer to that question. The debate will continue as long as the process is split between the legislature and the judicial branches.

---

2. Justice Scalia argues for a broadened textualist approach that permits courts to look to other sources in construing the ambiguity, but such sources are not on the public policy plane but rather are still on the rule or text plane: the dictionary definition of the word at the time the statute was adopted, if the word or phrase was used in other statutes about the time of the statute in question, and how the word or phrase was interpreted in those statutes.

PART IV

Conclusion

Historically many law students have complained that legal education is like teaching you how to swim by throwing you into the deep end of the pool and telling you to swim — that too little guidance is given to how to read and analyze a case, how to brief a case, how to understand the Socratic dialogue, how to outline, and how to take a law school exam. I prefer to use the analogy that learning how to think like a lawyer is like learning how to ride a bike. At first you will struggle, you will "fall off" the bike and skin your knees — sometimes in front of your classmates. Do not worry. Pick yourself up, dust yourself off, and get back on the bike. With time, with repetition, with trial and error, you will learn how to think like a lawyer. The purpose of this book is to offer a set of training wheels for that process to help you learn how to think like a lawyer more quickly and with fewer bruises.

The three-planes model to legal analysis provides an overview and an analytical scheme for how to think like a lawyer. That model is inherently flexible. The key is the interaction between and among the planes. Which plane you should be on, at which point in the legal analysis, and looking in which direction, depends on the arguments and analysis being performed at that point in time. *Be flexible* in your approach to legal analysis. It is not a formalistic, mechanical formula — it is a fluid process.

Likewise, IRAC and IRRAC provide a game plan, a structural model, with respect to how to write a well-written law school exam. But as the different variations of IRACs within IRAC, parallel IRRACs, and competing IRRACs show, *be flexible* in your approach to writing your law school exams. These models show you the structure and sequencing, but do not feel compelled to follow that structure and sequence literally. While the classic treatment of a "slam-dunk" element may be two sentences, if you feel the need to vary from that number of sentences, do so. The number is sentences you use is not important. What is important is the substance of the information within your sentences. Focus on what you are writing more than how many sentences it is taking you. Modify the game plan as you deem appropriate. It is a game plan to help you succeed in law school, but you should feel free to adapt it as you deem appropriate for your particular circumstances and your particular style of legal analysis.

Each student has his or her own learning style. Each professor has his or her own teaching style. Feel free to modify and adapt the ideas and techniques set forth in this book to fit your circumstances.

Be flexible, enjoy the ride, and enjoy law school.

CHAPTER 18

Miscellaneous Law School and Exam Taking Tips

Your professional reputation begins the day orientation starts. When you start practicing law, you will come to learn that when a new matter comes into the firm, the partner handling the matter usually sends around a conflicts memo to everyone in the firm to make sure that there is no conflict that would prevent the firm from taking on the new business. Often the partner who sends around the conflicts memo will list the opposing attorney and ask if anyone in the firm can tell the partner about the opposing attorney. If the opposing counsel went to law school in the area, and the firm is a medium to large firm, there is probably a good chance that one of the opposing counsel's classmates works for the firm. The classmate's best recollection of the opposing counsel will be the type of person and law student the person was during law school. Your professional reputation is one of the most valuable assets you have, and unlike your grades, it is something over which you have complete control. Law school is competitive, but there is productive competition and destructive competition. Always err on the side of the productive competition. Treat your professors and classmates the way you want opposing counsel to treat you. Both inside and outside of the classroom, behave in a manner that does justice to the type of person and lawyer you want to be and you want to be known as.

Actively participate in orientation. Law school is stressful. It is important to have a social group with whom you can relax, with whom you can enjoy yourself, and with whom you can vent when necessary. Most first-year social groups form in the first few weeks of classes. Be particularly active the first few weeks of classes. Find the group with whom you are most comfortable, and then settle down and focus on the task at hand—learning how to think like a lawyer.

Read all the assignments before you go to class and attend all the classes. That may sound obvious, but you will be surprised at how many students quit reading or cut classes for one reason or another. Most law professors prefer to treat their students as adults. They do not quiz you to see if you have done all the reading. They may or may not take attendance to see who is present every day.[1] If you think you can get through the class by taking the low road, that is your choice.

---

1. The American Bar Association imposes an attendance requirement on law students that each law professor is supposed to apply, but different law schools and professors apply it differently. Some may pass around an attendance sheet, while others take attendance visually, noting only those students who are regularly absent.

But most students who stop reading and/or cut classes find that it comes back to haunt them when it comes time for the final. Be the best student you can be. It will make the practice of law that much easier and more enjoyable.

In class, err on the side of taking copious notes, but do not be a stenographer. In class, you want to listen critically to the discussion while at the same time getting down as much of the discussion as you can without letting it affect your ability to listen critically. That sounds circular, but it is critical that you listen and think during class. The purpose of the Socratic dialogue is to help you develop that little voice inside your head that will help you analyze issues when you are a practicing lawyer. But some students think that listening critically means they cannot take notes at the same time. Not true. You want to do both, to listen critically and to take copious notes. You want to take copious notes because often you will not understand everything that is being said. You may think you do, but often a professor will throw out an idea, a concept, or an argument and not connect it up until days or even weeks later. If you have a good set of notes, it will help you make that connection. If you have no notes or few notes, it is less likely that you will make that connection.

A good set of class notes is also important because it tells you the depth that the professor expects you to know the material. Every issue, every rule, can be covered either in great depth or rather superficially. The degree to which the professor covers an issue or rule in class is often indicative of the degree to which the professor expects you to know the material for the exam. A great professor once said that outlining is nothing more than cleaning up a good set of class notes. There is much wisdom in that view of outlining.

Keep some balance in your life. If you are not careful, you will quickly find that the study of law, particularly the first year, can become all-consuming. Do your best to keep some balance in your life or you may burn out by the time exams roll around. If you like to work out, make time in your schedule to keep up your workouts. If you like to go shopping, make time in your schedule to keep up your shopping—even if you do not have any money to buy anything! Shoot to schedule one "free weekend" a month. Try to get ahead in your readings so that you can pick a weekend and from Friday afternoon until Sunday night you do not talk or think about the law. That will be difficult, if not impossible. You will not be able to get law school completely out of your mind even if you get away from the school—but do your best. At a minimum try not to do any law school work that weekend. When you come back to school on Monday you will be surprised at how refreshed and re-invigorated you will feel. You will be more productive in the long run. But you can only take a free weekend if you get ahead in your work. You do not want to come back on Monday behind in your readings. Time management is critical. The sooner you develop your legal analysis skills, the easier time management becomes.

The key to performing well on an exam is the quality of *your* outline. You have to produce your own outline. Creating your own outline is a hard and labor-intensive process that forces you to be honest with yourself about how well you know the material. See the relationship between your outline and the final. Write the material in your outline so it facilitates its use on the exam. Write in full sentences; that is how you write on the exam.

Memorize your outline to the point where all the relevant rules and rule elaboration just roll off your tongue the day before the exam. Your goal is to be able to recite orally each rule and each rule elaboration statement, perfectly, without hesitation, so if the rule and rule elaboration come up on the exam you can download that knowledge from your memory with minimal hesitation and slippage in quality.

When you enter the exam room, your mind set should be you *want* to take this exam. You should be excited about the opportunity to take the exam. Taking an exam is analogous to stepping into the batter's box in a game of baseball or softball. If you step into the batter's box afraid of the pitcher and the pitches, the chances you will strike out increase significantly. If you step into the batter's box confidently, wanting to take your turn at bat, the chances that you will get a hit increase significantly. An exam is analogous to the game. The fact pattern is going to throw you some slow easy pitches, some fastballs, and some curves. Your job is to hit as many pitches as you can, as well as you can. A positive attitude helps. Batter up!

Read the exam twice, noting the issues you spot in the margin by writing the name of the rule (in abbreviated form) that you think applies. After you read the exam twice, you arguably are ready to start writing. If you have written the name of the applicable rule (in abbreviated form) in the margin next to each issue, you have outlined your essay. Start at the top of the page with the first issue, IRRAC it, and then move on to the next issue, IRRAC it, and so on down the page. What more do you need to outline? Remember, every word you write in your outline you have to re-write — or re-type as the case may be — in your exam essay. Every moment you spend outlining takes away time that you could be spending elaborating more on your rules, rule elaboration, or analysis. *Now, you have to be true to yourself. If you need to outline before you start to write, do so.* But try to keep your outlining during the exam to a minimum — unless the professor has specifically allocated time to outlining. In that case, assuming you cannot start writing during that time, take all of that time to outline as many issues as you can.

Do not change your writing style to fit your different professors. You will hear stories on the student grapevine that one professor likes her exams written this way and another professor likes his exams written that way. Before you are done with law school you will probably take two dozen or so exams. You do not want two dozen different writing styles — you want only one. Develop a writing style that works best for you, practice it, perfect it, and then use it on all of your exams. One polished writing style used across the board will get you better grades in the long run than attempting to master over twenty different writing styles. But do not take this admonition too literally. Feel free to "tweak" your writing style for a given professor, but do not change it. Tweaking involves minor modifications that can be achieved with minimal effort and consciousness. A good example of that is if a professor says that he or she only wants you to analyze the elements that are in dispute, not every element. Complying with that instruction would affect what you write, but not how you write it. Once you perfect your writing style, apply it across the board. As long as it is a clear and effective writing style, every professor will like it.

After the exam, avoid the post-exam debates outside the exam room. Some students love to stand around and discuss the exam, questioning each other about one issue or another and how they analyzed it. Such debates usually do more harm than good. There is no way to know how well — or how poorly — you did on an exam based on these debates. As a general rule, law school grading is relative. The top ten to twenty percent of the class gets an A, the next sixty to seventy percent or so of the class gets a B, the bottom ten to twenty percent of the class gets a C or below. Unless everyone in the class joins in the debate, you have no way to assess your performance. And much of your grade turns on how you *write* your analysis. It does not matter how well you can argue it after the exam. All that matters is how well you wrote it during the exam, and no student is in a position to assess his or her performance on any given exam. Only the professor, reading all of the exams in context, can make that assessment. Therefore, do not waste your time and emotional effort trying to do so. Once an exam is over, consider it water under the bridge and move on to the next one.

Admittedly it is easier to say "move on to the next exam" than it is to do in reality. You need to develop a strategy for getting over an exam. Take an hour or two off and go do whatever it is you enjoy doing the most. If it is working out, go to the gym and work out. If it is running or hiking, go for a run or a hike. If it is shopping, go to the mall and let yourself wander in and out of stores. If it is being with friends, get a group of friends together and go out to lunch — but the ground rule has to be that no one will talk about the exam. Identify that activity that helps you relax and get the old exam out of your head, thereby preparing you physically and mentally to start the process all over again for the next exam. The sooner you can get one exam out of your head, the sooner you can start to study for the next exam. You can rest after the last exam.

Remember that law school is only three years. Most law firms hire out of their summer internship program. The best chance of getting the job of your choice is to get that job during the summer between your second year of law school and your third year. When do the law firms interview for those positions? Typically, during the fall of your second year. Hate to say it, but your first-year grades are by far your most important grades. You want to get out of the gate fast. A good first semester sets up a good second semester, which sets you up to get the summer job of your choice, which sets you up to get the job of your choice. There is a domino effect to law school and it all starts with first-year grades. That is one of the primary reasons you do not want to leave mastering legal analysis to chance.

The first key to doing well in law school is learning how to think like a lawyer. The second key is knowing how to express that analysis effectively on your exams. The purpose of this book is to try to ensure that you have every chance to let your true abilities shine through on your exams and that you have every chance to get your dream legal job.

Good luck!

Index